P9-EEO-890

CALIFORNIA - WESTERN AMERICANA

Santa Clara County Free Library
California

Alum Rock   Milpitas
Campbell   Morgan Hill
Cupertino   Saratoga
Gilroy
Los Altos { Main
             Woodland

Reference Center-Cupertino
For Bookmobile Service, request schedule

BORAX PIONEER

BORAX PIONEER:

Francis Marion Smith

by

George H. Hildebrand

SANTA CLARA COUNTY LIBRARY

3 3305 22008 0067

679156

SAN DIEGO |Howell -North Books| CALIFORNIA

SANTA CLARA COUNTY LIBRARY
SAN JOSE, CALIFORNIA

Borax Pioneer: Francis Marion Smith copyright © 1982 by Howell-North Books.

All rights reserved under International and Pan American Copyright Conventions. No part of this book may be reproduced in any manner whatsoever without written permission from the publisher, except in the case of brief quotations embodied in reviews and articles.

First Edition
Manufactured in the United States of America

For information write to:

Howell-North Books
P.O. Box 3051
La Jolla, California 92038

Library of Congress Cataloging in Publication Data

Hildebrand, George Herbert.
  Borax pioneer.

  Includes index.
  1. Smith, Francis Marion, 1846–1931. 2. Pacific Coast Borax Company. 3. Businessmen — United States — Biography. I. Title.
HD9585.B674P334   338.7′6223633′0924 [B] 81-6281
ISBN 0-8310-7148-6   AACR2

1 2 3 4 5 6 7 8 9 85 84 83 82

To Evelyn Ellis Smith, whose courage, intelligence and devotion made all the difference when these qualities meant the most to her husband and their children.

Contents

List of Illustrations

Plaque posthumously commemorating Francis Marion Smith, presented by the Key System at their Founders' Day Luncheon, Oakland, October 24, 1933. (Designed by Andrew T. Hass; executed by William Gordon Huff.)

Preface

This book can be read from two points of view: as a study in western history centering upon the life of a very unusual man, and as an illustration of the basic principles of entrepreneurship, as exhibited in the life of that same man.

There is a large measure of agreement that entrepreneurs are a special and rather rare group of people who provide the driving force for economic growth and expansion in the relatively few rich economies of the world, all of which are based upon private enterprise. Entrepreneurs are to be distinguished sharply from managers, administrators, and mere trend-followers who happen to find themselves in charge of a business. The entrepreneur is the man who initiates, leads, and plays the creative role in the emergence and development of successful firms and industries. The central figure in this book, Francis Marion Smith, was such a man. His is a great story in many ways, but it has never before been fully told. Because he has been gone for 50 years, few of those living today will associate his name with Death Valley and the 20-mule teams, or be aware that in his day he was known to two generations as "Borax" Smith.

Over his 60-year career in business, Mr. Smith turned borax production from an artisan trade into a worldwide industry, with headquarters in London and operations in Death Valley. Intervening between Smith's beginnings as a woodcutter at Columbus, Nevada, in 1871, and the loss of his entire fortune in 1913, were other large enterprises on the Oakland side of San Francisco Bay — the Key Route transbay train and ferry system, the Oakland Traction Company, and the Realty Syndicate. But it was through "20-

Mule Team Borax'' that Smith made his wealth, and through the other ventures that he lost it.

Borax Smith was always an entrepreneur with many diverse business interests. One of them was the West End silver mine in Tonopah, Nevada, which by 1915 had proved to be an outstanding property, providing the capital that enabled Smith to return to borax in 1921. Before his death in 1931, his new borax company was already a modest success. Posthumously, it restored most of his earlier fortune.

F. M. Smith lived in ducal style and was famous for his two great mansions and estates, Arbor Villa in Oakland, and Presdeleau, at Shelter Island, New York. He was a warm and generous man, a lavish host, a good friend to all children, a lover of plants and animals, and an outstanding sportsman.

My interest in Borax Smith began in my childhood, over 60 years ago. I am a native of Oakland and grew up within a few blocks of Arbor Villa. Because the Smiths and my own family both belonged to the First Congregational Church, I saw F.M. Smith fairly regularly. Even in his later years, there were many news stories about him, and these stimulated my interest in his fabulous life and career, and in the tragedy that involved the loss of his first fortune. Unfortunately, the newspaper accounts often were incomplete and wildly exaggerated, thereby presenting a challenge: Who was Francis Marion Smith? What did he accomplish with his life? What really happened to him back in 1913? And what was it in his psychological make-up that drove him on to build a second fortune, even at the age of 75?

Following his death in 1931, I had the good fortune of becoming a friend of his widow, Mrs. Evelyn Ellis Smith, who was always willing to talk about her famous husband. After her death in 1957, her four children invited me to begin serious work on this memorable man's life. Over the ensuing years and despite other obligations, I found that a very remarkable story was waiting to be pieced together from interviews, photographs, newspaper accounts, articles, company records, letters, a few books, and many legal documents. As the story took shape, I made it my business to visit all important sites associated with Borax Smith—from his boyhood home in Richmond, Wisconsin, through Teel's Marsh and Tonopah, Nevada, to the two locations of Ryan in Death Valley, and the famous camp at Borate in the Calico Mountains. On the personal side, I saw the splendor of both Arbor Villa and Presdeleau before they were demolished.

In expressing appreciation to the many people who made this book possible, Evelyn Smith tops my list. Next are her four children: Dorothy (Mrs. George T.) Bayley, Mildred (Mrs. Freeman A.) Nicholls, Evelyn (Mrs. Eugene H.) Beck, and Francis Marion Smith, Junior. They have entrusted to me everything of possible significance, have accorded me many interviews, and much kindness. Mrs. Bayley's son, Robert Bayley, has been most helpful about the Smith yachts and the architecture of Presdeleau. Evelyn Smith's brothers, George C. and Norman P. Ellis, granted me important interviews and turned over valuable documents, including Borax Smith's own scrapbook of newspaper clippings.

One of the several sad aspects of the work has been the loss of the three wonderful ladies who grew up at Arbor Villa with F. M. Smith and his first wife, Mary R. Smith. Of these remarkable women, Marion Smith Oliver (formerly married to Roland Letts Oliver) was their foster daughter, born in 1882, while Anna Mae Burdge (Mrs. Bernard P. Miller) and Sarah Winifred Burdge (Mrs. Walter Cole) were from their childhood wards of the Smiths. To the Burdge sisters, the Smiths were always Uncle Frank and Aunt Mollie. These three ladies were my only link to Smith's personal life before 1895, and to Mary R. Smith, who died at the end of 1905. Through many interviews and handwritten recollections, they proved to be invaluable sources as well as warm friends. In this connection, I also wish to thank Mrs. Miller's daughter, Mrs. Elizabeth Scott, for providing very important data and photographs.

It was never my privilege to know the eldest Fred Corkill, who was F. M. Smith's close friend and mining engineer for over thirty years—one of the "Nevada Circle," as I like to think of them. However, his daughter Mabel (then Mrs. A. P. Fulcher) was a great help with information about Borax Smith, her father, and the great camp at Borate. She also generously provided me with many of her father's fine photographs of Smith's many mines.

Lorena Edwards (Mrs. Earl) Meadows also deserves special recognition, for *A Sagebrush Heritage*, her fine biography of her father, Ben F. Edwards; for her friendship and encouragement; and for photographs, letters and personal information about Chris Zabriskie, who married Ben's sister, Margaret. Both Zabriskie and Edwards were also part of Smith's Nevada Circle.

Because borax, after all, was the foundation of F. M. Smith's long career in business, I want to give particular recognition to the unstinting help provided to me by Smith's old companies, Borax

Consolidated Limited, of London, and its subsidiary, United States Borax and Chemical Company, of Los Angeles. Mr. Norman J. Travis, Chairman of BCL, generously accorded me access to Smith's correspondence with his British partner, Richard C. Baker, and the letters of Zabriskie to Baker and Edwards. Mr. Travis provided me with superb working facilities in BCL's handsome offices in London, along with numerous other kindnesses—some excellent conversations and an opportunity to meet with several of BCL's directors and with Mr. E. John Cocks, historian of Borax Consolidated and its subsidiaries.

I owe much to Mr. James M. Gerstley, whose father was one of F. M. Smith's British partners, and who headed U.S. Borax until his retirement. Mr. Gerstley graciously provided the introduction to Mr. Travis, and arranged for me to obtain much company material. As a borax historian in his own right, Mr. Gerstley wrote A Reminiscence of My Father and Borax Years, 1933–1961, both valuable sources of information providing insights into the workings of a large business concern. I wish to thank Mr. Gerstley for personal copies of these books and for much other information. I am also indebted to Mr. Joe Kern, Manager of Public Relations at U.S. Borax, for much published material on company history as well as several photographs.

The Bancroft Library of my alma mater, the University of California at Berkeley, has been of great assistance in granting me access to the Frank C. Havens Papers, to the correspondence of William Lovering Locke and of George C. Pardee, and to old issues of the Oakland Herald and the Oakland Tribune. The State Historical Society of Nevada and the Nevada Historical Society have generously allowed me to examine their documents and photographs. The Historical Section of the Oakland Public Library has been unstinting in its help regarding local history and newspaper materials.

Numerous other persons have granted me interviews or exchanged correspondence: Lillian Ninnis, Virginia Edwards, Henry Hellmers, Horace Albright, Dr. John Connolley, Vernon Sappers, Albert Norman, Mr. and Mrs. Elmer Wendorf, Ollie Wells, Tom Young, Herman Budelman, Roland Oliver, J. Fred Corkill, Tom Gilmore, Warren E. Miller, and Raymond Emge. To all of them, my warmest thanks and appreciation. To David F. Myrick, dean of writers on western railroads, I owe a special debt for his careful reading of the manuscript, his meticulous criticism, and his valuable suggestions.

The task of completing the research and manuscript was made considerably easier by the patience, help, and continuing interest of my secretary, Mrs. Verma W. McClary. I also wish to thank the Center for the Study of the American Political Economy at Cornell University for helping to make this work possible.

I wish to thank Mary Lu Moore for a superlative job of editing, which was consistently accomplished with unfailing patience and good humor.

Finally, I want to express my deepest appreciation to my wife, Margaret, for her own keen interest in Borax Smith's story, and for her constant help and encouragement—inspiring me to bring that grand old pioneer's story to life.

George H. Hildebrand
Maxwell M. Upson Professor of Economics
    and Industrial Relations *Emeritus*
Cornell University
Tucson, Arizona
March 23, 1981

And your young men shall see visions,
And your old men shall dream dreams . . .
Acts II:17

. . . my life has been more along pioneer lines. To exploit a situation
where there is an opportunity to build has always appealed to me.
Francis Marion Smith

1

An Introduction to Borax and to "Borax" Smith

Francis Marion Smith, later known on two continents as "Borax" Smith, made the first great discovery of borax in the United States, then went on to turn the production of that ancient salt into a large and important industry with worldwide markets. Borax Smith's long life spun out enough adventure, accomplishment, and tragedy to supply a dozen novels. In fact, Jack London partially based the central figure in *Burning Daylight* upon F. M. Smith.

To understand Smith, what he achieved, and how he did it, the first requirement is some knowledge of borax itself—its chemistry, its long history, and the relatively recent discovery of the many uses of the boron compounds.

Concerning Borax

Americans of a generation ago will recall a very popular television serial known as "Death Valley Days." They may also remember that President Ronald Reagan—then an actor—played a central role, although the focus of interest in the show was on the famous 20-Mule Teams and the formidable region known as Death Valley, in which those teams toiled to haul forth a chemical called "borax."

Borax is described by the *Oxford English Dictionary* as a native salt known to inorganic chemists as sodium borate ($Na_2B_7O_7 \cdot 10\ H_2O$), a boron and oxygen compound with 10 molecules of water. When pure, it takes the form of a transparent crystal or a white powder. Over the centuries, crude borax coming out of central Asia has been called *tincal*, which is derived from the much older Sanskrit word *tincana*. Borax itself is one of a group of boron ores that includes other borates as well: *kernite* ($Na_2B_4O_7 \cdot 4\ H_2O$);

1

colemanite ($Ca_2B_6O_{11}$ • 5 H_2O); and *ulexite* ($NaCaB_5O_9$ • 8 H_2O).[1]

Some basis exists for believing that borax was known to the Babylonians 4,000 years ago, later to the ancient Egyptians, and then to the Greeks and Romans of classical antiquity. Indeed, it is thought that the Romans operated mines at Bandirma, in Asia Minor near the Sea of Marmora, where a form of borax now known as pandermite is found. All of these people used borax as a soldering material for making gold ornaments, while the Chinese employed it before A.D. 300 for glazing pottery.[2]

The word "borax" itself is of some interest. In its present spelling it has been traced back to medieval Latin, where it was also called "baurach." However, the origin of the word seems to have been Arabic, where it took the form of "bauraq" or "boraq." To the Greeks and Romans, the salt was known as "chrysocolla" (literally, "gold solder"), a term that has been a source of confusion over the centuries because the same word was also applied to hydrous silicate of copper. Georgius Agricola (1494–1555), the German author of the first treatise on mining, *De Re Metallica*, published in Latin in 1556, called borax "chrysocolla," but as Herbert Clark Hoover and Lou Henry Hoover point out in their famous translation, Agricola was always careful to supplement his references to chrysocolla with the words "which the Moors call borax." Unfortunately he himself confused the two minerals.[3] The Venetians perpetuated the confusion—perhaps deliberately for their own purposes—for they employed borax after Marco Polo returned from Asia with samples in the thirteenth century. The Venetians used it as a gold flux and probably as a glass hardener. Because their products were the finest in Europe, linked as they were later with the illustrious name of Benvenuto Cellini (1500–1571), they had an incentive to conceal the ingredients of their processes. In any case, they used the word *chrysocolla*.[4]

The element *boron* is less known than its compounds. It was discovered on June 30, 1808, by Sir Humphry Davy. Boron is one of the lightest elements, fifth in the atomic series, and quite similar to carbon in several respects. It is not found isolated in nature but always in combination with sodium, calcium, or magnesium. It is non-metallic and it can be either crystalline or amorphous.[5] Other pioneering names associated with boron are Sir William Ramsay, Alfred Stock, and H. I. Schlesinger. For more than a century after

Davy's discovery, these men were instrumental in opening up a whole new field in borate and borane chemistry. They made these chemicals most useful for industrial civilization.[6]

Borax as such was first useful to man as a gold flux, a pottery glaze, a glass hardener, and a burial preservative. If boric acid, the other borates, boric oxide, and boron fibers—to name some principal components of the boron group—are included, and if attention is shifted from handicrafts to industrial products, then the list becomes long indeed.[7]

The biggest user is the glass and fiberglass industry, where boron compounds add strength and brilliance to glass and strength to the fiberglass used in boat hulls, auto bodies, and aircraft sections. Next, there are the porcelain enamels used for stoves and refrigerators. Here borax contributes brightness, resistance to cracking, and bonding for teflon coatings. Then there is the older and more familiar field of soaps and detergents for household and commercial uses, where borax cuts excessive alkalinity, freshens and deodorizes, and serves as a mild anti-bacterial agent.

Boron compounds are used in automobiles and aircraft to add power to fuels, kill fungi and bacteria in fuel lines, prevent corrosion, and facilitate lamination of epoxy resins. In ceramics, borax is still heavily used for glazing pottery, tiles, and chinaware. Cosmetics and medicines also make extensive use of some of these compounds. In building materials, borax and boric acid serve as fire-retardants for lumber, wallboard, and fiberglass, as well as for control of termites and rot in lumber. Fireproofing is provided for products such as paint, draperies, and mattress fillings.

And still the list continues. Boron or its derivatives are used as weed killers as well as for slowing the growth of grass and shrubs on large tracts. They strengthen adhesives, improve the sizing of paper, harden the hard abrasives, make easier the plating of copper and lead, improve the quality of control rods in atomic reactors, serve as an additive to balance agricultural fertilizers, and aid plant growth by altering the chemistry of soils.

There can be no doubt that borax, an ancient and rather unexciting chemical, actually has led the way to a multitude of diverse uses for the boron group. Despite its pedestrian quality, this remarkable salt nonetheless has commanded much popular interest over the years, mainly because of the strange and remote places in which it has typically been found in nature. The three oldest-known borax deposits are those in the Kunlun Range of northern Tibet, in the Ladakh region of Kashmir in India, and near the Sea of Marmora in Turkey. Doubtless there are other borax lakes or desert sinks that were also exploited in ancient times, for much of Asia is geologically and climatically suited for the presence of borate compounds.

The exploited locations were remote from centers of use, and required transport over difficult routes. It is known that borax from Tibet was taken over the high passes of the Himalayas down to Calcutta for shipment by water, and that Calcutta was also the port of export for borates coming down from Ladakh. However, Calcutta was founded in A.D. 1690 and thus could not have provided port facilities in ancient times. But the Turkish pandermite deposits would have been accessible by sea to the Egyptians, Greeks, and Romans. Another ancient artery for borax would have been the Great Silk Route, which passed through what is now Iran, then Afghanistan, then over the Pamirs into Sinkiang, and finally to Peking. In the west, there was access to the sea via Turkey and Syria. It may be surmised, therefore, that the ancient Chinese obtained their borax (they favored a black variety) from locations in the Kunlun Range or their northwestern extension, the Pamirs. Meanwhile, the Romans could have brought borax westward from these same places.[8]

In 1777, the presence of boric acid was observed in the hot gases and vapors (soffioni) emerging from the fumaroles (vents) and boiling springs of the Maremma region of western Tuscany. About 1818, a French chemist by the name of Francois Larderel began production of boric acid there, at a location now known as Larderello. Soon the Maremma became Europe's main source of borax. Even today this site continues in production, with boric acid as a by-product from thermal generation of electric power.[9]

Borates, to use the collective term for boron-oxygen compounds, are found in three principal forms: as an ingredient in lakes, hot springs, and geothermal gases; as surface incrustations and ball-shaped extrusions on desert playas, sinks, and dry marshes; or as embedded geological formations. The first form is the direct product of volcanism. Geological opinion holds that the latter two forms also have originated in volcanism. Where the borate is insoluble in water, as with colemanite (borate of calcium), the material thrown up from below takes a sedimentary form and is resistant to leaching. By contrast, the two sodium borates, tincal or borax and kernite, because they are water soluble, could have been leached out of older deposits, or have been the residue of evaporation from their water-borne origins. Finally, there is the curious double salt, ulexite, which is part sodium and part calcium, and therefore can be partially the product of sedimentation and also of leaching.

Borax is typically found in desert regions such as those of western Tibet, Asia Minor, the deserts of Chile and Peru, the dry lakes of western Nevada and southern California, the mountains around Death Valley, the central Mojave Desert, and southern Nevada.[10] Deserts naturally convey notions of remoteness, inaccessibility, and harsh conditions for travel and living. They also suggest that an arid environment is helpful to the formation of borax deposits. The imprint of the desert has given this unusual group of chemicals an aura of mystery and romance. They have always come from far places. It has always been difficult to live and work in such locations, and, until the last 60 years, to transport the product to market. More than this, over most of its lengthy history and until a little over a century ago, borax was always a useful rarity, rather like the ambergris of the sperm whale, known and used by artisans in the glass and gold trades who had to import it in small quantities from distant places.

Shortly after 1860, small lots of borax began to be produced in the United States, although even in 1867, the peak year before 1873, only 220 tons were refined, for a value of $156,137.[11] As W. A. Gale says, "... the real U.S. borax industry may be said to have actually started in 1872, with the discovery of crystalline borax (tincal) at Teel's Marsh ... [Nevada]."[12] Gale goes on to describe the deposit as the first commercially profitable one yet developed within the United States. By 1873, when mining at Teel's was in full operation, refined output reached 1,000 short tons, with a value of half a million dollars. Borax had become an industry at last. The man who accomplished this feat was Francis Marion Smith, soon to be known as "Borax" Smith.

Borax Smith

Francis M. Smith left his father's farm near the hamlet of Richmond, in Walworth County, Wisconsin, in 1867, when he was 21 years old. His goal was to seek his fortune in the West. Over the next five years he prospected at various mining camps in Montana, Idaho, and Nevada, but failed to strike it rich. In the fall of 1872 he was working in the hills above the town of Candelaria, Nevada, cutting wood on a contract with one of the small borax refineries on Columbus Marsh, some 20 miles to the southeast. Looking to the northwest, he was able to glimpse the gleaming white surface of a place called Teel's Marsh. Curiosity soon led him there, where he collected samples of a whitish substance that accounted for the unusual color of the marsh.

It soon turned out that Smith had found the richest borax deposit in western Nevada. By speedily filing his locations, he gained title to the marsh and before the end of the year had a small refinery in operation. This was the true dawn of the borax industry in the United States. It was accomplished by the vigor and initiative that Borax Smith was to display throughout his long life. Within less than 20 years he had increased production nearly five-fold and established himself as the dominant figure in the industry. During those years he pioneered borax mining in Death Valley, switched ore recovery to underground mining, and made himself a multimillionaire. How he made those millions, and what he did with them over the course of an incredible business career of six decades are what this book is about.

2

A Wisconsin Farm Boy Goes West

When Charlotte Paul Smith bore her fifth child, on February 2, 1846, she decided to name him Francis Marion. Her purpose in conferring this distinguished given name was to commemorate his status as a direct descendant of the "Carolina Swamp Fox," Francis Marion, who had waged brilliant guerrilla warfare against the British during the American Revolution. Before long, of course, young Francis Marion Smith became just plain "little Frank" in the large family to which he belonged. Four decades later he would be known on two continents as "Borax" Smith, the prospector who had become a multimillionaire mining man. From then until his death in 1931, the press and the public knew him as Borax Smith, although to family and close friends he was always called "Frank." There is evidence, however, that he drew a considerable amount of pride from his sobriquet. Frank was the fifth of six children born to Henry and Charlotte Smith between 1840 and 1857. Of the others, Frank was closest to Byron and worked with him until Byron's death in 1911. For a time he was also associated closely with Julius, his other older brother, but in 1884 they ended their partnership and became permanently estranged.

Henry Grovier Smith, his father, had been born on September 9, 1810, at White Creek, New York, in Washington County close to the Vermont border. Not much is known of the Smith side of the family except that Frank's grandfather Abram was a captain in the War of 1812, and that his great grandfather, Jeremiah, fought as a soldier in the Revolutionary War.

As a young man, Henry Smith moved to Chili, New York, to take up farming. There he met Charlotte Paul, daughter of Zebulon Paul, who had been born in Chili on April 30, 1822. The Paul family was

7

Charlotte Paul Smith, mother of Francis Marion Smith, about 1867. (F. M. Smith collection.)

Henry Grovier Smith, father of Francis Marion Smith, about 1885. (F. M. Smith collection.)

Boyhood home of Francis Marion Smith, built at Richmond, Wisconsin, about 1848, as it looked in 1978. (Courtesy of Mr. and Mrs. Elmer Wendorf.)

large and locally prominent. Like the Smiths, they too were "York State Yankees," with origins in Taunton and Dighton, Massachusetts, and with a genealogical record extending back for six generations.

Henry Smith and Charlotte Paul were married on March 28, 1839. They first settled on a farm at Shelby, near Medina, in Orleans County, New York. Their first four children—Julia, Ella, Julius, and Byron—were all born there. But Shelby did not prove attractive. As it happened, the Paul family held extensive lands in southern Wisconsin, mostly acquired by purchase from the federal government. It is recorded at Elkhorn, the seat of Walworth County, Wisconsin, that on October 5, 1842, Charlotte Paul Smith purchased 200 acres of land located near the hamlet of Richmond from her father, Zebulon Paul, for the sum of $800. The Smiths had already built a log cabin on the property, and about 1848 constructed a substantial farm house built in the Upstate New York style of the period. The house faced directly west, overlooking Rock Prairie from the hill on which it rested. Probably to reduce the heat of the Wisconsin summer sun, Henry Smith planted several straight rows of soft maple trees in front. They are still there today, partially obscuring the house from the road some 200 feet below.

The trip from Shelby to Richmond had to be made by horse and wagon, over a distance of 600 miles. Upon reaching Chicago, the family paused to visit some Smith relatives who had settled there. Although the Smith cousins urged Henry to stop right there because Chicago was now a boom town, despite its muddy streets and raw qualities, the family continued on to Richmond, some 90 miles to the northwest, just over the state line. In his own "Autobiographical Notes," dictated many years later, Frank Smith found his relatives' advice "undoubtedly good," and then added with some regret that Richmond was "located too far away to maintain any close association" with them.

The land on which the family settled was on the east edge of Rock Prairie, about 1¼ miles south of Richmond. By the time the new house had been built, Henry Smith's holdings had increased to 400 acres, extending into Sections 20 and 28 of Richmond Township. Wheat was the main crop, and it had to be hauled 50 miles to Milwaukee, where it sold for as much as 40 cents a bushel. Despite two hired hands, soon joined by three growing boys, Henry Smith regularly complained that "the more farming he did the poorer he became."[1]

Young Frank was his mother's child, with the same quick perception, restless energy, and warmth of spirit. Always an observer of sharp intelligence, Frank early decided that farming was not for him. As he stated in his recollections, he was first inspired to go West when he was fifteen.

> I was coming home from my day's occupation on my father's farm and, as I watched the sun setting in the West, I was thinking of a man who worked for my father and had several years before gone to California. Now he had returned. Apparently he had an ample supply of this world's goods, and to my young and inexperienced eyes he was a great hero. The golden, setting sun in the West reminded me of the golden state, and I resolved there and then, that when the right time arrived, I would seek experience that could not be obtained on a farm.

Even then, when Frank Smith decided to do something, he usually did it. In his own words: "To exploit a situation where there is an opportunity to build has always appealed to me." Although the family did not know it, by 1861 Frank had already made up his mind to go West.

All of the Smith children, including the youngest, Charlotte Ida (born in 1852), attended the Richmond district school nearby. As they reached high school age, they transferred, one by one, to Milton Academy (now Milton College) at Milton, about 16 miles west of Richmond. Grandfather Paul then offered to send one boy to college, but it was the time of the Civil War and this plan was disrupted. When Frank finished at Milton, probably around 1864, his father sent him to Allen's Grove Academy, a few miles to the southwest, "for better discipline, I suppose." Frank Smith was known for his strong will and his stubborn ways throughout his long life, although these qualities were belied by a mild and friendly outward manner.

At that time the family belonged to the Methodist Church and adhered to its strict tenets about card playing and gambling. On one occasion the minister appealed for public confessions of faith. Frank recorded that he never forgot the experience of having his "very soul" aroused, causing him to go down to the front seat. Nor could he explain the episode. But he added that it "did not last." Not until 1884 did he again profess his faith, this time at the First Congregational Church in Oakland, California.

While at Allen's Grove, he engaged in a transaction that would have been fully understood by Tom Sawyer. He made a deal to saw stove wood at $2.50 per cord, then subcontracted the work for $2.00, "making a clean profit of 50 cents without any effort upon my part." He now saw himself as "a successful engineer and contractor in the near future."

Henry Smith apparently sensed a certain restlessness in his youngest son, for he tried hard to interest him in farming. To encourage him, he gave Frank a colt that grew up to become an excellent young horse. Frank then traded the horse for a pair of oxen. In those days oxen were the heavy work animals of the midwestern farms, used to break raw prairie and to pull heavy loads. But young Smith had a larger object in view than raising oxen. He had reached his majority in February, 1867. Once spring had arrived he intended to make the trip west that had been on his mind since he was fifteen. So he sold the team for $155 in cash that April. "With high hopes and bright dreams," as he recalled it many years later, he was now ready to depart. He was not to return home for another eight or nine years, but when he did he was a success in

Francis Marion Smith in 1867, when he was 21 years old. (F. M. Smith collection.)

the borax business, because he told of gifts of jewelry to his mother and three sisters "that made their eyes snap."

Frank Smith Leaves Home

Mother Smith performed the traditional maternal chore of packing his trunk for him, including, without telling her son, "a fine big cake on the top tray." Unfortunately, after checking the trunk to Denver, he changed his plans. When, two months later, he finally opened his trunk in Helena (then Helena City), Montana Territory, he concluded that while cakes were a luxury on the frontier, this one clearly was not.

To start the trip, the family drove him a few miles south to Delavan, Wisconsin, where he caught the train for Chicago. On arriving, he went to the theater for the first time, to see "Ben Bolt." The next morning he boarded a train for Denver, probably the Northwestern line, because he speaks of its progress being blocked by spring floods at Clinton, Iowa. After waiting in mounting frustration for a day or two, Smith set out on foot for Omaha. On the way he fell in with a group of young men who were planning to take a steamer some 1,200 miles up the Missouri, from Omaha to Ft. Benton, Montana, where a gold rush was underway. One of the party offered a spare ticket to Smith at "a liberal inducement." As Smith tells it, the deal was that if the ticket was honored on the boat, then he would pay the agreed-upon price on arrival at Fort Benton.

Meanwhile, in preparation for the river journey, he had bought a Colt rifle—a somewhat finicky and unreliable weapon that Smith described simply as "the worst shooting iron I have ever seen, in fact, dangerous to have about." The steamer trip would take six weeks. At various times a member of the party would ask him for payment, but Smith refused to pay until he had been delivered at Fort Benton.

At Yankton, Dakota Territory, Smith went ashore—then found himself left behind because in yearning for exercise, he had walked too far. By taking a shortcut at a bend in the river, he caught up with the boat. The steamer was now entering Indian country. Wars were raging among some of the tribes and also against the white man for occupying choice hunting grounds. The new Henry (later Remington) rifle was already in use, and arms were made available to the passengers. To avoid the dangers of tying up on shore, the boat began operating through the night as well. Finally the boat arrived at

Fort Benton. After one of his companions ventured an unneeded show of belligerence over the still unpaid-for ticket, Smith laid down his goods, took out his wallet and handed over the money—to the evident disappointment of some onlookers, who were hoping for a fight.

Smith's next move was to board a Concord stage for the ride to Helena City. Unlike dreary Fort Benton, here was a town awash with human life, all dedicated to placer mining. Frank tried his hand at it at Last Chance Gulch, but the results could not have been notable. He next tried his luck farther out in the country in a couple of locations, then worked briefly at a shaft-sinking job. He returned to Helena City, where he was hired and then fired as a dishwasher—all in one day.

Again Smith tried prospecting, this time at a place called Boulder Creek. Again the pickings apparently were slim, although he got his first look at some Indians of the Nez Percé tribe. There were several hundred, migrating from Oregon to the Yellowstone Valley for hunting and fishing. The women and children were numerous, with the former leading ponies which dragged travois composed of tent poles for a frame, and loaded with blankets, food, and youngsters.

Young Smith had now been wandering for about five months, spending most of his time in Montana prospecting—with little success. By early fall he was ready to move on and boarded a stage for Salt Lake City. His ultimate destination was Austin, Nevada, an active quartz camp at the time. However, Austin offered little, and nearby White Pine no more, so he traveled to Dayton, farther west. In those days Dayton was a milling center for the Virginia City ores, and the first great boom on the Comstock Lode was already under way. The exit to the Sutro Tunnel was nearby, although the tunnel itself was far from completed. Frank succeeded in bluffing his way onto the tunnel crew for a few days until he found a better job at the Imperial Mill.

After working at the mill until early winter, Smith moved on again, this time northwest to the Truckee River, in the vicinity of what is now Reno. The transcontinental railroad was still two years away from completion and the location was no more than a stop on the road from the railroad construction camp to the Comstock district, some 50 miles to the southeast. Adjoining the hotel was a small building housing a restaurant. Smith bought a half-interest, perhaps to disprove the earlier claim of a French cook that he would never even make a good dishwasher. Unfortunately, the land and building in which he had acquired the interest turned out to be located on one of the Central Pacific's mile-sections under its federal land grant, and the carrier decided to lay out the townsite of Reno right there. The little restaurant was found to be sited in the middle of the street. Smith and his partner had to buy a lot and move their building to the new location. Frank later sold out at a loss and moved east to the railhead, where he opened another restaurant in a tent. Within a short time he abandoned this venture for still another restaurant, at Wadsworth, which was an important camp on the Central Pacific line east of Reno. However, eating houses did not appeal to Frank Smith—he disliked the business and the roughnecks who were his patrons. Finally, he gave up the venture and returned to prospecting.

The Southern Mines of Nevada

One can only surmise how Smith spent the next five years. All we know is that he was "following different mining strikes," as he told it. Given the location of Wadsworth in the western Nevada desert, we can guess that these camps probably included the Virginia City district in western Montana, the Virginia City or Comstock district in western Nevada, and the so-called "Southern Mines" situated in the Marietta-Belleville-Candelaria district in Mineral and Esmeralda Counties, Nevada, adjacent to the California line. The Marietta-Belleville-Candelaria district was based originally upon silver, most of which was taken out of two famous mines, the Holmes and the Northern Belle. In any case, it was silver that eventually drew Frank Smith to the region. But luck still eluded him as a prospector, so he became a woodcutter instead, providing spruce and pine cut from the surrounding hills for use as mine props and as a source of charcoal for smelting.

The story of how Frank Smith became a woodcutter in western Nevada is of interest. As noted, Smith's first five years in the West were not profitable ones. About 1871 or 1872, he had presented himself to the management of a borax refinery operated at Powell and Chestnut Streets in San Francisco by Joseph Mosheimer and Emile K. Stevenot. He told them of his interest in borax, in hopes of getting a job. As there was no opening in the city, Stevenot offered him employment at Columbus, Nevada, as a woodcutter. Large quantities of scrub pine found in the Candelaria Hills and in the Excelsior Mountains were needed for the boiling operations by which cottonball borax was concentrated. Mosheimer and Stevenot had a small borax concentrating plant there. Frank Smith seized the opportunity and soon found himself providing wood to Stevenot's plant at Columbus. It would not be long before the plant would belong to Smith himself.[2]

There is a geological peculiarity in this region that Smith noted after he arrived there about 1872. At the base of its several ranges there were at least four important dry lakes or salt marshes. One of them, Rhodes Marsh, lies just a few miles south of the town of Mina. Columbus Marsh is just below the famous silver camp of Candelaria, founded in 1865. A few miles south of Columbus Marsh is Fish Lake Valley, a very large desert sink surrounded by rugged peaks. Finally, there is Teel's Marsh, about ten miles northwest of Candelaria, in a broad and desolate desert valley. It was in this wild and remote location that Frank M. Smith finally was to strike it rich on October 12, 1872, after a five-year odyssey through the western deserts.[3]

From Woodcutter to Borax Man

To carry on his woodcutting operations, Frank had built a simple board-and-batten cabin at the head of a narrow gulch, "commanding a fine view of the outlying country."[4] He says in his own account that he could see both Columbus and Teel's marshes from this location. This means that the cabin had to be fairly high in elevation, because there are intervening hills and ridges between Belleville and Columbus Marsh, and a substantial range from Belleville to the northeast, lying on the Belleville side of Teel's Marsh. The location that best corresponds to Smith's description is Miller Mountain (elevation 8729'). This peak is south of Belleville, southwest of Columbus and Candelaria, and faces open desert flat into Teel's Marsh on the northwest. It has a substantial growth of scrub pine on its upper reaches, while the hills and ridges to the northeast are barren. Finally, Miller Mountain alone affords direct views of both Teel's and Columbus marshes.[5]

Soon after moving in and starting as a woodcutter, Smith had to confront a challenge that was to prove the resourcefulness and inner strength that served him well throughout his business career. One morning, three choppers came onto his property and began cutting down his trees, sawing them up and stacking them to be picked up later. Given the odds and the lack of police protection and weapons, Smith had to go to Columbus (10 miles distant) to obtain a rifle, along with but four available cartridges. Returning at nightfall, he found his best stand of trees neatly piled up in stacks awaiting shipment the next morning.

At sunup Frank and his chopper ate breakfast, whereupon he sent the man off to work, not counting on him for help. Soon the timber thieves appeared—four men with 21 pack animals. In the meantime, Smith had taken his "position on the hillside, just out of close shooting range with small arms, and some 125 yards from the woodpile." He took aim and ordered them to clear out. After plenty of cursing, the gang offered to bargain, proposing to take only the wood it had already cut. No deal, replied Smith. Finally they left, sending back a delegation the next day, again proposing compromise. Smith "had no compromise to make." Having stood his ground, he had no further trouble with claim jumpers.

Frank Smith Discovers Borax at Teel's Marsh

On bright days during the dry season, Smith could see the "gleaming white" of Teel's Marsh from his little cabin high up in the hills. At last he could restrain his curiosity no longer, and took two of his choppers to visit the place. On arrival, they found that the crust was unusually thick at their chosen location, and seemed rich in borax. The party staked out a preliminary site, then collected samples which Smith immediately took to Columbus for assaying. Smith quickly returned to the marsh, established a camp, and had his men begin the task of laying out more locations. Smith himself then returned to Columbus to get the assayer's report. From the assay certificate he learned that his samples were "the finest specimen of borate of soda" found up until that time.

Frank Smith was not the first man to discover borax in the United States. That honor belonged to Dr. John A. Veatch, who found it at Tuscan Springs in Tehama County, California, in 1856.[6] In that same year, Dr. Veatch also found borax in what came to be called Borax Lake, in Lake County, California, a region similar to the geothermal district in western Tuscany, at Larderello, Italy. By 1864, the California Borax Company had begun operations at Borax Lake, an undertaking that lasted only four years before being ruined by flooding.

In the same period, in fact, a man by the name of William Troup (or Troop) had been searching for "cottonball" borax, a form of ulexite—found in dry marshes—that constantly renews itself from below. After searching throughout most of the 1860s, he finally found it at Columbus Marsh, about 1870 or 1871.[7] Moreover, John W. Searles, for whom Searles Lake in San Bernardino County, California, is named, had discovered borax at that location in 1865, although he did not undertake production there until many years later.[8]

With the Troup and Searles discoveries, the borax industry moved into the "playa" or dry marsh phase, in place of the earlier lake period. Thus borax deposits and production were known in the United States some 15 or 16 years before Frank Smith made his famous discovery. What distinguished him from all of his predecessors was that he was the first American to turn borax into a major mining industry.

Collecting two associates, Smith set out for Teel's Marsh a third time, anxious to forestall any other locators. The party pressed on after supper, arriving at the marsh after midnight. Here they met with the two men Frank had left on guard, plus a friend of the assayer who had been tipped off about the discovery. When the newcomer asked Smith where Teel's Marsh was, he was told that there was an alkali flat about 20 miles distant, and that at first light Smith would send a man along with him to guide him to the place. On the pair's return three days later, Smith already had the best locations all staked out, even saving one for the assayer himself, who had showed up despite his faithlessness toward Smith.

The original document constituting an agreement for the division of the claims is still in the possession of the F. M. Smith family. Dated at Columbus, Nevada, on October 29, 1872, the agreement provides that "the several locations of Salt Land for Borax" were to be treated as a unit, with 40 percent and two votes for "Francis M. Smith," and 20 percent and one vote each for Ira P. Hale, Louis A. Engelke, and W. D. Shaver. The instrument was witnessed by J. J. Spencer and John Kinsella.

Then came a legal blow: the Mining Commissioner ruled that borax lands constituted placer claims, limited to 20 acres for each locator. Hitherto these lands had been classified under the saline law, which allowed 160 acres per person. Smith was compelled to relocate all of his claims, and to enter claims in others' names, merely to retain his best holdings. Many neighbors and old friends back in Walworth County, Wisconsin, had the peculiar experience

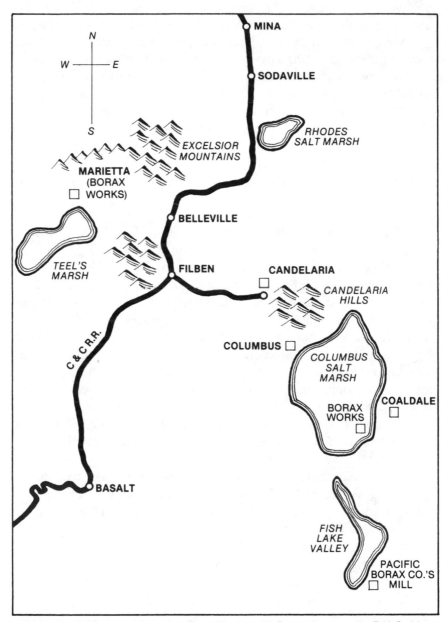

MAP 1. Teel's Marsh and Columbus Borax District, with Properties owned by F. M. Smith, 1872-1890. Scale: approximately 2 in. = 10 miles. (Prepared by David F. Myrick.)

of receiving an unexpected dollar each from Henry G. Smith for 20-acre deeds taken out in their names for lands they had never even seen.

After considerable further trouble with claim-jumpers and much litigation, Frank Smith finally established control over the richer portions of the marsh. His next step was to arrange through his brother Julius to have the firm of Storey Brothers of Chicago build a refining plant, and to join him in the development of the property. At the age of 26, Frank M. Smith had now become "Borax" Smith and a promising mining figure. For a partner he had his older brother, Julius Paul Smith, who settled with him in Marietta, the townsite for Teel's, and remained there until 1884.

Building an Industry

By early 1873, the firm of Smith Brothers was technically ready to start production.[9] The first step in turning cottonball into borax began with the raking up of the material and its underlying crusts in windrows, for shoveling into wagons. The material was then taken to large wooden tanks, each of 3,500-gallon capacity, partially filled with water. Steam was then introduced into the mixture to heat up the concentration of the solution to the critical level, after which it was allowed to stand. Surface scum and impurities were then skimmed off, while the underlying solution was drawn off in India rubber tubes for deposit in crystallizing tanks. About 10 days were required for the liquid to cool to 77°F. Then a valve was opened in the lower section of the crystallizer to draw off the mixture of mother liquor, large crystals, and mud. This mixture was washed in another tank, while undergoing manual agitation. The crystals were then ready for refining. A six-inch layer of borax and other salts normally remained in the bottom of the crystallizer, to be chopped out with a pick, allowed to dry out for a few days, and then placed in sacks for shipment.[10]

It is somewhat ironic that the nearest railhead for shipments from the little plant was Wadsworth, Nevada, 160 miles distant—the same Wadsworth where Borax Smith had reluctantly tried his hand at restaurant-keeping some five years before. In later years there were disputes among historians over who invented the famous 20-mule team for freight haulage. The *Scientific American* reported in 1877 that Smith Brothers shipped their product in a 30-ton load, distributed between two large wagons, while a third wagon was attached to carry food and water for the men and animals over the long stretch of desert. To haul the entire load, 24 mules were used, probably in paired fashion, although this is not stated, nor is it indicated whether horses were used as wheelers and leaders, as in the later operations in Death Valley.[11] In any case, it is clear that Borax Smith was thoroughly familiar with the use of long freight teams as early as 1877, some six years before he introduced them into Death Valley.

Besides its isolation, Teel's Marsh was a windy place, subject to frequent sandstorms that polluted the new company's product. To solve this problem, the Smith brothers built a small refinery on the Oakland side of San Francisco Bay, for final processing of their borax. Not long afterward they shifted their refining to a plant in West Alameda owned by William T. Coleman, who was later to become closely associated with Borax Smith in borax operations in Death Valley.

In addition to the refining problems, the Smiths soon had to face another one involving marketing. By 1875 the American economy was depressed. Moreover, borax was not then widely known. Thus the problem was the classical one of creating demand. Fortunately, Frank Smith was equal to the challenge. His solution was to go east himself and open a small store and office in New York City, at 185 Water Street. Here he began a vigorous campaign to sell borax to the public. His claims in its behalf were pardonably exaggerated for those more tolerant times. Borax, his literature proclaimed, would clean black cashmere, cameos, and coral. It was ideal for the laundry. It would keep milk and cream sweet. A borax shampoo would cure "nervous headache." Mixed with water, it was a preventative against "diptheria, lung fever, and kidney trouble."[12] Significantly, Smith's claims did not extend to industrial uses, for these were to come later.

3

Branching Out:

The Death Valley and Mojave Deposits

Teel's Marsh gave Smith the necessary base on which to build his industrial career. However, Frank and Julius Smith were primarily producers of a relatively new and unknown product. They were not distributors. They had no markets and no knowledge of how to find them. Thus they badly needed an experienced marketing organization if they were to succeed in their new venture.

The Association Between F. M. Smith and W. T. Coleman

Fortunately, there was such an organization at hand—the firm of William T. Coleman and Company, of New York and San Francisco. Its head, William Tell Coleman, had long been engaged in the borax business, as a selling agent for Veatch and later for Troup as much as 15 years before Smith went into production. Coleman had also acquired an interest in the Pacific Borax Company about 1872, after this firm had started work at Columbus Marsh.[1] In 1875 Pacific Borax built a second refinery at Fish Lake Valley, under the management of Rudolph Neuenschwander, a close associate of Coleman's. By late 1875, the firm was in financial trouble. In August 1876, it closed down. Coleman then sued the company in bankruptcy for $45,000.[2]

As of 1873 Smith and Coleman were competitors. The date at which they joined forces cannot be fixed with certainty, and indeed the relationship is made all the more complex because they continued to be competitors in some places while working together in others. The U.S. Borax and Chemical Company, which is the lineal corporate descendant of Smith Brothers, has in its possession hand-out cards, which it dates around 1876 or 1877, and which advertise the many virtues of the Smiths' product—for washing, starching, preventing moths and cockroaches, dressing wounds, softening chapped skin, bathing, cleaning clothes, and preserving milk and cream.[3] Very likely F. M. Smith himself used these very cards in his opening sales campaign in New York City in 1875. The cards declare on their face that W. T. Coleman and Company are the "exclusive selling agents" for the Smith Brothers' product.

There was much more to the Coleman-Smith association. In the early 1870s, Coleman had bought a former soap factory in West Alameda, on the eastern edge of San Francisco Bay, and converted it to a borax refinery. Soon the Smiths were shipping their product to Coleman instead of to their own small plant. Then, in 1880, Frank Smith, acting alone, bought the Pacific Borax Company, probably by paying off or taking over that firm's indebtedness to Coleman. No doubt this move was inspired by a strong recovery in the borax market after 1878, and, more importantly, by the impending completion of the narrow-gauge Carson and Colorado Railroad

Columbus, Nevada, where F. M. Smith began his career in borax, as it looked in 1886. (Courtesy of Lorena Edwards Meadows.)

into Candelaria in early 1882. About 125 miles to the north, this line connected (at Mound House, Nevada) with its broad-gauge parent, the Virginia and Truckee, which in turn provided a direct link to the Central Pacific at Reno. Borax now could be produced at Columbus and Fish Lake marshes, hauled but a few miles to Candelaria, and then be taken by rail, with transloading at Mound House, all the way to West Alameda. The operations at Teel's Marsh were also beneficiaries of these improvements, and the new railroad company established a station and loading dock at Teel's, a few miles west of Belleville at a point where entry into Teel's Marsh could be made over flat ground all the way to Marietta.

Smith always had a roving eye for new business opportunities, and his urge for expansion was still unsatisfied. This time his goal was to construct a large works at the north end of Fish Lake. By the end of July 1882, the new plant was dedicated in the name of the Pacific Borax Company. It was the largest refinery in the state. Combined with Smith's property on Columbus Marsh (the original Pacific Borax Plant) and his half-interest in Smith Brothers at Teel's,

Mercantile store in Columbus, Nevada, owned by F. M. Smith's Pacific Borax Company and managed by Byron G. Smith. 1886. (Courtesy of Lorena Edwards Meadows.)

he was now the foremost man in Nevada marsh borax production.[4] In that year, refined borax production in the United States had reached 2,118 short tons, for a value of $340,000. Borax Smith's dominance in the industry was then strengthened further by the sudden departure of Julius Smith from the firm in 1884. The reasons for this rupture have never been disclosed, although it has been suggested that conflict between the two men's wives was a factor. In any case, Julius moved to California at the time, continued as a borax dealer for a short period, and then established the Olivinia Vineyard at Livermore.

While these many changes in the ownership and structure of the industry were going on, Smith undertook his first important merger by consolidating the Columbus and Fish Lake properties under the name of the Pacific Borax, Salt and Soda Company in 1888.[5] In that same year, a prominent San Francisco businessman, Joseph Wakeman Mather, lost a son, and decided to return east. He persuaded F. M. Smith to open a New York office at 48 Wall Street, and to appoint him to operate it. After taking this step, Frank made Joseph Mather president of Pacific Borax, Salt and Soda. Smith was constantly in need of added capital to finance the growth of his business, while Mather had excellent banking connections of obvious use to Frank. Despite their mutual need for each other, the fact remains that Smith had done a very large favor for Mather in providing him with the job that he wanted. It was an act of friendship, soon to be followed by others, although Mather was to repay them in rather odd fashion some years later.

Evidence suggests that F. M. Smith and W. T. Coleman had never pooled all of their holdings to become full partners. Rather, they had begun as business associates standing in the roles of principal (Smith as a producer) and agent (Coleman as a distributor), with Coleman also serving as Borax Smith's financier. As matters progressed, they became friends and close business associates, conducting much of their affairs in a rather informal way, as the following episode illustrates.[6]

A couple by the name of Aaron and Rosie Winters had settled in the late 1870s at Ash Meadows in the Amargosa Desert, just east of Death Valley. A passing prospector from the Nevada borax district, Harry Spiller, told the Winters about borax. Pretending ignorance, the Winters pumped Spiller thoroughly for information. As soon as he had departed the next morning, they started the long trip to the salt flats in Death Valley, making camp at what is now Furnace

Creek Ranch. There they gathered samples from the marsh, made the traditional burning test with alcohol, got a green flame, and knew at once they had found cottonball.

Winters' next move was to send a sample to Coleman, who passed it on to Smith for his opinion. The latter was very favorably impressed, and sent two trusted Nevada employees whom he had inherited with Pacific Borax, William Robertson and Rudolph Neuenschwander, to Ash Meadows to meet with Winters, look at his deposits, and possibly buy them. They paid Winters $20,000 for what he called his "right of discovery"—meaning that he had no legal or patented claims but only a secret location. Legal rights to the area would have to be established subsequently by the buyers.

Whose money was used for the purpose? It could have been Coleman's, or Smith's, or a joint fund, or even an order by one of them to pay out funds. It really made no difference, for Smith and Coleman fully trusted their representatives. It was also a typical way of doing business in the Old West. Frank Smith had built up credits with Coleman by shipping him borax. By selling the borax, Coleman covered his debts to F.M., paying him cash as required, and keeping a margin of profit for himself.

Ever anxious to expand, with the ultimate goal of dominating the market, Smith was impatient to start exploiting the deposits. Back went Robertson and Neuenschwander to Death Valley in 1882, to build a bunkhouse for the work force that was to construct the Harmony works.[7] During 1881 and 1882, saline claims had been filed on the marsh in the names of Coleman, Smith, Robertson, and Neuenschwander. These claim books are on view today at the Furnace Creek Ranch Museum. Later, Smith and Coleman organized the Harmony and the Meridian Borax Companies to operate the properties, reserving controlling interests for themselves.[8]

However, a minor obstacle now appeared. Harmony had no water supply because canny Aaron Winters had retained the water rights for himself by filing claims on them after selling the borax bed. It was all perfectly legal—Robertson and Neuenschwander had simply overlooked the need for water. Coleman and Smith had to pay an additional $2,500 to get control of Furnace Creek.[9] In 1883 the Harmony works began operations, continuing in production until 1888, with J. W. S. Perry as superintendent. It was here also that Perry designed the great wagons that were hauled by the famous 20-mule teams to the railhead at Mojave, 165 miles to the southwest.[10]

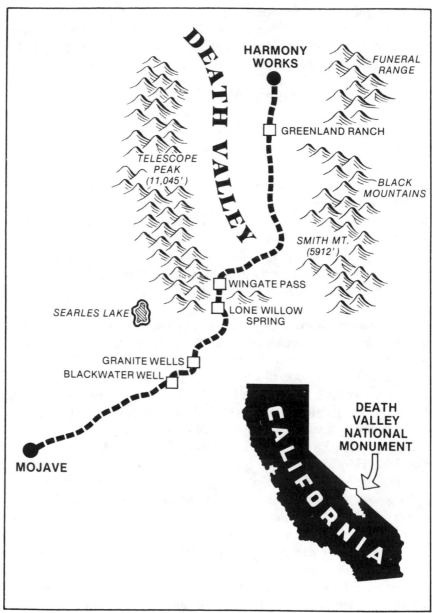

MAP 2. F. M. Smith's and W. T. Coleman's Harmony Works in Death Valley, with route of Twenty-Mule teams to Mojave (1883-1888). Not to scale.

The Harmony Works and
the 20-Mule Teams

As noted earlier, the use of long teams in the West did not begin with the hauling of borax from Harmony in 1883. Similar teams had commonly been used in the copper diggings around Bisbee, Arizona, even earlier. What was new at Harmony were the specially built wagons designed by Superintendent Perry. He sought a vehicle that could haul a large enough load to keep the price of borax competitive when shipped over long distances, and that could withstand the destructive effects of a hot, dry climate. It also had to be a wagon that would hold together through constant use over the roughest of desert tracks, while the wheels had to be of large tread and diameter to permit the hard-working animals to drag them through long sandy stretches. Perry had 10 wagons built at Mojave in 1882, at a cost of $900 each. Each weighed 7,800 pounds and could take a payload of just over 10 tons. In dimensions, the wagon bed was 16 feet long, 6 feet deep, and 4 feet wide, while the diameters of the front and rear wheels were 5 and 7 feet, respectively. Each wheel had an iron tire, 1 inch thick and 8 inches wide.

The teams went into service in 1883, following a standard route to Mojave, and making the round trip of over 300 miles in 20 days. Leaving Harmony, the team headed straight south past Furnace Creek Ranch (then called Greenland) to Bennett's Well and the abandoned Eagle Borax works. To the east towered the Black Mountains, close to 6,000 feet high. At the Eagle works the team turned southwest, heading up Long Valley out of Death Valley, leaving Death Valley through Wingate Pass in the Slate Range, an exit known to the old timers as Windy Gap. After traversing the pass, the team turned south again, passing Lone Willow Spring and Granite Wells, to the south of Searles Lake. Here it turned southwest again just before Blackwater Well, heading almost in a straight line for Mojave.[11]

There is general agreement that the first driver was a man named Edward Israel Stiles, but there is no consensus about who conceived the first team for use in Death Valley. Some say Stiles.[12] John Delameter, who built the wagons, claimed the honor for himself.[13] Some years later, an inquisitive itinerant reporter found himself unsatisfied with these versions. To resolve the issue, he called on Ed Stiles, who was now retired and living on a ranch near San Bernardino, California.

When asked the question, Stiles is said to have replied that in 1882 he was driving a 12-mule team between Isadore Daunet's Eagle Borax Works in Death Valley and Daggett. A man in a buckboard drove up and asked if the team was for sale, and according to the writer, Stiles advised him to write a Mr. McLaughlin, the assumed owner. Fifteen days later Stiles had returned from his round trip, and he met the same man in the buckboard, plus an eight-mule team with a red wagon and a driver named Webster. The man in the buckboard showed Stiles a bill of sale for the team and wagon, then hired him on the spot. The two teams were taken to Greenland, "where Al Maynard, foreman for Smith and Coleman," told Stiles to remove the tongue from the new wagon, substitute a trailer tongue, and on the next day assemble all 20 animals in a string of pairs and attach them to the two wagons, with a water wagon behind. That is Ed Stiles' recollection of how it all began.[14] The buckboard still survives at the museum at Furnace Creek Ranch. According to Stiles' account, the man in the buckboard was Borax Smith. There is the ring of truth in all this, including the role of F. M. Smith. He had been using long teams at Teel's several years before Harmony opened in 1883. Smith was an entrepreneur. While entrepreneurs rarely invent anything, they are alert to fresh syntheses that unite old ideas with just-created ones. This takes a special kind of vision and imagination, which Smith possessed throughout his life.

The great teams were withdrawn from the long haul to Mojave by 1888, when Harmony closed permanently. But their demanding labor was not yet over. In their years of service, the 20-mule teams brought great quantities of borax out for the world, and in freighting this highly useful commodity to market they established one of the most famous corporate trademarks and brand names ever devised. Indeed, it proved so serviceable that over the next four decades the company regularly sent its teams to expositions, fairs, and other events where "The Twenty" could strut their stuff once more.

The Calico Deposits

During the early 1880s, borax deposits were being opened up at almost an explosive rate. These developments were reflected in increased production (see Table 1).

The opening of the Harmony plant in 1883 shows up clearly in

Table 1
Borax Production in the United
States During the Harmony Period

Year	Output (lbs.)	Dollar Value (thousands)
1882	4,236,291	$338,903
1883	6,500,000	585,000
1884	7,000,000	490,000
1885	8,000,000	480,000
1886	9,778,290	488,915
1887	11,000,000	550,000

Source: Engineering and Mining Journal, LI:1 (January 3, 1981), p. 14. These figures compare with the official ones in Mineral Resources of the United States, as cited.

these figures. After 1884 prices fell as production grew. By 1887, borax was selling at only five cents a pound, as against eight cents in 1882.

For F. M. Smith, one of the discoveries in the early 1880s was the great lode of borate of calcium found in the Calico Mountains, at a site soon to be named Borate, near what later became the railroad town of Daggett. Its discovery in 1882 was of great importance because it made possible a shift from marsh operations to much more productive hard-rock mining. This new form of borax came to be called colemanite, for W. T. Coleman, although Coleman had proposed "smithite" instead. (Colemanite's chemical formula is $CaB^6O^{11} \cdot 5 H^2O$.) It was the dependable William Robertson who bought the claim for the two partners.[14]

Again there was a degree of obscurity surrounding the transaction. Henry G. Hanks attributed the Calico purchase to "Wm. T. Coleman & Co.," while Gilbert Bailey, a state geologist writing in 1902, linked Smith with Coleman. Probably the most reasonable interpretation is that the two men each had a share in the ownership, as they did at Harmony. In any event, Calico was developed for mining by Smith alone, starting about 1889, after Coleman had left the industry.[15]

W. T. Coleman's departure was not voluntary. On May 7, 1888, the House of Coleman was forced to make an assignment of all of

F. M. Smith's borax works on Columbus Marsh, Nevada, 1886. (Courtesy of Lorena Edwards Meadows.)

its assets, "in view of pressing engagements in New York" and "to prevent a dissipation of our property."[16] The firm's spokesman, Frank S. Johnson, a partner, reckoned its assets at between $4 and $4.5 million, and liabilities at $2 million. The borax properties alone were valued at $2 million, but their sale was blocked when Congress put borax on the free list in a new tariff bill. This was a fatal blow, for it threatened a fall in the domestic price of borax, and thus a corresponding decline in the capitalized values of all American borax deposits.

Initially, Coleman's failure was treated as a temporary matter, but it soon became apparent that the firm would not reopen its doors. Showing the characteristic integrity that made him one of the most highly regarded men in San Francisco, Coleman liquidated his personal holdings and devoted the few remaining years of his life to paying off his creditors in full.

In the assignment, the Coleman interests in Meridian Borax, Harmony Borax, and the West Alameda refinery were segregated for separate treatment under the custody of A. L. Tubbs.[17] In March 1890, Borax Smith acquired the borax properties and the Alameda refinery as well.[18] The reported price for the Death Valley properties alone was put at $400,000. Smith undoubtedly borrowed heavily for this purpose, which may have been one reason why Joseph Mather began to sour on his employer. Mather disapproved of extensive debt, and also had the unhappy job of raising funds for Smith. Borax Smith, by contrast, had great ambition, and was only too glad to borrow money in the service of these larger ends.

Formation of the Pacific Coast Borax Company

Even before his financial collapse, Coleman had begun preparations for mining colemanite at Borate. Smith fully agreed with the wisdom of the move, so by 1890 Borate was in production. The time had now come for consolidation of his several borax companies. The Pacific Coast Borax Company was created on September 10, 1890, with Smith as president and majority stockholder. The age of colemanite had begun, while that of marsh extraction was virtually over. "PCB," as the new company soon came to be known, lost no time in winding up its marsh operations and in closing its mercantile stores in Columbus and Marietta.[19]

Borax works at Columbus Marsh, Nevada, in 1886. (Courtesy of Lorena Edwards Meadows.)

In taking this step, however, Smith made a deal with his old Candelaria banker friend, Ben F. Edwards, to continue operations on a smaller scale at Teel's, Fish Lake, and Columbus marshes, where profitable borax still remained. To carry out the deal, Edwards made an interesting arrangement with a Chinese labor contractor with the unlikely name of Billy Ford, under which Ben would pay Ford $65 per ton of sacked borax, providing the sacks and shovels, while Billy would feed, clothe, and house his crews. In turn PCB would pay Edwards $75 per ton.[20] Ford's Chinese laborers lived in little wooden shacks barely three feet high. Some of them are still intact today. In a speech to the PCB sales force in 1905, Borax Smith declared that production was still continuing at Teel's at that late date, with a total cumulative output of probably 17,000 tons.[21]

Before leaving this harsh, desolate, isolated and yet wildly beautiful region of the Nevada borax marshes, it is appropriate to take account of the many close friends and talented people whom F. M. Smith found there. Undoubtedly part of his business genius lay in his ability to select loyal and competent associates, to whom he readily delegated authority and responsibilities as rapidly as they could handle them. Some of these people came from Columbus or Teel's, but most of them lived in Candelaria. For convenience, they're referred to here as the "Nevada Circle."

Of the whole group, there were four men of outstanding ability, three of whom were to spend the rest of their careers "in the profitable service of Borax Smith."[22] In no particular order of preference, the first one was John Ryan, the Irish bachelor from County Clare, whose loyalty, natural intelligence, courage, and common sense made him Borax Smith's right-hand man for almost 40 years. He first went to work for Smith at Teel's Marsh in 1873, and stayed with him (save for three years in South Africa) until Smith quit PCB in 1914. Ryan was a rugged desert man and hard-rock miner with the natural leadership qualities of a top superintendent. Smith used him for everything from chasing claim jumpers in Death Valley to supervising a big camp at Borate and building and then operating the Tonopah and Tidewater Railroad. So far as John Ryan was concerned, Frank Smith was the boss. Anything he ever asked John Ryan to do he did, and did it the way "Mr. Smith" wanted it.

Next, there was Fred Corkill, superintendent of the Holmes Mine (a silver property) near Belleville, Nevada, in 1885. Later he became Borax Smith's mine superintendent, first at his borax properties in Nevada, then at the great colemanite camp at Borate, and finally at Smith's West End Consolidated silver mine in Tonopah. Corkill was a mining engineer of rare ability, who had emigrated from the Isle of Man. He rose in the service of PCB, first at Borate, then at the Lila C (Old Ryan), and finally at "New" Ryan, on the east side of Death Valley. Both his son, Frederick W., and his grandson, J. Fred Corkill, became key men in PCB. However, the first Fred Corkill stuck with Borax Smith, leaving PCB for Smith's West End silver mine in 1914, when Smith himself severed all connections with the company he had founded.[23]

Then there was Benjamin Franklin Edwards, of Welsh descent, born in California in 1865 and 20 years later a young miner in Candelaria.[24] Edwards was a man of diverse talents, all of which attested to outstanding business ability. Undoubtedly he knew Borax Smith by the mid-1880s, through that tireless empire-builder's many trips to look over his three big properties in the

Bunkhouse built by F. M. Smith at Monte Blanco claim in Death Valley, 1882. The building now serves as the Furnace Creek Museum. (Fred Corkill collection.)

Abandoned Harmony Borax Works, Death Valley, about 1890. Harmony was operated by F. M. Smith and W. T. Coleman from 1883 to 1888. (Fred Corkill collection.)

western Nevada district. When PCB decided in 1891 to get out of "marsh farming" for borax mining, Smith picked Edwards as his agent and contractor to keep the properties going on a smaller scale. By this time Edwards was also a banker and merchant in Candelaria. Edwards and Smith would continue their business association until 1917, when they disagreed over management issues. Yet they remained friends until the death of Borax Smith in 1931.

Finally, there was Christian Brevoort Zabriskie, probably the most important of the whole group in terms of influence upon Smith. Chris, as he was universally known, was of Dutch and Polish descent. He was the son of an army officer, Captain Elias B. Zabriskie, and was born in 1864 in Fort Bridger, Wyoming.[25] Later the family moved to Carson City, where he grew up. Chris Zabriskie had good looks, charm, brains, plenty of ambition, and a measure of opportunism in his character. He worked in and around Candelaria in the early 1880s, and soon caught the sharp eye of Borax

Part of Greenland Ranch, now Furnace Creek Ranch, Death Valley, about 1890. (Fred Corkill collection.)

Smith, who was on the lookout for exceptional men. Toward the end of 1884 or early in 1885, Smith offered him the job of superintendent of his Pacific Borax Company works at Columbus Marsh. This connection seems not to have lasted very long, for the local papers carried reports of his doing various jobs in various places. In the fall of 1888, Chris Zabriskie married Margaret Louise Edwards, who was Ben Edwards' sister.[26] Toward the close of 1892, the Zabriskies and their year-old daughter moved to Oakland, where Chris entered the real estate business.[27]

Advertisements in the local paper disclosed that Chris was selling lots in the northwestern section of Oakland, near the Emeryville line. Of more importance was the claim that the lots would be conveniently close to the proposed "new ferry terminal" for San Francisco. This was the first public revelation of Borax Smith's great dream for a transbay electric railway and ferry system—a project that would not come to fruition for another 10 years.

From Ulexite to Colemanite

With the formation of PCB in 1890 and the stripping off of the marsh properties by the sub-contract with Ben Edwards, F. M. Smith was now a producer of colemanite borax with his mines at Borate. In picking up the remains of Coleman's fallen empire, Smith acquired two very important undeveloped colemanite deposits, one known as the Lila C (for Coleman's daughter), at Old Ryan on the east side of the Greenwater Range; and the other a collection of colemanite claims, the so-called Hillside group, on the west side of this range, 3,200 feet above the floor of Death Valley. In time, these claims would become mines, to be known as the Widow, the Played Out, the Grand View, the Biddy McCarthy, the Monte Blanco, and the Lizzie V. Oakley.[28] But these properties were reserved for the future, for Smith as an outstanding mining man was always careful to keep his proved ore reserves well ahead of current production.

Colemanite is a very different type of mining proposition from the ulexite gathered from marsh beds. Ulexite, as noted in Chapter 1, is classified by chemists as a double salt, sodium-calcium borate. By contrast, colemanite is one of the calcium borates. It is found in granular masses or in white or gray crystals.[29] Ulexite and the other salt-bed borates are believed by geologists to have been derived from hot springs and leaching from older deposits. As for colemanite, it is generally thought today that it was derived from the elevation and folding of salt-bed or playa deposits during the Tertiary period in geological history. Subsequent drainage over millions of years leached out the sodium borates, leaving behind zones of mineralization composed of calcium borate (colemanite), which is insoluble in water.[30]

How, then, was borax to be extracted from colemanite? Smith's initial step was to build a new refinery at West Alameda in 1889. It was a crushing, reduction, and refining plant all in one. Its most unusual feature was its mode of construction. It was the first structure in the United States to be built with reinforced concrete. It was typical of Smith's daring spirit to bet his funds on a new material. For several years he had been financing an inventor by the name of Ernest L. Ransome. The building was constructed according to Ransome's own process, which was also used to build the Ferry Building in San Francisco in 1896. Ultimately, Ransome and Smith joined forces to form the Ransome Concrete Machinery Company of Dunellen, New Jersey, as well as two producing firms.

Operations at Borate were a case of genuine underground mining, with shafts, drifts, cross-cuts, and stopes. Mineralization was not continuous, but was scattered through zones or pockets that the miners called "kidneys."[31] The colemanite was sorted by hand, then sent to the surface through shafts of depths up to 600 feet. Twenty-mule teams then hauled the ore out of the deep and crooked canyon and across a dry lake to the railhead at Daggett, 12 miles distant. After arrival at West Alameda, the ore was crushed to a fine powder and treated with a hot sodium carbonate solution. By continuous agitation the precipitated calcium carbonate was removed and the remaining solution was placed in crystallizing tanks, where the borax was crystallized on suspended wires, then recrystallized to become a finished product.

But Smith was unhappy with the operation, first because it continued to require mule teams, and second because hand-sorting was the only means of eliminating waste material ("beneficiation") at the mine, which added to the shipping cost to Alameda. In 1894, to solve the transportation problem, Smith tried out a Daniel Best

The West Alameda borax refinery as it looked about 1890. This was the first concrete building in the United States. (Fred Corkill collection.)

Borax Smith's steam tractor, "Old Dinah," at work at Borate in 1894. (Courtesy of U.S. Borax & Chemical Corporation.)

steam tractor, known locally as "Old Dinah." The experiment was a failure, although many of these machines had proved successful in lumber camps and under other more favorable conditions.[32] In any case, Borax Smith was a stubborn as well as a determined man. This time he met the need for transportation by building the Borate and Daggett, a narrow-gauge line of about eight miles in length. It was opened in 1898, and hauling power was supplied by two geared engines of the Heisler design, known respectively as the "Francis" and the "Marion."[33] Four miles from the new road's junction with the Santa Fe Railway at Daggett, the company built a modern calcining plant. This location was named Marion.

The objective of the new plant was to solve Smith's second problem, that of better ore beneficiation. The plant was based on the principle that colemanite flies apart (decrepitates) when heated. By appropriate screening, the waste rock can be separated at 1200°F, leaving the fine particles as borax freed from the calcium carbonate. The process requires a roaster to effect the decrepitation, with screening to isolate the fines.[34]

The Executive Organization of the
Pacific Coast Borax Company

At this point, it is appropriate to examine in further detail the operating organization of the Pacific Coast Borax Company in the 1890s. The head office was in San Francisco. Although it was an incorporated firm, it was a business completely dominated by a single man, F. M. Smith himself. The board of directors was composed of Borax Smith nominees because Smith held most of the voting stock. Mining and refining were entrusted to superintendents who were loyal Smith lieutenants, such as Fred Corkill, Billy Smitheram, and J. W. S. Perry. Sales were headed by Smith himself, with Joseph Mather in a similar capacity at the New York office.

In 1892 Joe Mather's son, Stephen Tyng Mather, a young man of twenty-five who worked for the *New York Sun*, had an idea that aroused Smith's interest. Stephen Mather was convinced that there was a great story in borax, and he could not understand why it had never been written. He persuaded his father with his proposal, and together they got Borax Smith to finance it. Through his newspaper connections, Steve Mather recommended a reporter named John R. Spears to do the writing. The result was Spears' *Illustrated Sketches of Death Valley and Other Borate Deserts of the Pacific Coast*, which had a major impact in its time.[35] More than that, it convinced Smith that Steve Mather would make an excellent advertising and sales-promotion manager for PCB. It was one of the best investments he ever made, for young Mather was a natural salesman, with an attractive personality, much energy, and a superb imagination. It was he who persuaded Smith to expand the package business, and to add the label "Mule Team Borax" to go with a sketch of the famous 20 already on the box.[36] Smith demurred initially, but eventually consented to adding the label "20 Mule Team Borax" to go with the famous trademark. In this way borax became a household word all over the country.

In the summer of 1894, Steve Mather and his wife traveled to California to see Borax Smith. Mather's goal was to persuade him to open a Chicago office. Smith agreed to think the proposal over, but sent him back with the question unresolved. Not long after, however, Smith wrote his approval, requesting that Mather meet him in Chicago "prepared to organize the distributing office you recommend," and enclosing $1,000 for the expenses of his California trip. Soon the new office was in business, with Mather putting on a series of successful promotions that created a large new market for borax.[37]

The future looked bright for Steve Mather, but his father took a different view. The year was 1896. Steve had sought his father's advice about buying some PCB shares, to which Joseph Mather's gloomy response was that he was "tired of Mr. Smith's style of business," that he had watched Smith invest impulsively, and that he was now "hampered for money to meet his pressing obligations." Joseph Mather then announced his retirement.[38]

Smith managed to get Steve Mather to take over the New York office long enough to train the new man, Chris Zabriskie, after which Mather would return to Chicago. Meanwhile, Thomas Thorkildsen, Stephen's Chicago assistant, would hold the fort there. The least noticed yet most important feature of the whole transaction was Joseph Mather's stern disapproval of F. M. Smith's ready reliance on short-term borrowing, for up to a point it was an accurate observation with ominous portent for the future.

Frank Smith was to lose Thorkildsen almost immediately upon Mather's return because Smith had suspected Thorkildsen of back-dating customers' bills to give them lower prices. This suspicion led to an acrimonious dispute and Thorkildsen's departure. Mather stayed on with PCB until the spring of 1903, when he suffered a nervous breakdown. In a rather thoughtless action, Smith immediately severed him from the payroll. In return, Mather wired him his resignation at the end of 1903,[39] at the same time getting off a telegram to Thorkildsen accepting a job in the latter's new borax company. This firm opened mines first at Frazer Mountain in Ventura County, California, and then at Soledad Canyon, near Lang, California. It also had a refinery in Chicago.

Relevant to this entire incident, it should be noted that even before Mather's illness, while he was still an employee of Smith's, he had arranged to borrow $10,000 from his father to invest in Thorkildsen's new borax enterprise.

Meanwhile, trade was dull during this period, and Smith decided to take a trip to Europe in 1896 in search of new markets. At its conclusion, he would be in control of a new multinational company.

The Pacific Coast Borax Company's famous photograph of the 20-Mule
Team in action in Death Valley, about 1887. (F. M. Smith collection.)

4

Creating A World Market:

Formation of Borax Consolidated, Limited

hen F. M. Smith undertook his first foray into the European market in 1896, he found himself on board the same vessel as Lewis Gerstle, a San Francisco friend and president of the Alaska Commercial Company. As it happened, Gerstle had a young nephew in London by the name of James Gerstley. James had begun his business career in the late 1880s with a wholesale firm that handled "fancy" goods as they were then called. More importantly, he also engaged in the export of small packets of boric acid.[1] About 1890, James Gerstley had met a man by the name of Richard C. Baker on a steamer en route from Canada to England. At the time, Baker was helping to finance a borax refinery in England that was to use a process developed by a Professor Iltyd Redwood. Greatly impressed by Gerstley's intelligence and his knowledge of French and German, Baker persuaded him to join the new firm of Redwood and Sons,[2] which had established a factory at Belvedere Wharf, on the south side of the Thames. Baker was also a member of the firm of Burton, Baker and Company, which manufactured a food preservative called "Preservitas."

The PCB Merger with Redwood's Chemical Works

On shipboard, Lewis Gerstle learned from Smith that he was looking for foreign markets, and thereupon offered to introduce him to his nephew James. By happy coincidence, Redwood's at that very time was searching for a new source of supply of borax and boric acid. Accordingly, a meeting was arranged among Smith, Baker, and Gerstley.[3] In the meantime, Frank and Mary R. Smith took the Orient Express to Istanbul (then Constantinople), where

44

they stayed at the Pera Palace Hotel, operated by the *Wagon Lits* Company. This excursion enabled Smith to visit the pandermite mines at Bandirma, which he saw in "a blinding snowstorm."[4] Smith always liked to keep an eye on the competition.

When Smith, Baker, and Gerstley finally met, they hit it off surprisingly well, given the sharp differences in their personalities and backgrounds. After all, Borax Smith came from virtually another culture and was used to dominating all business situations in which he participated. Baker was of the English upper class, more reserved, keenly intelligent, and inclined to be carefully analytical toward new proposals. There is reason to suppose that James Gerstley's qualities of tact, graciousness, and patience provided the essential lubricant that enabled things to move forward so smoothly.

The three men worked all day, and, it is said, throughout the night. In any case, by the end of their discussions they had reached agreement to combine their properties. Both Baker and Gerstley were new to Smith. Both were able and experienced businessmen, well endowed with common sense. On his side, Smith was always receptive to a good opportunity, and was never one given to procrastinating or brooding when important issues had to be resolved. As he himself used to say, "I am not a detail man." On the contrary, he was quick to make decisions, inclined to brush aside questions of risk, and always impatient to get going with any project to which he had committed himself.[5] Besides, he had strong incentives working in favor of the deal. Sales were slow at home and he was in need of ready cash for improvements at Borate and to pay for the completion of his elaborate Oakland mansion, Arbor Villa.

On August 26, 1896, F. M. Smith signed an agreement to convey the entire assets of Pacific Coast Borax Company to the new concern, The Pacific Borax and Redwood's Chemical Works, Limited, which held a British charter. Baker and Gerstley put in their properties, and before long the trio had become a foursome with the addition of Federico Lesser. Lesser was an able executive who brought to the new concern outstanding talents as a linguist and important connections with borax dealers in South America.

The capital structure of the company consisted of £200,000 of 6 percent preference shares at a par of £10; and £310,000 of ordinary (common) shares, also at a par of £10; for a total initial capitalization of almost $2.5 million. Moreover, first mortgage bonds of £100,000 were also provided, for future issue as needed. Among the members of the board of directors were Sir Alexander Wilson, chairman of the new company and an investment banker; R. C. Baker, who was named managing director in Europe; and F. M. Smith, who became managing director in the United States. Because of the large capitalization of Pacific Coast Borax, which of course Smith controlled, he became the majority stockholder in the London firm as well.[6]

There are reasons to believe that the promoters of the new concern had in mind the larger goal of eventual acquisition of other companies in the industry, rather than a simple consolidation of the two original ones. But this larger objective called for much more capital than could be raised at the time, given the firm's pressing needs simply to finance immediate improvements.

Their immediate goals were important enough. One was to link the PCB mines at Borate by rail with the Santa Fe. The second was to build the roaster and concentrator plant in the desert flats just outside Daggett. Third, the partners wanted to build a new refinery on the east coast, to serve most of the American market more cheaply than from Alameda. Smith, acting for the group, chose a location at Bayonne, New Jersey, arranging also to use the Ransome process of reinforced concrete for the structure.[7] Lastly, the group wanted to develop further its markets in Europe, and at the same time acquire new sources of supply to supplement the output of the Calico mines in California. Such sources already were being exploited in Turkey, Italy, Chile, and Bolivia. In addition, the new company held title to the undeveloped deposits acquired by Smith in 1890 from Coleman's trustees in bankruptcy.

The rail and reduction plant projects at Borate were initiated together. In 1898 the plant was completed, but it gave rise to technical problems that were not fully resolved until 1900.[8] Also in 1898, the railroad was extended eight miles up the canyon to Borate as a narrow-gauge line, while a third broad-gauge rail was added between Marion and Daggett.

In the same year, construction of the new refinery at Bayonne, New Jersey, was undertaken. When the project was publicly announced, rumors circulated that Smith intended to close the Alameda works entirely, but this was stoutly denied by Smith's associates. However, Smith did transfer Charles Pickett, his superintendent at Alameda, to Bayonne, where he was to supervise construction and then direct a force of 200 employees, as compared with 80 in Alameda. Note was also taken that the Tariff Act of 1896 imposed a duty of $60 a ton on imported borax, from which the immediate result was a flood of business for PCB, making the new works at Bayonne necessary for expansion.[9]

Smith estimated that Bayonne would cost $100,000, or $200,000 including land. As usual, he intended to use the most modern methods available. Thus separate electric motors would supply the driving power in place of a steam engine with a single main shaft. The ore was to be milled to a fine powder, taken by screw conveyor to the upper floor, dumped into 100-ton tanks—to which sodium carbonate would be added—and the solution would then be boiled with water. Next, it would be taken to settling tanks, and then the clear solution would be conveyed to crystallizing vats equipped with rods on which the crystals would form. After removal from the rods, the deposits would be crushed, screened, and sacked. By this time, packaged borax had come into its own, and special production lines were provided for this purpose.[10]

Another noteworthy development in this period was an earnest effort, primarily conducted by Baker, to buy up small competing companies and independently owned deposits, in places as widely distant as Bandirma, Turkey; Larderello, Italy; Arequipa, Peru; and Ascotan, Chile. Apparently Smith had some reservations about this policy, because it absorbed scarce capital; also, as he put it, "When it comes to tariff legislation these outside companies are of great assistance in securing high tariff."[11] On other occasions, however, he expressed warm approval of Baker's successes as a negotiator.

What was gradually emerging after the merger of 1896 was a large multinational company dedicated to the production and distribution of borax and its derivatives. This was to be another bit of pioneering by the partners. Given that communications were less efficient three-quarters of a century ago, the successful expansion of so widespread an enterprise was indeed remarkable. It had another consequence as well, suggesting the analogy of an eclipsing binary star system. Each star rotated about the other, both were locked together by the same forces, and to a distant observer one of the pair would be visible and dominant at one time, and the other star at another. Thus Baker and his colleagues managed corporate financing and the acquisition of new properties abroad, while Smith and Zabriskie concentrated upon the American side. Yet both sides worked well together, kept constantly in touch, and alternated in taking initiatives. The next step was obvious: a still larger combination better designed to serve all of these purposes. By January 1899, it had come into being.

Formation of Borax Consolidated, Limited

During 1898, the railroad and roaster plant at the Borate complex both had been completed, as had the new refinery at Bayonne. Seemingly it was working so well that Smith was moved to describe it enthusiastically as "a hummer" in a letter to Baker, although two more years were to pass before its break-in troubles were fully resolved. At this time Baker was concentrating his own efforts upon acquisitions of other producers. Of these, the largest was the Borax Company (formed in England in 1887), which controlled the Turkish pandermite deposits, along with the *Société Lyonnaise* and *Maison Lafitte* in France. There were also a German syndicate and two important South American properties with which Baker undertook negotiations.

As noted earlier, Smith favored these acquisitions in principle and had faith in Baker's negotiating skills, but was uneasy about the financial implications. His concern stemmed not from caution or small-mindedness, for in money matters Smith was anything but small-minded. Rather, he did not want these properties to be paid for out of dividends, or by issue of common stock that would compel the partners to share their profits. He also wanted to make sure that adequate funds would be set aside for new refineries, aggressive advertising, and research into new uses for borax.[12]

Smith's restless personality had little time for these laborious European negotiations that so fully absorbed Baker's ample energies. As Smith described the matter quite candidly, Baker's efforts involved "a class of work that you have a taste for—certainly you have a talent for. Personally, I have neither taste nor talent for arranging details of this character, in fact, I am a poor detail man anyway."[13] Nonetheless, Smith was generously endowed with managerial talents of his own, although they were of a different order. He was above all an innovator, a builder, and a producer. Financial abstractions were difficult for him to understand, continually tried his patience, and harassed him—by way of cash flow problems—throughout his business career. Handicapped throughout most of his life by eye trouble, probably deriving from muscular imbalance, he could not spend much time on documents of any kind.

To understand Smith's real abilities, one need refer only to his success in becoming the world's major borax producer by 1890— less than 20 years after he entered the industry.

Table 2 (below) provides evidence of the growth of the American borax industry during the period of his leadership, when his companies accounted for probably 85 percent of the national output. Between 1873, when Smith had his first full year of production, and 1890, when Pacific Coast Borax was formed, he brought down the implicit price by 74 percent per pound. Here was felt the full impact of his advance to dominance in the industry. By achieving something very close to a domestic monopoly, Smith was steadily driving down the price of his product through a powerful combination of technological improvements, exploitation of richer deposits, development of a world market, increased production and sales, and outstanding leadership. To be sure, the price became relatively stable between 1890 and 1898, but at the same time total output increased by 68.4 percent. Obviously, Smith was neither restricting production nor pushing up price in these years. On the contrary, he was using a temporarily monopolistic position to build up a large industry.

Smith could be a very tough negotiator. For example, in 1898 he drove the Santa Fe Railway into cutting tonnage rates from $8 to

Table 2
Production of Refined Borax in the
United States, Selected Years, 1873—1898

Year	Production (short tons)	Total Value	Value Per Pound
1873	1,000	$ 500,000	$0.250
1880	1,846	280,000	0.087
1890	4,750	620,000	0.065
1891	6,690	870,000	0.065
1892	6,750	900,000	0.066
1893	4,350	650,000	0.075
1894	7,340	970,000	0.066
1895	5,959	600,000	0.050
1896	6,754	680,000	0.050
1897	8,000	1,080,000	0.066
1898	8,000	1,120,000	0.070

Source: Department of the Interior, United States Geological Survey, Mineral Resources of the United States, 1915, Part II, "Nonmetals" (Washington: Government Printing Office, 1917), p. 1017.

$7.50 to New York or Galveston, regardless of ultimate destination. His purpose here was to throw dust into the eyes of the Santa Fe traffic managers, distracting their attention to forestall an eventual demand for higher rates once the road had learned that PCB was diverting its shipments from Alameda to Bayonne. At the same time, he took care to direct the attention of the Santa Fe people to the large new furnace he had ordered shipped into Marion over their line, describing it with much detail but leaving out its real purpose, which was to concentrate the ore more intensively. The reason for the omission? Greater beneficiation of the ore would increase its value per ton, and the higher value would supply the Santa Fe with grounds for raising its rates to the company.[14]

Because PCB again enjoyed tariff protection with the Republican resurgence in 1896, Smith became keenly sensitive to imports coming from cheap foreign sources, particularly those involving re-export of borates initially sold to Europe below the American price. During the early part of 1898 he worried over the activities of a large American chemical company; he suspected them of buying substantial quantities in London for re-export to the United States. Repeatedly he warned, even ordered, Baker not to sell that company any product, and not to give any credence to its threats that it would develop its own borax properties either in South America or in the United States unless Pacific Borax would sell it crude borax in London instead of in the United States. Smith well knew, through his scouts and by his own observation, every significant deposit in North and South America. Thus he could detect a bluff immediately, as in this case. He could, therefore, dictate his own terms: the type of borax he would sell (fully refined), the monthly rate at which he would provide it, and, of course, the price. It goes without saying that the buyer was also compelled to take delivery of American borax exclusively. This coup made a profound impression upon Baker. Borax Smith revealed his business philosophy when, with unreserved candor, he wrote to Baker the following:

> You will probably think the position I have taken rather an aggressive one, but the final result will show that my position is the true and correct one. My policy and conviction with borax has always been aggressive, and, I have believed, correspondingly successful. I believe in this business it pays to fight, and I believe when you come to see matters as they exist here, and as expressed above, you will quite agree with me.[15]

Early in June 1898, F. M. Smith and his family left Oakland for their annual summer stay at their home on Shelter Island, New York. By this time, Baker had already started on the complex task of acquiring new subsidiaries and organizing and financing a new and much larger company to take over Pacific Borax. Smith himself planned to go to London in September or October, on the expectation that the successor company would then be in place or could be put in place soon after his arrival. His letters during these intervening months reflect a concern over the lack of a market for his preference shares, which he evidently hoped to sell to raise fresh capital for his now numerous as well as diverse business ventures. As he put it himself, "I have abundant use for funds personally; in fact, I took up some improvements, thinking there was no question about our having a market for the preferred . . ."[16] On the very next day he wrote Baker again, proposing formation of a syndicate to take over a block of the preferred so that he would be able to "fulfill my engagements."[17]

Baker's response evidently expressed some concern at Smith's desire to sell, for we find Smith reassuring him that he did not intend to sell a large amount, although he had had "a good many demands upon me this last year" and also wished to be prepared if "an unusually large demand" should come up.[18] As usual, Smith was encountering cash flow problems. The underlying reason was that he was buying up four street railway companies in Oakland and developing a huge land syndicate as well.

In late September, Smith wrote Baker that he planned to sail for Europe—possibly on October 11—on what he called the "Big William," referring to the steamship *Kaiser Wilhelm der Grosse*. His party was to include Mrs. Smith, their adopted daughter, Marion, and Miss Evelyn K. Ellis, Mary Smith's private secretary.[19] The Smith party landed in Europe by mid-October and then began a month's tour of Western Europe. On this trip they ordered Aubusson tapestries and carpets of custom design, and acquired some antique French furniture for their new Oakland home, Arbor Villa.

This pleasant diversion came to an abrupt end on November 22, 1898, in Paris, when Smith received a letter from Baker, written the previous day, providing an extensive explanation for further necessary delays in organizing the new successor company, the advent of which Smith was anxiously awaiting. Apparently the major irritant to Borax Smith was the prospect of an indefinite further delay, together with a request from the lawyers that valuations be disclosed for each of the components of the blocks of assets that each partner contributed. This infuriated Smith, leading him to say that he now wanted "to do my financing on new lines" and to "drop the whole business outside of what we have committed ourselves to."[20] After expecting to have the new company functioning by October when he returned, Smith complained, he now was told that the consummation might not take place until January.

Evidently Baker managed to cool Smith down in some fashion, and after a futile search of Paris for a Thanksgiving turkey dinner, Smith and his party left for Vienna, planning to proceed from there to Venice and Rome. In a letter to Baker just before Christmas, Smith now referred to news from Baker that the financing would be completed early in January, expressing his desire to be in London at that time and "to get hold of some money before I return . . ."[21] Perhaps deliberately, because of Baker's recognition of Smith's problem, Baker sold some of the old preference shares just before receiving Smith's letter from Rome.[22] Baker was an astute and perceptive man who depended upon the good will and cooperation of his highly individualistic and somewhat temperamental majority stockholder. Unless he could placate Smith, the whole enterprise would be in jeopardy. Also, Smith had been gone from Oakland, the seat of his business operations, for some seven months. Thus it was not unreasonable for him to be impatient with all these delays, all the more so because those operations required money and constant attention.

Borax Consolidated, Limited, came into being in January 1899. The company was capitalized at £2.4 million sterling, or just under $12 million, of which £2.2 million in securities was to be raised immediately after incorporation, and £200,000 was to be held in reserve. The capital structure consisted of £600,000 in voting common shares; £800,000 of 5.5 percent cumulative preferred; and £1 million in first mortgage debentures at 4.5 percent, of which £800,000 was issued upon formation of the company.

Control, obviously, lay with the common, or "ordinary," shares. These represented 25 percent of total capitalization and thus enjoyed considerable leverage. Smith, of course, was the majority holder. The partners also acquired portions of the preferred and the debentures, which gave them a source of future financial liquidity through their sale without impairing their voting control. Significantly, none of the common was offered for sale, while more than half of the preferred and of the debentures were placed on the market. The remainder of these securities were used to pay for acquisitions of independent concerns and for assets turned in by the partners themselves.[23]

Thus began a multinational company that today has marked its 80th year of existence. Its founders had built well, but at the outset of 1899 many problems confronted them. They had to coordinate activities over what were then vast distances. Their principal source of supply, Borate, was beginning to show signs of playing out. A choice had to be made of the next deposit to develop, and this was most likely to call for a return to the Death Valley region, which had not been seriously exploited since Harmony closed down in 1888. But re-entry into the valley on a scale comparable to the great camp at Borate posed transportation problems not hitherto encountered.

Organizational Structure, 1899–1914

As BCL began its corporate life in 1899, the central fact of its existence was that Borax Smith owned a majority of the voting stock. This gave him the ultimate powers of the initiative and the veto on all major questions, although he usually deferred to Baker on financial matters, and also sought his advice on many other questions as well. Smith had entered BCL with a large going concern in the United States. Here was the company's biggest source of supply and largest contributor of income and profit. Moreover, Smith had long since built up a large group of executives, many of them old associates loyal to their chief.

On the production side at Borate and Marion, Smith had the services of the senior Fred Corkill, a member of the original Nevada Circle and the kind of exceptional mining engineer who could develop as well as exploit mines. The operating superintendent at Borate was Billy Smitheram, who had also come down from Nevada to join Smith, and who succeeded J.W.S. Perry, the original manager at Harmony. There was John Ryan, limited in professional education but highly intelligent, and capable of running the plant at Marion, of finding and evaluating new sources of ore, and of directing the construction of a major railroad. Associated with him on frequent assignments from Borax Smith was John Roach, superintendent of the roaster at Marion and a good friend of the Corkills. Less talented than Ryan, Roach was very capable around mines or in staking and testing claims. He, too, had originally joined Smith in Nevada. In addition, there was Clarence Rasor, who

John Ryan, F. M. Smith's right-hand man for over 40 years, quenches his thirst. The locale is probably Death Valley in the 1890s. (Fred Corkill collection.)

worked at Borate, would have much to do with laying out the company's 174-mile Tonopah and Tidewater Railroad, and eventually was to become chief engineer for American operations.

Besides the two refineries at Alameda and Bayonne, Smith maintained three sets of offices for marketing and financial purposes. The head office in 1899 was in San Francisco, at 101 Sansome Street, where it remained until the earthquake and fire in April 1906. After that catastrophe, Smith transferred it to the Albany Block in Oakland, and about 1912 to the new Syndicate Building in that East Bay city, which Smith had had built to house his now-extensive group of enterprises.

Buckboard on the way to Greenland, Death Valley, in the 1890s. John Ryan was probably the driver. (Courtesy of U.S. Borax & Chemical Corporation.)

In order of priority, the second office was in New York, under the charge of Chris Zabriskie. Third was the Chicago office, headed by Steve Mather, who did a remarkable job of developing the household package trade.

This is the major outline of the American organization at the time BCL was formed. At its head was F. M. Smith himself, who enjoyed certain advantages over Baker. He had voting control of the company. He possessed an outstanding group of associates, all of them with many years in his service. Sheer geographic distance both weakened the cohesiveness of BCL in London, because of the slowness of communications in that day, and necessarily enlarged

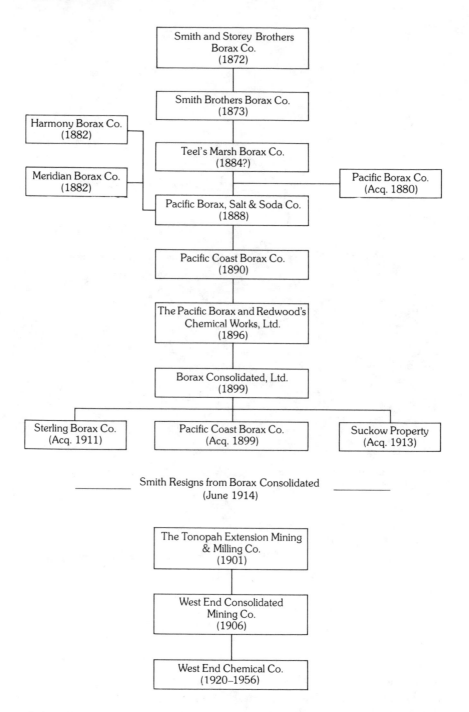

Fig. 1. Corporate History of Borax and Silver Mining Companies Controlled by F. M. Smith, 1872–1931.

the discretion available to the American group. In Borax Smith the American side had a leader who had enjoyed a free hand from the time he had entered the industry. Smith was very much the classical figure of the commanding, risk-taking entrepreneur. He was not about to change the habits of a lifetime simply upon the emergence of BCL. Meanwhile, his British co-manager, R. C. Baker, who was the actual administrator of Borax Consolidated, was compelled to depend for his information upon the mails (letters took at least two weeks each way), coded cables for urgent matters, and an annual tour of the American properties.

Clearly, communications were a handicap for Baker in managing the central office of a multinational company. However, despite the nearly autonomous character of Smith's management of the American operations, it must be noted that in the ensuing 15 years before Smith resigned from BCL and its subsidiary, PCB, Baker compiled an impressive record of accomplishments.

From the opening stages of the relationship between Borax Smith and R. C. Baker, a theme in Smith's letters reflects his customary assumptions of complete autonomy; indeed, his desire to preserve and extend it. This theme manifested itself in diverse ways. One of them was Smith's proposal that he attempt to acquire control of Stauffer Chemical Company. In broaching the idea, he went on to speak of "gathering in" properties in the United States, doing so in his own name and on his own responsibility, with BCL to take them over afterward "if they choose."[24]

A little over a year later Smith brought up another idea: that a new American company be created to take over his interest in BCL and the PCB portion of BCL's assets. In Smith's view, this would not affect Borax Consolidated itself, but would provide him with collateral for borrowing purposes. Smith would then control the new holding company, which in turn would control BCL. In this way Smith could reduce his actual investment without loss of control.[25] What he seems to have had in mind was a form of "pyramiding" by means of holding companies. A year later, Smith raised the same proposal a second time, adding that he would go forward only if Baker were fully in accord and if it would involve no hardship for the English side.[26] In a somewhat fuller elaboration, Smith described what today would be called a holding company that would deal in stocks of other borax companies, in that way exerting control without full ownership.[27] By the end of 1901, he again modified his proposal: why not move BCL headquarters to New York City? This would put the company in the center of the world's money market, and it ought to make no difference to Baker whether he lived in New York City or in London—or so Smith thought.[28]

Baker seems not to have been enthusiastic about any of the various versions of Smith's idea, so his superior ceased to press the matter beyond suggesting that an American company could be useful in taking over "the large holdings" (presumably his own) of BCL common stock. This would enable Smith to raise additional fresh capital, which probably was his primary purpose all along.[29]

The theme of autonomy asserted itself for Smith in another form toward the end of 1899. He had disclosed rather abruptly to Baker that he had been lending PCB's surplus funds on the call loan market, making good returns in this way. As he described it, the loans went to himself, to certain Oakland associates, and to banks. Following the advice of Lafayette Hoyt DeFriese, BCL's able legal counsel, who happened to be in town, Smith proposed that the BCL board pass a resolution authorizing him to make short-term loans with company funds, because such loans would earn more returns. Given the possible conflict-of-interest problems implicit in these actions, particularly under English company law, DeFriese must have urged the directors' resolution as a means of protecting all concerned. However, Smith could see no problems in their granting him "as free a hand in this direction as possible."[30]

Baker seems to have resisted this proposal, for in his next letter Smith told him that he had not wished to embarrass the board, and had not known that his proposed discretionary resolution allowing short-term lending or surplus funds, including anticipated forthcoming dividends, would make the directors personally responsible for any losses incurred.[31]

The ultimate fate of F. M. Smith's proposed resolution is unknown. However, in a letter written in 1904, Smith refers to the requirements of the BCL board as regards his accounting procedures, adding that "I realize that I have drifted away from the exactness required by English auditors. However, all loans and advances have been and are abundantly secured, as the statement will show."[32] Apparently the board did not prohibit Smith's lending policy, but did insist upon adequate security and full disclosure. In any event, the statement shows loans totalling $600,000 in 1904, involving a 60-day demand note of $250,000 to Oakland Transit Consolidated; a 60-day demand note of $150,000 to San Francisco, Oakland and San Jose Railway (Key Route); $50,000 to Henry Wadsworth (another Nevada associate now involved in Smith's Oakland ventures), secured by 1,000 shares of Realty Syndicate stock (par value $100); $50,000 to Ernest A. Heron against a 60-day demand note for $50,000; and $100,000 to Frank C. Havens against a 60-day demand note for $100,000.[33] Wadsworth was a director of Smith's traction properties in Oakland, while Heron was president of the traction companies, and Havens was both a director and Smith's closest associate in the Realty Syndicate. Heron's and Havens' notes, Smith stated, were fully secured at over double their value.

Borax Smith's endless pursuit of autonomy within the otherwise rather conservative precincts of BCL was due to his remarkable abundance of energy, his lively imagination, and his unappeasable hunger to expand and diversify his business interests. His more cautious British colleagues simply had never encountered a man like this and doubtless had plenty of trouble trying to understand him. His predominant traits imposed upon him an insatiable need for more liquid capital. Put a little differently, his personal net working capital was usually perilously thin. He never seemed to have found a substantial alternative to massive and increasing short-term borrowing as a means, albeit temporary, of protecting his solvency in the pursuit of further expansion, despite the large and continuing increases in his total wealth and net worth, year after year. The basic problem from which he suffered throughout his career in business was lack of liquidity, brought on by the method of financing upon which he chose to rely. More than this, Smith was an individualist in the classic mold. His activities were wholly inner-directed.

As his brother-in-law, Norman P. Ellis (who was very close to F. M. Smith in his last years and who understood him unusually well), once described him, he was "a borrowing capitalist," a man who built great ventures largely upon short-term finance and who regularly "sweated blood" at the end of each year as his notes fell due.[34] His failure to develop adequate permanent financing for his many different enterprises was ultimately to prove his undoing. But if finance was Borax Smith's Achilles Heel, his qualities of farsighted vision, his abilities as a builder, and his capacity for imaginative synthesis through which he could assemble the parts into the whole—these were the factors that made him great.

5

Borax Consolidated, Limited:

The Period of Control by F. M. Smith
in the United States

With the exception of two families, those of Fred Corkill and "Wash" (William Washington) Cahill, the great camp at Borate was an all-male community. Rough board and batten buildings and even caves served as housing in that bleak, dry, and rugged country. When F. M. Smith made his frequent visits to Borate, he took his meals with the Corkills.

One of the peculiarities of Borate was a white, shingled structure perched high upon a hill above Mule Canyon and tied down at all four corners by stout guy wires against the stiff winds coming off the Mojave desert. It was called "Smith House" because it served the top man as the traditional guest house found in isolated mining camps as accommodations for important visitors. Borax Smith was a frequent and regular visitor because he liked to keep a watchful eye on all of his properties.

Soon after Smith's return to the United States following the establishment of BCL in January 1899, and after a very rough Atlantic crossing on the *Majestic*, he undertook a lengthy inspection trip, first to Borate, then up to the hillside colemanite claims in Death Valley, then on out to Rhodes Marsh in Nevada, and home at last via Reno. In those days, Smith usually traveled by buckboard, stopping at dry camps set up by Ryan or Roach. If he were in a hurry, he would use relays of horses. On this trip it was buckboard all the way to Nevada, where he could board a Carson and Colorado train for the trip north to Reno. The C and C was usually called the "Slim Princess" by local residents because it was narrow gauge. Chris Zabriskie had worked as a relief telegrapher on this road at Belleville in the 1880s.

Ore bin for No. 1 hoist at Pacific Coast Borax Company's mines at Borate, California, in the Calico Mountains. About 1898. (Fred Corkill collection.)

Borate in the 1890s. White building at upper right is the Smith House, while the house at upper center was occupied by the Fred Corkill family. (Fred Corkill collection.)

Looking down the canyon from Fred Corkill's house (immediate foreground), Borate, about 1894. (Vernon J. Sappers collection.)

The Decline of Borate Begins

By 1900 the underground workings at Borate had reached the 600-foot level and there was some concern that the property might be beginning to be worked out.[1] Hints at this possibility began to appear in Smith's letters to Baker following his trip in February

1899. He found the mine looking poor in some places and better in others.[2] In March 1899, he wrote Baker at much greater length, providing a thorough review of the problem of ore supply, together with his proposals for long-term future development of new sources of borates. Here Borax Smith demonstrated his abilities as a mining man. He began by noting the "immense demand" upon the property at Borate. No mine should be overtaxed, for if it were, known reserves would be drawn down and shortages would necessarily follow until mine development could catch up with the excessive extraction rate. At Borate, Smith noted, four different openings (shafts or drifts) were currently being worked. If the quantity and quality of their yield should decline simultaneously, the mine superintendent would become upset by inadequate production, and problems of swelling ground and crushed timbering would also follow. Smith concluded:

> My idea is that we should make the other developments from other properties, so as not too largely [to] tax any one property, even though the profits were not quite as large as they would be when the ore is taken from Daggett [Borate]. In fact, we should begin to look toward Death Valley . . .[3]

The roaster and calciner plant at Marion, near Borate, about 1898. The Heisler locomotive at center was the "Francis" of the Borate & Daggett RR. (Fred Corkill collection.)

A 20-mule team hard at work, at Borate about 1894. (Courtesy of the Nevada Historical Society.)

Another view of a mule team at work at Borate in the Calico Mountains, about 1894. (Vernon J. Sappers collection.)

He went on to reassure Baker by citing good things about the mine, yet injected the observation that average ore value had declined, and that there was an "enormous" amount of richer colemanite at the company's claims on the west side of the Greenwater Range, overlooking Death Valley. All that was needed to open up these deposits was a railroad to bring out the borax.

Almost exactly a year later, following another visit to Borate, Smith returned to this theme: the mine was being overtaxed to maintain a high rate of output. Accordingly, ore values were declining.[4] This time, however, he urged that the Lila C mine should be developed because it "is an exceptionally good one" and it was only 135 miles from the railhead on the Ivanpah (formerly Manvel) branch of the Santa Fe.[5] He then buttressed his argument with a detailed description of the visible ore body. Two months later he returned to the theme, describing the "Lila C and Ash Meadows" as

Train with Heisler engine at work on the Borate & Daggett, transloading borax to a Santa Fe boxcar, about 1894. The engine was named for Borax Smith. (Vernon J. Sappers collection.)

"a great property" with very high ore values. Once BCL was fully established and monetary conditions favorable in England, "we ought to take hold of this proposition."[6] Two years later he wrote Baker that although the Borate properties looked good, timber and roaster costs had gone considerably higher, while "The quality of the ore is far inferior to the Lila C colemanite." He closed by referring to the valuable silver discoveries at Tonopah, which "sooner or later" would bring in a railroad.[7]

During this period Smith was developing doubts about how long Borate could serve as a primary source of ore supply. As a prudent mining man he was always concerned about available known reserves. Because the ore at Borate was uneven in quality and scattered in "strings" and "kidneys," the reserve question constantly reasserted itself. Borax Smith's reasoning moved naturally to the second stage: the Lila C ought to be developed without delay

A close-up of the "Francis," one of the Heisler locomotives operated by Borax Smith's Borate & Daggett Railroad to haul colemanite from the mines at Borate to the calcining plant at Marion. About 1898. (Courtesy of U.S. Borax & Chemical Corporation.)

because it afforded a large supply of colemanite and was the most accessible of the company's sites except for Borate itself. Hence the third step in his thinking: provision of transportation for bringing out the product at competitive costs.

It was Smith himself who deserved the credit for diagnosing the problem, then pushing the company into providing a full solution. Moreover, that solution was to establish Smith as the man most responsible for opening up Death Valley to the world.

Development of the Lila C Mine

During 1903 and 1904, Borax Smith sent both John Ryan and Fred Corkill to the Lila C deposit at Old Ryan to prepare careful estimates of the size of the ore body, its mining characteristics, its ore values, and costs of extraction in that particular location. The general finding was that the Lila C could serve as a replacement for Borate, had a prospective life of six years, but posed a serious transportation problem. An official report of the U.S. Geological Survey for 1906 described the Lila C as a colemanite vein some 2,000 feet in length, from six to eight feet wide and very steeply inclined. Between 1903 and 1906, the company had opened 3,000

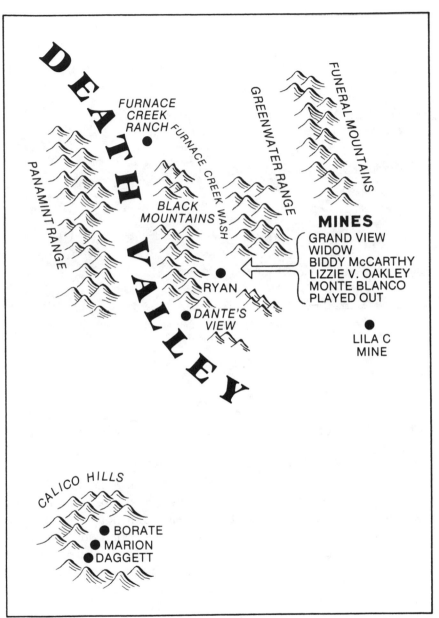

MAP 3. Later Borax mining operations developed by F. M. Smith in Death Valley region and at Borate (1890-1914). Not to scale.

Old Ryan and the Lila C mine, near Death Valley Junction, about 1907. The railroad was a branch of F. M. Smith's Tonopah & Tidewater. (Fred Corkill collection.)

feet of shafts and drifts, blocking out enough ore to provide an annual output of 30,000 short tons of high grade borates for some years to come.[8]

Smith put Fred Corkill in charge of the mill and roaster when the mine began production in June 1907, and assigned Billy Smitheram to serve as mine superintendent. By this time a seven-mile railroad was under construction from Death Valley Junction to the Lila C, and in August 1907, the main line of the Tonopah and Tidewater Railroad was opened for connection between Death Valley Junction and the Santa Fe at Ludlow. By 1908 the big camp of Borate, after serving since 1890 as PCB's primary source of production, had been abandoned.

Ore extraction at the Lila C was accomplished by means of five inclined shafts. However, the ore body, while rich in average value, proved to be shallow, with a maximum depth of only 300 feet.[9] After hand-sorting to cull the best ore, the remainder was crushed in the mill and then passed through rotary roasters to decrepitate the ore, which yielded a fine flour for shipment.[10]

Hand-sorted borax awaiting shipment from the Lila C, about 1907. (Fred Corkill collection.)

So pressing was the need for a new supply of ore to replace the declining production at Borate that the company had started production at the Lila C in June 1907, before overland railroad connections had been completed. For two months Smith returned to the use of 20-mule teams to haul the Lila C borates south about 30 miles to the T&T railhead at the station of Zabriskie.[11] As ever, the faithful animals performed reliably. Presumably, they had been kept at pasture or for odd jobs at Borate. When they ended their duties at the Lila C in August 1907, their hard task was finished forever, although the company continued until 1940 to use the teams for advertising purposes at various events around the country.

Because of its shallow depth, the Lila C was destined to be a short-lived mine, lasting barely seven years. But once again Borax Smith proved equal to the problem, for among the Coleman claims acquired by him in 1890 was the rich scattering of hillside deposits overlooking Death Valley, discovered in 1882–83, and examined by him at that time, and again with more care in 1899 and 1900. It remained for Smith to solve the transportation problem in the Death Valley country.

Smith Becomes a Railroad Builder

When Borate began in 1890, F. M. Smith had been compelled to revive the 20-mule teams for the 12-mile haul to Daggett. As noted earlier, in 1894 he had bought a Daniel Best steam tractor in hopes of supplanting the teams. But Old Dinah, as the tractor was called, could not negotiate the steep grades and sandy tracks that the sure-footed mules could readily overcome, so the tractor was put aside. The teams had staved off technological unemployment for a few more years.

As Borate began to show signs of exhaustion after 1900, Smith began bombarding Baker with various transportation proposals, all with a view toward making mining at the Lila C feasible while keeping PCB free of exclusive dependence upon any single railroad company. These proposals included a standard or narrow gauge railroad, steam tractors, and even a monorail. The starting point of Borax Smith's thinking was an anemic little railroad known as the California Eastern, which took off from the Santa Fe at Goffs (then called Blake) and ran to Barnwell, about 29 miles northwest. About 1901 the Santa Fe obtained the line and extended it to Ivanpah. Probably the new owners viewed their acquisition as a way to divert the route of the San Pedro, Los Angeles and Salt Lake Railroad, which Senator William Andrews Clark, the copper magnate, was planning to build.

To F. M. Smith the obvious move would be to build a railroad from the Lila C to a point called Manvel, which had been the terminus of the Santa Fe branch before its extension to Ivanpah.[12] Perhaps his idea seemed too expensive to his English partners, or, equally possible, he had simply returned to his earlier notion of steam tractors, for a year later he was writing Baker about the savings from using tractors and a graded road that eventually could be converted to a railroad.[13] Nothing happened for another year, when again Smith urged that BCL consider either a railroad or a "steam wagon road" from the Lila C to a mainline connection somewhere.[14] A few months later he came down hard on the need for a railroad from the mine to the Ivanpah branch, proposing that BCL take up the question seriously, and suggesting that a decision be reached by fall 1902.[15]

Given that Smith was putting on the pressure for some kind of solution to the transportation problem, we can only surmise that his English colleagues were still not ready to undertake the heavy financial commitment involved. But Borax Smith was stubborn and a man of strong will. Either he wrung consent out of London or just went ahead on his own, for by summer 1903, he wrote Baker that he was building a "traction road" (hard-surfaced road) between the Lila C and Ivanpah. He then went on to describe a new type of tractor, to be driven by a gasoline engine, that would generate electric power to be conveyed to motors geared to the rear wheels of the borax wagons—essentially the modern principle of diesel-electric traction.[16]

Unfortunately for Smith, this so-called "Gibbs engine" had yet to be designed and tested. When it was, it proved impracticable. It was now early 1904. Having spent $100,000 on the traction road, Smith turned back to the Best steam tractor, hoping that this time it would work, given a proper roadbed. So Old Dinah was refurbished at Borate, shipped to Ivanpah by rail, greeted there by John Ryan, and put on the ground. Wagons were attached. After firing up, it started off with its load of empties trailing behind. Fourteen miles out, at State Line Pass, the engine blew out a boiler flue and the experiment was over.[17]

But Borax Smith was no quitter. He had now proved his case for either a railroad or for some feasible substitute. This time his tack was to propose building an independent railroad with "dummies" on its board of directors to conceal the real control, guarantee it the borax traffic at rates favorable to BCL, and have BCL guarantee the line's bonds, so that they would be salable.[18] Finally Baker was won over, for Smith now wrote of his pleasure at getting Baker's "hearty approval" of the railroad project. He then disclosed that the new road was already being incorporated in New Jersey. It was to be called the Tonopah and Tidewater Railroad, to which Smith added the query, "How does that sound, broad enough, is it not?"[19] On July 19, 1904, the new road received its charter. However, the big question was still to be answered: What route would it take?

At the outset there were two possibilities: a line southeast from the Lila C to Ivanpah, or a line straight south to Ludlow, a siding on the Santa Fe 121 miles south of what later was to be called Death Valley Junction. At this point matters became somewhat obscure. Smith chose the Ludlow route and arranged for rails and ties to be dumped at Siding 10 (later called Crucero) on the Clark road to Salt Lake, about 30 miles north of Ludlow. He also began to run surveys for the preferred route. It can be inferred from his letters as well as from his penchant for expansion that Borax Smith had the boom camps of Bullfrog, Rhyolite, Goldfield, and Tonopah very much on his mind as potential sources of freight and as ultimate destinations for the new T&T. Hence the choice for Ludlow, which was much closer to "Tidewater" (Los Angeles) than Goffs (formerly Blake).

F. M. Smith's business instincts were right. A railroad was essential, but in that isolated and desolate country it could well be a loser unless it could augment its borax freight. The only way to do this was to build to the booming gold and silver camps. One evening in April 1905, fate intervened to alter the whole course of events. F. M. Smith had chosen to dine alone at the Pacific Union Club in San Francisco. Following dinner he lighted his usual cigar, with its toothpick in the inner end, and started to relax over a brandy. By sheer chance he encountered a fellow millionaire whom he knew fairly well. He was William Andrews Clark, U.S. Senator from Montana, copper magnate and currently builder of the San Pedro-Salt Lake railroad. The two men sat down for a visit. Clark began with an enthusiastic account of his vision of the future of Southern California and the role his new line would play in it. In response Smith observed with what perhaps was only seeming modesty that he, too, was building a railroad, a small affair that would run north from Ludlow on the Santa Fe to the Lila C.

The scene must have been rather like a poker game in the Old West, for neither man was entirely without guile in business dealings. Indeed, Clark already knew that Smith had incorporated the T&T nearly a year before, and the very name itself suggested, as the borax king intended it should, that he had no mere short line in mind. Perhaps Clark hoped to forestall Smith's construction, for reasons of his own. Alternatively, his purpose may have been to add to his new road the borax traffic soon to come from the Lila C.

Whatever Clark's motive, he proposed that Smith forget about Ludlow and, instead, build northwest from the new town of Las Vegas. The route to the Lila C would be shorter. It would pass through open country all the way, reducing both construction and operating costs. And it would be quicker to build. Smith reacted with a seemingly sincere enthusiasm. Soon the two men had laid out a route on paper. Then Smith began to display reluctance, mentioning his deal with the Santa Fe for the supply of rails and ties at a favorable price. After suitable hesitation, Clark agreed to match the other road's terms, adding a special tonnage rate for borates as well. Smith thought he had an oral contract, shook hands on it, and set out for his home in Oakland.[20]

Within a month Borax Smith sent John Ryan, Clarence Rasor, and Wash Cahill to Las Vegas, where they put up a tent for living quarters and began assembling a construction crew. Their plan was to set up a camp at Corn Creek Ranch, 20 miles west, and then to start grading from there in both directions. Work was to begin at Las Vegas so that a connection could be made with Clark's road. In this way track could be laid northwest to carry construction trains bringing in carloads of supplies from the main line.

However, when the Smith crew began preparations to install the connecting switch, Clark's chief counsel, C. O. Whittemore, emerged from a nearby private car to read the group a legal document that turned out to be not a written version of the Clark-Smith verbal agreement, but an order not to trespass on the right of way of the Clark road.

Meanwhile, Smith himself had not been idle, for he seems to have been expecting something of the kind. After Clark had failed to send him a written agreement for signing, Smith had an investigation made, probably by Chris Zabriskie in New York. It revealed that the Senator had been touring Europe and now was en route home. Smith immediately sent John Ryan, who could think clearly as well as argue brilliantly, to confront Clark when he landed. In no time at all Ryan found his man. Like the bulldog he was, Ryan soon extracted from Clark the admission that in his opinion Smith and he had made no contract that evening at the Pacific Union Club, and that while touring Europe the idea had suddenly come to him that he might as well build northwest himself, which would force Smith to turn over his borax traffic at a connection close by the Lila C. Thus was born Clark's Las Vegas and Tonopah Railroad.

Even before the "trespass" incident in August 1905, there had been signs of what Burr Belden has accurately called "an historic double-cross."[21] Clark had begun months before by organizing the Nevada Rapid Transit Company to build a hard-surfaced auto road parallel to Smith's intended route. Then, when T&T supplies began arriving in Las Vegas, the shipping rates turned out to be much higher than those promised by Clark in his meeting with Smith. By October 1905, Clark finally showed his hand, by starting construction of the LV&T. On October 26, 1907, the line was finally completed to Goldfield.[22]

Upon Clark's disclosures to Ryan—virtually at the gangplank in New York Harbor—the tough little Irishman at once wired the news to Smith in San Francisco. Borax Smith, too, had been educated in the hard school of the mining camps of the Old West. Accordingly, he proceeded at once to make an agreement with the Santa Fe for the Ludlow connection, railroad construction supplies, and eventually, through passenger and freight service when his road was completed.

What was the explanation for Clark's singular behavior in this curious episode? The more cynical hypothesis would be that his real purpose at the Pacific Union Club was simply to stall Smith's railroad-building from either Ludlow or Las Vegas—dangling before him the prospect of a cheaper version of the mainline rail connection that he already knew Smith had to have. Delay obviously would work in Clark's favor; he had a reputation as a crafty operator, and so this explanation cannot be rejected. The second possibility is that Clark had made his original deal in good faith because it would provide shipments for his traffic-starved new road. Later, after he had begun thinking about the boom camps of Bullfrog, Rhyolite, and Goldfield—all at their height in early 1905—along with the already well-established silver mines at Tonopah, the Senator concluded that much traffic was to be had there. Why give it to Borax Smith when he could build his own road and even get there first?

Although this breach of trust gave Clark the advantage over Smith, it was only temporary, for the T&T already enjoyed through connections to both Goldfield and Rhyolite, established with completion of the Bullfrog Goldfield Railroad at Gold Center, on June 18, 1907. Even this modest gain seems to have given Clark a twinge of conscience, for he directed officials of the Salt Lake road to repay Smith $30,000, to cover money expended and for the abandoned grade out of Las Vegas.[23] But Frank Smith was unforgiving—the T&T was strictly a Santa Fe affiliate for as long as he was associated with BCL, so far as traffic exchanges were concerned. He was to enjoy further revenge in 1914, when the LV&T gave up its line from Beatty to Goldfield, leaving the route to the Bullfrog Goldfield Railroad—a T&T affiliate. Smith's revenge was complete when in 1918 the LV&T abandoned the rest of its line, between Las Vegas and Beatty, although by this time the event was purely symbolic. Borax Smith was by then no longer in either the borax or the railroad business.[24]

Whatever the explanation for this melancholy affair, Smith's problem now was how to build the T&T before Borate was ex-

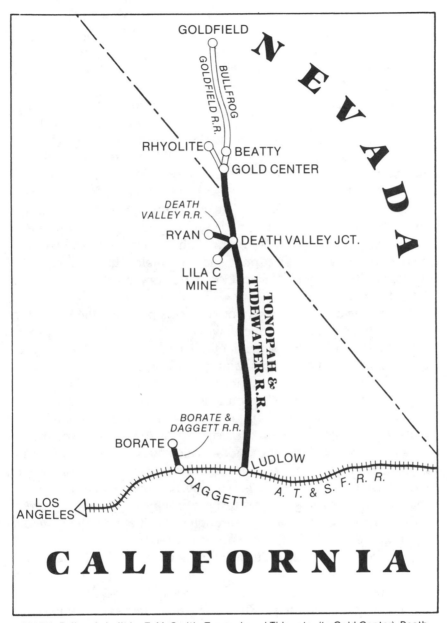

MAP 4. Railroads built by F. M. Smith: Tonopah and Tidewater (to Gold Center), Death Valley, and Borate and Daggett—1894-1914. Segments between Gold Center and Rhyolite and between Gold Center and Goldfield operated by Tonopah and Tidewater after 1908. Scale: approximately 1 inch = 65 miles.

hausted. Again Ryan, Rasor, and Cahill were the field generals in charge. Construction began in November 1905, at Ludlow, where the company's shops and general offices were to be located. The first 78 miles to Sperry were fairly routine going. Then came the extremely difficult and costly 12 miles through Amargosa Canyon to the Tecopa district, followed again by easy going to Death Valley Junction and the branch to the Lila C. By November 1907, the T&T was completed to Gold Center, two miles south of Beatty, Nevada. About six months earlier, on June 18, 1907, the Bullfrog Goldfield had been completed to Beatty, with a line south to Gold Center and a branch to Rhyolite.[25] Thus the Smith road and the BG made their connection at Gold Center. The BG provided the T&T with a through connection north. It had been built by the Bullfrog Syndicate, a group headed by John and Arthur Brock of Philadelphia. It also controlled the Tonopah and Goldfield Railroad and the Tonopah Mining and Milling Company, operators of Tonopah's largest mine.

Within a year the Bullfrog boom had collapsed and the BG was in financial difficulties. The outlook was also poor for the T&T, except that previously Smith had prudently persuaded his BCL colleagues in London to have the company guarantee the bonds of the railroad, as to principal and interest. His British associates came to regret that guarantee with mounting bitterness down through the years until the road's abandonment in 1940, because the line consistently failed to earn interest, and, at times, even operating expenses. But without the T&T—which had many of the same faithful qualities as the company's mules—there was no other way except with mule power to exploit the rich colemanite deposits in the Greenwater Range. In this respect Smith's decision was correct, although his dreams of a large through traffic that he claimed would "put the T&T on velvet" were never to materialize.

An accord was made in June 1908, by which the T&T would take over management and operations of the BG, although the accounts would be kept separate.[26] The T&T could now advertise itself as "The Nevada Short Line." Ryan and Cahill were sent to Ludlow as general manager and general superintendent, respectively, of what was to become an historic railroad—the original means by which Death Valley was opened to the world. William R. Alberger, who headed Smith's traction system in Oakland, was appointed traffic manager, while Frank M. Jenifer, who would later become president of PCB (long after Smith's time), was brought in from the Santa Fe as general freight and passenger agent.

In a peculiar way, the T&T revealed an attractive aspect of the complex personality of Borax Smith—his predilection for commemorating those who stood highly in his affections by naming stations after them.[27] Thus the *Official Guide of the Railways* (for July 1911) includes the following stops in consecutive order northward from Ludlow: Rasor, Baker, Dumont (Harry Dumont of the San Francisco office), Sperry (Charlotte Grace Sperry, niece of F. M. Smith), Zabriskie, Gerstley, Evelyn (for Evelyn Ellis, who had married Smith on January 23, 1907), Horton (the T&T's trainmaster) and Ryan (for the successive termini at the Lila C and then at the large group of mines high up on the western side of the Greenwater Range, at the end of the Death Valley Railroad).

The Tonopah and Tidewater was one of those unusual properties that still commands much interest among railroad *aficionados*. Partly this arose from its lonely existence and remote operations in the far deserts of the West. Partly, too, its appeal in Smith's time and even until 1928 lay in its ability to offer through rail service, by means of connections, all the way from Los Angeles to Goldfield and Tonopah, for a total route of 467 miles to Tonopah. Indeed, until the late 1920s the company operated a Pullman with buffet facilities, departing (in 1911) from Los Angeles on No. 18, the Santa Fe's Arizona accommodation, at 2:00 P.M., reaching Ludlow at 8:45 P.M., where the sleeper was transferred to T&T No. 9 for the night run to Death Valley Junction (2:40 A.M.) and on to Beatty, arriving at 5:40 A.M.. At Beatty the Pullman terminated, but the T&T's reclining chair cars ran through all the way from Ludlow to Goldfield. This service operated northward daily except Saturday, and daily except Monday to the south.

Over the years the quality of the service declined, first with the advent of the automobile, then with the transfer of all of PCB's borax mining operations from Ryan to Kramer in 1927, and lastly with the breaking of the Goldfield link by the abandonment of BG in 1928. The Pullman was taken off and service was cut to three trains a week between Ludlow and Beatty, with transfer to a rail motor car north of Death Valley Junction. Passenger service was now incorporated in mixed trains, and the run was made in the torrid daylight hours, without buffet service.

Old timers recall that in the early years it was not unusual for the northbound passenger train to include Frank Smith's *Hauoli* (Hawaiian for "Delight"), and John Ryan's *Boron* in the consist. Both private cars would be cut off at Death Valley Junction, and taken over the Old Ryan branch to the Lila C. On arrival at about

3:00 A.M., both men would promptly appear, fully dressed and ready for an inspection trip. That is the way Borax Smith liked to do things.

Over the years, the hoped-for traffic in and out of Rhyolite, Goldfield, and Tonopah failed to materialize. Rhyolite played out within three years, while Goldfield also entered an early, although more protracted, decline. There was no point in shipping Tonopah ores southward, and so the principal through business on the T&T, or "The Nevada Short Line" as its owners called it, was passengers, and they were not enough. Throughout its 33-year existence the T&T was primarily an originating and terminating carrier, with little bridge traffic, confined to hauling mining supplies and consumers' goods northward, and PCB borates to the south. When PCB quit its mining operations at (New) Ryan in 1927, the fate of the T&T was sealed. The road rocked along with heavy losses for another 13 years. Service was cut drastically, and the section between Ludlow and Crucero was taken up in 1933, leaving the old Clark road as the T&T's only connection to the outside world.

During the mid-1920s, a decade after F. M. Smith was gone from Borax Consolidated and PCB, R. C. Baker decided that the matchless scenery of Death Valley ought to make possible a substantial tourist trade. In this way, too, the Tonopah and Tidewater could create more business for itself. Accordingly, the company built the still-magnificent Furnace Creek Inn at the mouth of the wash, and a group of motel cabins on the site of the old Greenland Ranch. Then, after PCB moved to Kramer in 1927, it converted dormitories into hotels—the Amargosa at Death Valley Junction and the Death Valley View at (New) Ryan. Tours were established through Pullman service and connecting motor bus, and at last the public could see the wonders of this fascinating region.

Baker's idea was an excellent one, except for one factor: the T&T failed to get much of the new business, for the era of the automobile had dawned. And so the unlucky railroad resumed its slow decline. However, the borax company's contribution to tourism proved to be a permanent success.

Eighteen Days in Nevada

In March 1906, about four months after Smith had started construction of the T&T, he suddenly announced at the dinner table at Arbor Villa that he had in mind a trip to Nevada and Death Valley.

(Smith liked to provide pleasant surprises, and in addition was somewhat impetuous by nature.) Present were Grace Sperry and Evelyn Ellis.[28] When he asked if they might wish to go along, their response was ecstatic, even after Smith had warned them that they might well have to sleep over a barroom at some point.

On March 26, 1906, a stormy day in Oakland, Smith and the two young ladies made their way to the Southern Pacific station, arriving barely in time to catch Train No. 24, the *Tonopah Express*. Attached to the train was F. M. Smith's capacious and elegant private car complete with Chinese cook and waiter, the *Hauoli*, which was to be the party's home for the next day and a half. Snow and slides in the Sierra Nevada delayed No. 24 for many hours, bringing the train into Reno in the afternoon instead of mid-morning. Smith had planned to have the westbound portion of his party meet the *Hauoli* at Hazen, 45 miles farther east, where the Southern Pacific branch turned south for Mina and the Tonopah connection. But with Smith's train running over 10 hours late, the eastern group unexpectedly boarded at Reno. It included Chris and Margaret Zabriskie, and R. C. Baker, all of whom were quite surprised to find the two young ladies aboard for what was certain to be a very difficult journey. In addition, William H. Shockley, one of Smith's mining experts at Tonopah, put in an appearance, although lack of room compelled him to ride up ahead in the day coach. Through Shockley, the Oakland group learned that Ben Edwards, Mrs. Zabriskie's brother, had gone on ahead to Tonopah to secure rooms for the entire party.

The train finally arrived at Tonopah at two in the morning, with the temperature below zero. Unhappily, the supposed comforts of the *Hauoli* disappeared when the car's steam lines froze. Even with the dignified R. C. Baker under the car engaging in some half-hearted tapping with a hammer, presumably in hopes of finding the right pipe and valve, and with the always-impatient F. M. Smith lying on the floor above and joining in this futile exercise, no heat was forthcoming. Mrs. Zabriskie soon gave up, persuading Fred Corkill to give her his room in town, and leaving within another day for Bishop, California, with her brother's two young sons. Although wholly familiar with desert life and climate, having grown up in Inyo County, California, Maggie had already had enough of this trip.

The extreme cold persisted and Borax Smith, who was prepared for it, bought the girls two canvas blanket-lined overcoats to help them to endure the harsh weather. The party then visited the West

End Consolidated silver mine—controlled by Smith and in which Baker and Zabriskie were investors—with the girls bravely going below to look at a stope in the presence of Fred Corkill and the others. Next was a 50-mile automobile ride to Manhattan to look at more mines and mine prospects. Then on to Goldfield, some by auto and some in the *Hauoli*, with visits to 16 more mines. Frank Smith had been keenly interested in all of the western Nevada boom camps, pouring a small fortune into numerous properties, of which only the West End Consolidated would prove to be a substantial winner.

From Goldfield the group headed south to the Bullfrog–Rhyolite district, traveling by automobile over unpaved tracks in the Ralston Desert. At four in the afternoon they arrived at Beatty, where they were joined by Will Shockley and John Ryan. The weather had now turned very hot. The next morning found them in Rhyolite, where Smith, with his permanent abundance of energy, suddenly pointed to the highest hill in the area and persuaded part of the group to climb it with him, presumably for exercise.

The next morning the party started south by car for the 70-mile trip to the new Lila C mine. It was the first time an automobile driver had ever ventured into this forbidding country. But Smith and Ryan had driven through this region many times by buckboard or wagon, and nearby Eagle Mountain was a useful landmark. A book telling of their experiences, written by Ben Edwards and Grace Sperry, offers a good description of the principals on the trip:

> A word about these venturesome spirits! F. M. S.—American-Western—and the following pages tell the rest. R. C. B., supposed to be English, but in three days the "London" on his suitcase was the only means of identification. C. B. Z.—Western foundation with a heavy coat of New York veneering. This showed in his dressing principally (dress shirt and patent leathers for going down mining shafts). He was expert in desert neckties. J. R.—practically the party's most valuable asset. E. E. and G. S.—let the reader judge, for the other members of the expedition had long ceased to catalogue them. [29]

The whole group inspected the Lila C, walking an entire 2,000-foot drift to do so. The following day they boarded a wagon drawn by four horses, with Borax Smith at the reins. For Baker and Zabriskie in the rear seat, it seems to have been a harrowing ride. There was no way to get comfortable and no way to establish a fixed posture. In contrast, Smith was in his element and enjoyed every minute of it. At Shoshone Springs, named by him and now called simply Shoshone, they took lunch, and then drove on, arriving at 3:00 P.M. at the old Amargosa Borax Works, where they spent the night.

Early the next morning they set out for the T&T railhead at Silver Lake, where the steel and grading gangs were working—70 miles below the borax works. On arrival the party found the *Hauoli* and the *Boron* waiting. The tired travelers found the many comforts of the *Hauoli* quite welcome. They retired to the big car's spacious "back porch" (observation platform) to watch the miles roll by. One more day saw them back in Oakland, where, a little over four days later, R. C. Baker was to experience the San Francisco earthquake.

Borax Smith and Borax Consolidated: The Final Phase

By the time the Lila C was in production in June 1907, Borax Smith had announced that PCB would shortly begin looking for its next mining site. In making this disclosure, he already had a good idea of where that site would be: the large group of claims located in 1882–83 by Robertson, Neuenschwander, Ryan, and others acting as agents for Coleman or Smith, or for both of them together, on the west side of the Greenwater Range, facing west toward Death Valley—the so-called "Hillside claims" mentioned earlier. Their site was extremely difficult as a mining proposition.

To appreciate this point, as well as the grandeur of the setting, it must be realized that these claims lay at an elevation averaging 3,200 feet, except for the Monte Blanco group, which was somewhat lower.[31] Below the claims the ground dipped sharply for 800 feet to the floor of Furnace Creek Wash, while at certain points the valley floor itself, which is at sea level or below, was visible. From the claims down to the wash, and descending along the wash in a northwest direction for about 15 miles, one reached what the company originally called "Greenland" or Greenland Ranch—a place where the mules were kept and alfalfa was raised for their feeding, and where Borax Smith had planted some very tall palm trees. Today this location is known as Furnace Creek Ranch. Its elevation is 179 feet below sea level.

Looking southward from the hillside claims, one sees the forbidding profile of the Black Mountains. These form the southeastern border of the valley floor. At their southern extremity below Ben-

nett's Well, there is a massive uplift in the range called Smith
Mountain, 5,912 feet in elevation and named for Borax Smith.
Further north in this same range are Golden Canyon and, almost a
thousand feet above, Zabriskie Point.

From the turnoff for Ryan on the road leading south through the
upper neck of Furnace Creek Wash, a trip of about 10 miles brings
one to Dante's View. Here one can gaze at Death Valley in all of its
magnificent grandeur. Directly to the west and forming the western
boundary of the valley floor are the Panamint Mountains, a range
averaging over 5,000 feet in altitude and capped by Telescope Peak
at 11,035 feet. Directly below Dante's View is Bad Water, at an
elevation of −276 feet, which makes it the lowest point in the
continental United States.[31] Dotting the valley floor are the salt
marshes that brought about the establishment of the Harmony works
in 1883. Whatever the direction, the view of the valley is best either

Death Valley from Dante's View: Directly below is Bad Water, Furnace Creek
Wash is in upper right. (Courtesy of U.S. Borax & Chemical Corporation.)

Biddy McCarthy borate deposit (upper center and right), hillside claims,
Death Valley, about 1900. (Fred Corkill collection.)

at sundown or in early light, when the sun's glow will be a deep red
or an incandescent white, and deep purple shadows will bring out
the mystery and the vastness of the mountains. At these times the
air is clear, with a limpid violet cast. Above all, there is the awesome
silence of the entire great scene—silence accompanied by the
knowledge that so much of it is completely untouched by man.

In dimensions, Death Valley is a deep rift in the earth's crust,
about 135 miles long and no more than 14 miles wide at its
broadest point. In ancient times it was a lake, the later evaporation
of which is believed to have produced the salt beds. Some
geologists think that it is a fault-block valley, formed by the settling
of the central block, or what is now the floor, and by the related
uplifting of the ranges on the sides.

This, then, was—and is today—the setting for the hillside claims
that Borax Smith decided to develop in 1912 as one of his last great
contributions to the Pacific Coast Borax Company. His first problem
was that of access; it was brilliantly solved by the company's chief
engineer, Clarence Rasor, who laid out a railroad route from Death

Close-up view of Monte Blanco deposit, about 1900. (Fred Corkill collection.)

Early exploration and development of the Monte Blanco hillside claim, Death Valley, about 1900. (Fred Corkill collection.)

Valley Junction (20 miles to the east) to a terminus near the mines initially called Devair and soon after, Ryan. Smith had intended originally to bond the T&T for an additional $369,000 to build the branch, but an unimaginative State Railroad Commission blocked the move on the ground that the road was too weak to support additional debt.

To get around this needless obstacle, BCL incorporated a separate concern, the Death Valley Railroad Company, with R. C. Baker as president. This was in January 1914. Construction began at once with 325 men and 150 mules. Eleven months later the line was finished. It was three feet in gauge, with grades not exceeding 1.5 percent until the final, most difficult mile, when the climb to the ore bins and terminal rose to 3.5 percent.

At Ryan there was a cluster of mines awaiting development: the Upper and Lower Biddy McCarthy, the Played Out, the Grandview, the Widow, the Lizzie V. Oakley, and, six miles below, the Monte Blanco. Some were opened before the DVRR was completed. Initially, the mining method was of the quarrying type, in some cases with bottom openings ("glory holes") connecting to a drift below.[33] Later, underground mining by means of shafts, drifts, cross-cuts, winzes and stopes was substituted. Ryan was more than a group of mines, however. It was a well-organized community, planned and developed by Harry Gower (who joined PCB in 1910, staying on for half a century).[34] The town included dormitories, a store, a recreation hall, a church, a school, and other amenities unknown to those earlier borax miners who had to rough it at Borate, Marietta, and Columbus.

A roaster and calcining plant was built at Death Valley Junction. At Ryan, a one-mile extension of the DVRR was made to the Lower Biddy McCarthy, and an additional extension of four miles was proposed but never built to the Widow and Monte Blanco mines. Instead, a two-foot gauge line, the "Borax Baby Gauge" railroad, was added later to cover the five miles to the Widow mine.

In addition to the new camp at Ryan and the crushing and roasting plant at the Junction, F. M. Smith made another major contribution to PCB as the end of his tenure drew near: the purchase in 1911 of the Sterling Borax Company for $1.8 million. This company had been created in 1908 by Thomas Thorkildsen, as a segment of an earlier borax firm formed by him in 1897 to compete against PCB after he had quit Smith's employ. In 1898, while Stephen Mather was still PCB's sales manager under Smith, he had invested capital in Thorkildsen's new venture, becoming what his own biographer calls "a secret, silent, non-participating partner." The only aspect of this duplicitous arrangement to which Joseph W. Mather could find any objection was his son's failure to leave Borax Smith and to strike out on his own then and there. As for Stephen, he evidently decided to play it safe by sticking with Smith for a while longer, while at the same time financing a vindictive and highly aggressive competitor.[35]

After he had dropped Mather from the payroll, Smith wrote Baker that he had suspected for some time that there had been an alliance between Mather and Thorkildsen, adding that Mather was now using his influence "to get our business."[36] Meanwhile, the partners built up their mines at Frazier Mountain and later near Lang, both in Ventura County, California. In 1908 they merged these properties as Sterling Borax.

In selling out to Smith in 1911, they removed a sharp thorn from his side, and at a very good price. The deal included a 10-year agreement by PCB to supply Sterling with borax ore as needed. But although one might have expected the restoration of the partners' relationship with Smith to have led promptly to friction and conflict, there was a curious end to the episode. Acting on his own and not on PCB's account, Smith appointed Thorkildsen as president and Mather as vice-president of Sterling, which was continued as a separate company.[37] Either Smith had fully forgiven them or badly needed their knowledge and competence. Most likely, the true explanation includes a bit of both.

On October 24, 1913, during F. M. Smith's final year with BCL and PCB, a tantalizing bit of news leaked out, bearing the headline "Smith Said to Have A New Borax Find." The story got out when John Ryan filed a deed in Bakersfield, the county seat of Kern County, California, recording the transfer of a mining claim from a Dr. John K. Suckow to himself, acting as agent for Smith on behalf of the new owner, Borax Consolidated. Suckow had been drilling for water, then found a deposit of what he believed to be gypsum about 40 feet below the surface. When his samples were tested in Los Angeles, they were declared to be borax in colemanite form, not gypsum.[38] Ryan was immediately notified in Oakland, and proceeded to the site accompanied by Borax Smith's right-hand man, Fred Corkill of the West End and of Pacific Coast Borax. Their findings were positive and immediate purchase of the Suckow property was arranged, with Suckow said still to be under the

Portrait of F. M. Smith's British partner, Richard C. Baker, painted by Sir Edward Patry. (Courtesy of Borax Consolidated, Limited. Photographed from the original in London.)

impression that he had found gypsum. Smith and Ryan took particular pains to keep the acquisition secret, while exploitation of the property was deferred for another 14 years.

The actual location of this property was given as Section 22, Township 11, north range 8, West San Bernardino meridian. This puts it about 12 miles west of Kramer and four miles northeast of Rich station on the Santa Fe line between Barstow and Mojave. The land involved 160 acres on the edge of an old lake. The Suckow property ultimately became the basis of Borax Consolidated's present enormous American operation. Yet it was acquired for the company by Borax Smith when he was still in its service, in October 1913, at the very time that R. C. Baker, en route to London, had in his pocket an option to buy Smith's majority holding in BCL for only $4 million. When Baker drove that "hard bargain," as the *San Francisco Chronicle* termed it, did he know of Ryan's find? Perhaps not, given Smith's and Ryan's extreme efforts to keep it secret.

In any case, Borax Smith's remaining time with PCB and BCL had now grown very short. Between 1893 and 1912 he had involved himself very deeply in real estate and traction developments in the Oakland area, borrowing over $5.5 million on both short-term and call-notes in the process. With his credit already exhausted, the banks began calling in his notes, ostensibly under pressure from the State Bank Examiner. On May 5, 1913, F. M. Smith executed an assignment of all his vast collection of business assets to the "F. M. Smith Advisory Committee," a group of leading bankers in the San Francisco-Oakland area. At age 67, Borax Smith was stripped of his fortune.

However, he was still managing director in the United States for BCL. In the meantime, in spring 1914, R. C. Baker had the unpleasant duty of informing him that under British law a person who becomes insolvent cannot continue to hold a company directorship. Baker tried to soften the blow by inviting Smith to stay on as managing director, but Smith rejected the offer, thereby severing entirely his connection with the company he had helped to found and to lead for 15 years. Baker thereupon reorganized the executive structure of the company, naming himself head of the whole enterprise, and appointing Chris Zabriskie as vice-president to manage the American properties under his direction. The relative autonomy that F. M. Smith had enjoyed for so long was thereby ended.

The reasons for Frank Smith's resignation are not hard to understand. He was a rugged individualist, a proud man, and an entre-

Christian Brevoort Zabriskie, protégé, longtime associate and eventual
successor of F. M. Smith as the American head of the Pacific Coast Borax
Company. About 1920. (Courtesy of U.S. Borax & Chemical Corporation.)

preneur who enjoyed the exercise of business power. To him it was simply inconceivable that he should now become a paid executive, serving at the whim of a group of men he had once dominated through his majority ownership of the company's voting stock.

As for his great holdings in BCL, Smith seems to have expected, or at least hoped, that his "Advisory" Committee would help him to straighten out his financial affairs. But not these bankers. They wanted their money and they wanted it fast. Combing through Smith's huge portfolio to lay its hands on any liquid assets, the committee quickly found a substantial amount of gilt-edged BCL stocks. In spring 1914, while Borax Smith was still managing director, it sent committee chairman, Frank B. Anderson of the Bank of California, to London to negotiate a sale. Smith pleaded in vain for delay, then hurried to London himself, first in hopes of obtaining a better price for his shares, and then of getting an injunction to block their sale. He failed on both counts, and the stock passed into other hands.

Frank M. Smith was no longer Borax Smith. He was now simply Mr. Smith, capitalist and businessman, in apparently voluntary exile from the industry for which he had done so much and to which he had given most of his life. Still, the industry would hear from him again, for Borax Smith was a fighter. As he saw matters, he had just *begun* to fight.

6

The Diverse Personal Life of Francis Marion Smith

Frank Smith actually lived two, and for a good part of the time, three parallel lives. He had begun his long life in borax, and it would end in borax. In 1893, when his income was reported at $20,000 a month, his second career began as he started investing in his Oakland enterprises. His third life, of course, was his personal one. His first marriage, in 1875, brought about his first family, the building of his two great estates, and the beginning of his career as a yachtsman as well as his involvement in social and civic affairs.

First Marriage and First Family

During the first years of the property at Teel's Marsh, Borax Smith had to make fairly frequent trips to the Bay region, to conduct business relations with his agent and financier, W. T. Coleman. Each trip was an arduous one, because it meant crossing desert country by horse for some 140 miles, whether one got a train at Carson City or at Wadsworth, Nevada. Thus it was convenient to stay on the continental side of San Francisco Bay, both to shorten the trip, and, in Smith's case, to have more convenient access to the West Alameda refinery.

This made the Tubbs Hotel, on East 12th Street between 6th and 7th Avenues in Oakland, the logical place at which to stop—all the more so because it was the best one in town at the time. Even then Smith had begun to display a preference for the best in all things. The Tubbs turned out to have an even more important advantage for F. M. Smith, in that it enabled him to meet Mary R. Thompson Wright at a ball given by the hotel during one of his visits.[1]

Mary R. Wright was a young divorcée from Brooklyn, New York,[2] who recently had shed herself of a husband with a roving eye, and who had been brought west by her mother, Mrs. William (Mary Jane) Thompson, who maintained her daughter and herself by operating a small boarding house in Oakland, on West 12th Street.[3] Nothing is known about Mr. Thompson other than that he came from New Jersey, and relatively little about Mrs. Thompson except that she was a New Yorker, had an English father, and a mother whose maiden name was Clarissa Jacobs. She also had strong Manhattan Dutch connections, through the Janis, Ledbetter, and Stryker families.[4]

Mary Rebecca Thompson (Wright) quickly caught Frank Smith's attention that evening at the ball, doubtless because she readily qualified as a Titian-haired beauty, with a fine figure, an erect carriage, and a handsome face with broad, warm features. In these circumstances, Frank's extreme nearsightedness was no handicap once the couple were on the dance floor. But later that same evening, his eyes betrayed him (although in an innocuous way), for he perceived an attractive girl with auburn hair sitting alone. Persuading a friend to introduce him, he was embarrassed to find that it was the same Miss Thompson.[5] Evidently this was no barrier to a ripening friendship, for before long he was paying her calls at her home, and on occasion, enjoying a decent meal after months of harsh subsistence in the desert.

In time the young couple became engaged. On July 14, 1875, they were married in Brooklyn, New York. Both were 29. For their wedding trip they went to Richmond, Wisconsin, to visit Frank's parents, after which they traveled to western Nevada to undertake the 140-mile trip by buckboard to Marietta, on the edge of Teel's Marsh.[6] In those days, to reach Marietta one had to climb about a thousand feet from Belleville over a primitive dirt road to a pass through the Excelsior Mountains, descend a steep and winding defile to the floor of Teel's Marsh, and then head west for about five miles. This was Marietta—a town of some 50 buildings at the time, with a hotel, a daily stage, two large stores (one operated by brother Byron G. Smith), and a plenitude of bars to serve the tired and usually thirsty mining population.[7]

Teel's Marsh is a desert sink shaped rather like a dumbbell, with a main axis pointing southwest. Marietta, which is now a ruin, lies about a mile directly above the eastern tip. As of 1875, the biggest thing in town was Smith Brothers' Teel's Marsh Borax Works, which was the crude concentrating plant at which Frank and Julius Paul Smith refined ulexite to obtain their borates. Teel's Marsh was situated in a large U-shaped desert valley, open at the southwest end, and about 10 miles in width and depth. Although Frank had put up a two-room cabin for his bride, replacing the single-room one that had served him, the general ambiance offered by Marietta could hardly have held much appeal for a New York City girl. It was a wild and rough place, peopled largely by drifters and tough prospectors, and far distant from somewhat more attractive towns, such as Belleville, Candelaria, and Columbus. Apart from Julius and Sadie (Sarah) Smith, Alvin Potter, the local superintendent, and occasional visits from Byron Smith, John Ryan, John Roach, and other borax men, there was little social life available.

On one occasion, two men called at the Smith cabin to ask for directions. After it was learned that they were fugitives charged with murder, Frank strung up a system of ropes and bells so that his wife could summon help from the men at the plant. Mary also found the arrangement useful for household purposes, for example, when the water barrel on the roof had sprung a leak. Yanking on the bells brought a couple of fully armed workers rushing to her aid, only to find themselves drafted to repair the leak.

The climate was also far from ideal, for Marietta was a cold and windy place, beset by snowstorms in winter and desert cloudbursts at any time. On one occasion, when the Smiths were returning from Belleville after nightfall, the horse flatly refused to proceed down the pass. Investigation revealed that the road had been cut by a deep gulley formed from the runoff from a recent cloudburst.[8]

In the summer of 1878, the *Delavan* (Wisconsin) *Republican* later reported, Frank and Julius Smith persuaded their wives, Mary and 'Sate' (for Sadie), to join them on a trip to Yosemite. They traveled by horse and wagon. Each night one couple would sleep in the wagon, and the other in a tent. From Marietta the party slowly progressed northward, passing Whiskey Flat and then the old camp of Aurora, where Mark Twain had lived. Trotting along beside the horses was Frank's faithful dog Jeff, who soon became footsore and had to be left behind with a kindly rancher. Gradually the party worked its way over the steep Tioga Pass, and after several more days dropped down into the unspoiled magnificence of John Muir's Yosemite. The trip took over a month, but the experience proved so rewarding that the Smiths continued to tell about it for years afterward.

Mary Rebecca Thompson at the time of her marriage to F. M. Smith, July 14, 1875. (Courtesy of Mrs. Elizabeth Scott.)

Francis Marion Smith at the time of his marriage to Mary R. Thompson, July 14, 1875. (F. M. Smith collection.)

Mary endured Marietta for five or six years, during which time her husband was expanding his operations at Teel's, and a few years later at Columbus and Fish Lake Valley. By 1881, there was not much doubt that he was already the commanding figure in the business. This also happened to be within a year of when "The Slim Princess" (the Carson and Colorado Railroad) opened operations, providing direct connections from Belleville to San Francisco. It was also about the time when Mary decided that she wanted to have her home in Oakland. Her husband shared her wish, for he had grown strongly attached to the city and its long range of hills. Besides, the move was feasible in a business way. They could live in Oakland, and now he could get easily to any of his three Nevada borax works by rail. The couple moved in 1881 to what they called "the little gray house" on the north side of East 17th Street, between 9th and 10th Avenues. Mary Jane Thompson joined their household there.[9]

At about this time, an event took place that was to leave a profound impression upon Mary R. Smith for the rest of her life. She had badly wanted children, but had lost her first and could have no more.[10] However, she found her own solution to her tragedy, which was to bring children into her home to the extent that she could, and to provide homes for many more. Her great adventure began in 1883, when a tiny, auburn-haired infant-in-arms was brought to her and was given the name Marion Frances Smith—thus becoming their foster daughter. About a decade later, the two Burdge sisters, Anna Mae and Sarah Winifred, joined the family in their very early teens as wards, having no near relative to care for them. About 1895, Charlotte Grace Sperry, a niece of F. M. Smith through his sister, Julia Sperry, also became a ward following her mother's death.[11] Then, in the late 1890s, Evelyn Ellis joined the growing household as financial secretary to Mrs. Smith. Finally, Florence Nightingale, a young singer who had been trained abroad, also came to live at Arbor Villa for two or three years. With her addition, the "family" came to include six young women, whom F. M. Smith habitually referred to as the "Solid Six." They were a remarkable group in many ways—for their intelligence, their diverse talents, their good looks, and, except for Florence, for their good temper and their devotion to "Uncle Frank and Aunt Mollie," as they were taught by Mary to call their foster parents. Although in this unusual way Mary R. Smith did gather a kind of family around her husband and herself, and thus brought great happiness into their lives, her deep need for motherhood still went unsatisfied.

The Smiths lived on East 17th Street barely two years. Then, in 1882, F. M. Smith began a series of acquisitions that by 1892 gave him title to practically the whole of the Tubbs and Mathews ranches, for a total of 53 acres. This huge parcel was to become Arbor Villa. Long before the big house was built, Smith began development of the gardens. The first parcel was located on a knoll about one block east of East 24th Street, and two blocks north of 9th Avenue. (East 24th actually runs southeast.) On this site was built a solid and commodious two-story residence, known to the family as "the old red house." Although it was probably built of redwood, which was cheap on the Pacific Coast in those days, the house was more of a contemporary Midwestern or even Bostonian style than what is known in the Bay Region as Pacific Coast Redwood Gothic. It had large rectangular windows grouped in threes to form a bay for each floor, while each of the four bays ran up to the roofline. A certain similarity is evident with Oak Hall, built a decade later under the guidance of Mary's firm hand, and later universally known as Arbor Villa. The Red House still stands on East 24th Street between 8th and 9th Avenues.

By the acquisition of the two ranches, Smith put together a single great parcel of land[12] that on the south extended along 9th Avenue from East 28th to East 24th Street, then turned north for two blocks to 7th Avenue, then south again to East 23rd, followed by about a one-block northern indentation, then south again to East 22nd, and then north to what was then called 4th Avenue (now Park Boulevard). Fourth Avenue was actually a ravine that ran eastward for roughly eight blocks, emerging at what today is called MacArthur Freeway. Smith initially acquired roughly six blocks on the south side. His purchases soon embraced both sides of the ravine, and this acquisition allowed him to devote the southern portion to the estate (roughly 25 acres), while assigning the northern section to the cottages later to be built for the Mary R. Smith's Trusts.

The knoll on which the old red house stood provided a magnificent view of Lake Merritt, downtown Oakland, and San Francisco Bay. Just beyond the house itself, on the south side, were some extensive stables of remarkably good architectural design. The best place to build Oak Hall was obviously on this same knoll, as the Smiths themselves were first to recognize. But the time was not ripe, for the money was not yet at hand. Furthermore, the newly built red house would have to be moved or torn down when the time did come.

The west front of F. M. Smith's mansion, Arbor Villa, in Oakland, about 1902. (F. M. Smith collection.)

In 1886, F. M. Smith bought the southwest corner of 8th Avenue and East 24th Street, which was a parcel lying just outside the main property. He then had the red house moved to this new site, and this became the family's new address. While the move was going on they made their home in the stables. Construction of the mansion still lay in the future.

F. M. Smith borrowed $400,000 in 1888 to purchase the borax assets of W. T. Coleman and Company, which, as will be recalled, had gone bankrupt. Once these assets were in hand, Smith arranged a large-scale consolidation that brought together his Nevada properties, the Calico deposit (Borate), the Hillside claims in Death Valley, the Monte Blanco and the Lila C, the works on the valley floor, and the Amargosa property near Ash Meadows. In addition, in 1889 Smith enlarged the works at West Alameda, using Ernest Ransome's reinforced concrete techniques to build ribbed floors and supporting columns. This was the first concrete building in the United States.[13] On September 10, 1890, the Pacific Coast Borax Company took title to all of these holdings. Smith now accounted for a major share of the world borax production, while his competi-

Southeastern front of Arbor Villa in 1912. Dining room is at bottom center, with the conservatory at left. (Warren E. Miller collection.)

tion within the United States was, in comparison, almost trifling. In such circumstances, it would hardly be surprising if some upward revaluation of these assets were undertaken in designing the capital structure of PCB. Promoters' profits were the custom of the time, and Borax Smith was to resort to them more than once as a source of ready cash.

Arbor Villa

Preparations were now made to finance the building of the great house. Smith announced the project in January 1893, indicating that he expected to spend $100,000. But the job went slowly, was interrupted from time to time when money became tight, and did not reach completion until 1895. Even then, many of the costly furnishings were not added until another three years had gone by, while the grounds were not fully developed until still later. Originally the Smiths had intended to call the house Oak Hall, in recognition of its extensive oak paneling for the interiors. Together the house and grounds were to be known as Arbor Villa. Before long,

South, southeast, and east fronts of Arbor Villa, showing the conservatory, drives, and, in the foreground, the archery. (F. M. Smith collection.)

however, "Oak Hall" went out of use, and the whole estate became known as Arbor Villa.

The mansion itself was of the Queen Anne shingle style, huge in dimensions and unique in that region.[14] The west front alone was 114 feet wide, while the south side extended for 136 feet. The basic plan called for a reverse-L scheme. In keeping with the shingle style there were several eclectic features, such as an extensive use of reinforced concrete; diverse window arrangements and placements; studded copper facings on the twin gables around the house; and wherever possible a fine show of indifference to the principle of symmetry.[15]

Two persons share the credit for this remarkable mansion—Mary R. Smith, who had seen Queen Anne houses along the Atlantic coast and who was determined to have one; and the architect, Walter J. Mathews, builder of many great homes in the East Bay and a self-trained professional who had started his career as a carpenter.[16] Together they worked over the plans step-by-step dur-

The north and east sides of Arbor Villa, with the observation tower at left, Lilac Cottage at middle left, Park Boulevard in foreground—as seen from Van Dyke Avenue. (F. M. Smith collection.)

Front view of Arbor Villa, looking east from Eighth Avenue and East 24th Street. (*Oakland Tribune.*)

The front entrance to Arbor Villa, showing one of the two green lions, concrete work, and mahogany paneling. About 1902. (F. M. Smith collection.)

The central reception hall at Arbor Villa, showing, left to right, entrances to the library, the small reception room, the drawing room, and the main staircase. About 1902. (F. M. Smith collection.)

The library at Arbor Villa, showing paneling, cabinetry, and Maybeck-designed furniture, all in Koa wood. (F. M. Smith collection.)

The conservatory at Arbor Villa. The glass doors at center lead to the main reception hall, and those on the right, to the dining room. (F. M. Smith collection.)

ing the two years in which the house was under construction. In planning Arbor Villa, Mathews had to have been inspired by Henry Hobson Richardson, for Richardson was the greatest American exponent of the Queen Anne style.[17] He was an advocate of generous and open interior space, a great central hall around which the other rooms would be arranged, and an ingenious use of porches and entrances as part of the whole scheme. In designing Arbor Villa, Mathews carried out these principles with complete fidelity.

Of the more than forty rooms in the house, the central reception hall was among the most notable ones. It was octagonal in shape, with a ceiling open to the second floor. The walls were paneled in three-quarter-inch oak, while the floor was given an intricate parquet pattern, with a mahogany border enclosing an interwoven oak leaf design. This great room extended 36 feet across, terminating on its outer side against a series of full-length movable glass doors forming the wall of the octagonal conservatory. This surprisingly modern room also adjoined the oak dining room and the library, allowing visitors to see the Smiths' extensive collection of Hawaiian plants.

Perhaps the most beautiful room in the house was the library, where walls and ceiling were paneled throughout in Koa wood from Hawaii, with its lustrous reddish-brown shade. The furniture in this magnificent room, also made of Koa, was designed by Bernard Maybeck, later to become the Bay Region's most renowned architect.[18] He also designed the elegant oak cabinets, chairs, and big dining table for the main dining room, all during his early years with Charles Plum and Company in San Francisco. Also noteworthy were the parquet floors and their inlaid borders, which were composed of intricate designs brought to life with rare woods such as mahogany, prima vera, and amaranth. The firm of A. W. Kenney in San Francisco was responsible for these productions.

Mention must also be made of the drawing room, where mahogany was employed with specially made Aubusson tapestries and carpets, together with classical French furniture and Sèvres vases. Finally, there was the huge interior ballroom on the third floor, capable of accommodating three hundred people and containing a theatrical stage at one end. Overhead its ceiling was cleverly painted to represent a Japanese parasol. Access to the ballroom was provided in such a way that guests did not pass through the second, or family floor.

The grounds of Arbor Villa embraced nearly 25 acres, of which

20 were developed. They included a deer park on the north side, rose and grape arbors from which the property received its name, a birch grove, a lily pond, a tennis court, stables, innumerable flower beds, and many enticing pathways winding through the trees. To

Another view of the conservatory, looking toward the dining room doors. (F. M. Smith collection.)

The drawing room at Arbor Villa, showing the French furniture, the Sèvres vases, the Aubusson tapestry, and the onyx fireplace. (F. M. Smith collection.)

the east stood an observation tower that served for years as a landmark for the whole area. On the north side was a beautiful little building with a Dutch door, known as Lilac Cottage and used by the family for breakfasts on Sunday mornings. Most of the estate was surrounded by an iron picket fence, while there were three magnificent gates giving entry to the attractive red-gravel lanes running up to and encircling the mansion.

Very appropriately, and indeed entirely consistent with Borax Smith's character, was a small and well-weathered board-and-batten pioneer cabin found among the trees in the area just south of the big house. It was while living in this tiny structure in the year 1872 that Smith had discovered Teel's Marsh. Accordingly, he had it brought down to Oakland as a permanent reminder of his humble beginnings. Beside the door was a small framed card reading as follows: "This cabin was built in the year '72 by Mr. Smith, built with his own hands, lived in by him during the time of his early discovery of borax at Teel's Marsh, Nevada."

The property had many other artifacts as well—iron lions and elk on the sweeping lawns; small "cozies" hidden along the paths as places for resting and meditating; an archery range; fountains; gardeners' greenhouses; a large vegetable garden; and even a cattery.

Among the more charming features of Arbor Villa were its many and diverse pets. After all, Frank Smith had grown up on a farm and loved animals. First on the list were his horses from Normandy, of which his favorite mount was Voltaire. Then there were the innumerable dogs: "King" and "Queen," the two St. Bernards; "Barstow," a tough and loyal little mongrel picked up at the Santa Fe stop of that name; and "Hooligan," an airedale who was shot while routing some burglars. "Annie Rooney," a little donkey and friend of all children, must also be mentioned. There were two Manx cats acquired in the East, llamas imported by Smith from Peru, and the famous Arbor Villa peacocks, who daily could be seen strutting up and down the lanes, sounding their raucous cries.

To sum it all up, Arbor Villa was a wondrous place, created in simpler and more innocent times, the likes of which were not to be encountered again.

The ballroom and theater on the third floor. (F. M. Smith collection.)

Main entrance gates to Arbor Villa, on Park Boulevard at Van Dyke Avenue. (Warren E. Miller collection.)

South grounds of Arbor Villa, showing observation tower and stables. (F. M. Smith collection.)

Francis Marion Smith standing in the doorway of the cabin in which he lived when he discovered borax at Teel's Marsh, Nevada, in 1872. On the grounds of Arbor Villa, in 1915. (Courtesy of Pacific Coast Borax Company.)

The glory years of Arbor Villa under the dominion of Mary R. Smith extended from 1895 until 1905, when her health began to fail and she was forced to curtail her social life. Still, that unique decade added so much to the rather quiet residential town that Oakland then was that at least something must be said about it.

First, the personnel of Oak Hall included the five Chinese who ran the kitchen (splendidly) and who did the serving. In addition, there was a maid for each of the three main floors, and a butler in traditional formal garb. There was a footman, as well. The chauffeur, Gus Carlson, began his career by driving the landau, carriages, and tally-ho, succeeding later to Stevens-Duryea and Peerless motor cars. No one knows today how many gardeners and handymen there were, but the estimates range from five to 18.

Each business day at about nine in the morning, F. M. Smith would appear at the Park Boulevard gate in frock coat, wing collar, and silk topper, to start his daily walk with his silver-handled cane to the narrow-gauge station of the former South Pacific Coast Railroad, to catch the ferry train for San Francisco by way of Alameda

The rose arbors from which Arbor Villa got its name. About 1902. (F. M. Smith collection.)

Grape arbors at Arbor Villa, about 1902. (F. M. Smith collection.)

The birch grove on the west side of Arbor Villa, about 1902. (F. M. Smith collection.)

The path down from Lilac Cottage to the footgate opposite "The Lodge," at the corner of Park Boulevard and McKinley Avenue. (F. M. Smith collection.)

The original stables at Arbor Villa, illustrating the Queen Anne style. About 1902. (F. M. Smith collection.)

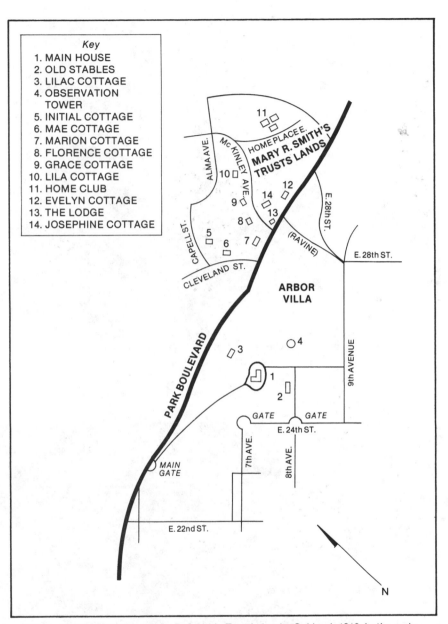

Key
1. MAIN HOUSE
2. OLD STABLES
3. LILAC COTTAGE
4. OBSERVATION
   TOWER
5. INITIAL COTTAGE
6. MAE COTTAGE
7. MARION COTTAGE
8. FLORENCE COTTAGE
9. GRACE COTTAGE
10. LILA COTTAGE
11. HOME CLUB
12. EVELYN COTTAGE
13. THE LODGE
14. JOSEPHINE COTTAGE

MAP 5. Arbor Villa and the Mary R. Smith's Trust's lands, Oakland, 1912. In the early years, Park Boulevard was known as Fourth Avenue and McKinley Avenue as Cottage Street. Note that East 24th Street actually extends southeast and northwest. Scale: 4½ inches = 2200 feet. (Courtesy of Thomas Brothers' Maps.)

The 20-Mule Team pays a visit to Arbor Villa in 1915, on the way to the Exposition in San Francisco. The second man from the left is John Ryan, while F. M. Smith is at right. (Courtesy of The Bancroft Library.)

F. M. Smith on his morning ride, near Lilac Cottage, about 1905. (F. M. Smith collection.)

Lilac Cottage, about 1902. (F. M. Smith collection.)

Point. By this time, Smith was on the portly side, but maintained an erect and vigorous stride, every inch a gentleman and a squire. Each evening Marion Smith would meet him at the same station, driving her little trap, drawn by a single magnificent black horse, with a groom to assist her.

But Borax Smith's day did not begin at nine. He regularly rose at five, then headed for the stables in the company of two or three of the Solid Six—most often the Burdge sisters. Voltaire and the other horses were already saddled and waiting. In those wonderful days the choices for riding were innumerable, but the favorite route led across the grounds eastward through the then-empty hills to Shepherd's Canyon and the top of the Contra Costa range. After three hours of riding, the party would be back at Arbor Villa for a farmer's breakfast, following which F. M. would set out on his walk to work.

Social life at Arbor Villa was frequent and diverse. Both of the Smiths loved to have friends around them, and Mary had the talents of an organizer as well as the graciousness of an exceptional hostess. She was superb at arranging small and intimate dinner parties for Frank's business friends and colleagues, such as R. C. Baker and

James Gerstley, or the old Nevada men such as John Ryan, Chris Zabriskie, Fred Corkill, and Ben Edwards. None of them ever left her table unrewarded or denied access to the finest wines that Frank could find.

Mary R. Smith was just as competent at arranging a ball for 300, or a theatrical production for the same number. She was also fully equal to organizing an exquisite "coming out" party for one of the Solid Six, or a marriage service such as the famous "Rainbow Wedding" of her adopted daughter, Marion, to Roland Letts Oliver. The "rainbow" was a multi-colored arch that extended up into the octagonal opening in the ceiling from both sides of the big reception hall. In social events of this kind, Mrs. Smith had a knack for flower and fern arrangements, with the full resources of her vast greenhouses at hand to allow her full scope for her talents. She also made special use of the conservatory, in one instance by having a tiny waterfall and brooklet built, and dozens of electric lights in dim green low candlepower, to bring out the full beauty of the plants at night.[19]

Yet the social events for which she is still best remembered three-quarters of a century later were her various charity fetes, which drew as many as 5,000 guests, and raised up to $10,000 through sales at the various booths or of tickets of entry into the observation tower and the first floor of the main house.[20] One of the most unusual of these affairs stemmed from her visit to a home for small children. It pleased her so much that she planned a little surprise for the youngsters, by arranging for a lunch and a whole day's visit for them on the grounds of the estate. When the day came, she personally led them on the tour, doubtless arranging also for rides on little Annie Rooney.[21]

Given that the Smiths were away in the East for three or four months each year, and that they also made numerous trips abroad for lengthy periods, social life at Arbor Villa was rather a stop-and-go affair. Moreover, in a certain sense the Smiths actually were not "society types." To be sure, they had wealth—so much that everybody who was anybody coveted their invitations. Also, there was no doubt that Mary was regarded as a leading hostess in the community. But it should be noted that the Smiths were not active party-goers themselves. When they wanted to attend a party, they arranged their own. And while they belonged to the top set, they paid little attention to the role—particularly Frank, who was modest in demeanor and preferred to stay quietly in the background.

Presdeleau

During the 1880s, the Smiths began taking lengthy summer vacations. At first they went to Castle Crag in northern California, where train service to San Francisco was readily available to F. M. Smith. Then Mary persuaded him to spend a summer at "The Antlers," on the southern end of Raquette Lake, in the Adirondacks. The following year they tried another Adirondack hotel on Saranac Lake. The purpose of all this was to find a summer home, or a site for one.

The solution came in 1892, when in response to some favorable descriptions, they decided to visit Shelter Island, on the eastern end of Long Island, New York. On a drive across the island they saw an old colonial house on the east side of the road, set low in a grove of trees and facing toward a beautiful little bay then known as Clark's Cove. "Aunt Mollie," as she was known to intimates, took one look and exclaimed, "That's the place I want." On the pretext of seeking a glass of water, they made acquaintance of the owner, a Miss Cartwright.[22] By the end of the conversation, Smith had bought the property, which consisted of some 40 acres. The year was 1892.[23] By the end of 1900, Smith had built up his holdings to 259½ acres, which now included a deer park west of the road, the main property leading down to the cove and east to a high cliffside, and a detached section known as Cedar Island Point, which was in the southern portion of Coecles Harbor and included a small island. Smith's parcel extended south on land to the road leading to the Nicolls property and terminating at Clark's Cove.[24] This entire area is known as Sachems Neck. It forms the headlands, south of which is Mashomac Point. The point itself is at the end of a long peninsula southeast of Clark's Cove.

The Cartwright house had been built about 1700, when the island was still a Quaker settlement. It was not large enough to accommodate Mr. and Mrs. Smith, the Solid Six, and other guests. Smith thereupon arranged to add a new house, to be joined to the old one, with a *porte cochère* running between them. Meanwhile, the Smiths lived at the Manhansett Hotel on the island.[25]

The builder of the new house was a local resident named Elias Havens Payne. Again the shingle style was used, but this time they were painted white while the windows were given shutters painted dark green. The placement of the four great columns along the porch of the main front, which faced south, gave Presdeleau a colonial appearance, although there was no strict rigidity of style imposed upon the building. For instance, the Cartwright section also had four columns, smaller in size, and topped by a classical Greek pediment, while the new section had its large columns terminating in support of a plate beam, above which were the hip roof and dormer windows of the third floor. At its eastern end, the porch of the house was formed into a large and graceful semi-circle. Inside, the first floor contained a living room and a dining room just behind the columns, paneled in solid oak, while the semi-circular end contained similar rooms, screened in and capable of closure for winter. On the north side, a kitchen and pantry wing, with servants' quarters above, was provided.[26] Many years later, a new section was added to the second floor of the new part of the house, including an outer screened porch over the semi-circular wing and two new bedrooms. At this time, the third floor already had five bedrooms, while its semi-circular section became a large open deck porch.

At its peak, Presdeleau consisted of 35 rooms and had cost approximately $250,000 to build. Many years later, in 1924, the old Cartwright wing was torn down, leaving the new house with linear dimensions of 50 by 150 feet. As always when F. M. Smith did any building, he used the finest of materials throughout. However, the glory of Presdeleau lay less in the splendor of the house and its furnishings than in the magnificence of its setting, particularly after the changes Borax Smith had made in the early years of his ownership.

At the water's edge of his property, there was a tidal creek leading in from the cove. "We ought to plant something there. What would go good in that location?" Smith asked Ollie Wells, one of his caretakers. The laconic reply was typical of the New England style of speech of the old inhabitants: "Well, why not salt water, then you could grow clams." After enjoying a laugh, Smith immediately saw the practicality of the idea. He then had tidal gates installed and some dredging done, and soon he had a permanent supply of clams, oysters, crabs, and eels.[27] His next move was to order some punts of the Cambridge style, from England, for use in this inlet. Then he turned to Ernest Ransome yet another time, to construct a Japanese-style arch bridge in concrete to cross the inlet at its outer end.

Piece by piece, more comforts were added—a cabin on Cedar Island for clambakes, bath houses along the shore, a landing dock for the captain's gig from the steam yacht, a float for swimmers, and a large second dock for landing coal and supplies. Smith also had a lengthy and massive sea wall built behind the margin of the beach, to check erosion by winter storms. Trees were planted all around the property. Along the Presdeleau section of the South Ferry Road, he had a neat row of poplars set along the entire length of the property, just as he had done for Arbor Villa along Park Boulevard.[28] A 12-foot wire mesh fence was built to enclose the deer park, and shipped in from California were deer whose descendants still roam the wilder parts of the island. Along the east side of the main road, Smith had a handsome, white criss-cross fence installed, adding further to the neatness and beauty of the estate.

Mention must also be made of two acts of kindness that well express the unostentatious generosity that typified Frank M. Smith. When he bought the Cartwright place, a retired schoolteacher, Miss Esther Sarah Havens, lived in a tiny house on a small enclave on the main property. F. M. Smith bought this little house, made a number of improvements to it, and then presented it to Miss Havens for lifetime use. There was also the story of "Old Man" Crooks, who lived in another small house on the Smith property. F. M. Smith made a similar arrangement with him. After Mr. Crooks' death, Smith moved this building closer to Presdeleau and enlarged it for a guest house. The Zabriskie family used it frequently thereafter.

With the completion of the landscaping, the big house, and the surrounding improvements, Presdeleau had been transformed into a glorious summer home, offering a superb climate from the beginning of May right into harvest time, and providing views of the cove and of Gardiner's Bay that were breathtaking on a clear summer day. Here the Smiths also shared their good fortune with their family and friends, but in lesser numbers and without the elegance that often accompanied social events at Arbor Villa.[29] Presdeleau was an estate for yachting, sailing, tennis, swimming, riding, and "taking the sun"—not for formal gatherings, even though these were held on occasion.

About the first of June each year, Mr. and Mrs. Smith, the Solid Six, the Chinese staff and the maids would leave Oakland for the East and Presdeleau. The trip required the *Hauoli*, the private car for the family, and a second Pullman of standard design to accommodate surplus family and the staff. At Chicago the original practice was to transfer by tally-ho to the Erie station, but after some hoodlums had stoned the Chinese cooks on one occasion, it was arranged for everyone to stay aboard the cars during the lengthy switching operation to Dearborn station.

The Erie route was slow, but it had two advantages. It passed

Panoramic photograph of Presdeleau, F. M. Smith's estate on Shelter Island, at the outer end of Long Island, New York. About 1900. (F. M. Smith collection.)

Close-up of the mansion at Presdeleau. Smaller structure at left is the original Cartwright house, while larger structure at center and right was added about 1895. (F. M. Smith collection.)

Looking north and west at Presdeleau. Summer porch at left.

through the beautiful Southern Tier country of New York State, and it terminated in Jersey City, where the Smiths had their steam yacht handily waiting to meet them. Then followed a trip of about six hours up Long Island Sound, passing Greenport, turning south into Gardiner's Bay, and entering Smith Cove, where the gig landed them on the passenger dock. Thus began a four or five months' summer stay, filled with yacht trips to Larchmont, Newport, Nantucket, the Thimble Islands, and even as far south as Chesapeake Bay. Although Borax Smith conducted much business while at Presdeleau, at times also making the three-hour train ride into New York City to his PCB offices at 100 William Street, it was essentially a summer home for rest and recreation. The pace of life was easy, the diversions many, and the setting so beautiful that business affairs were only unhappy distractions. In this connection, Smith was regularly urging his partner, R. C. Baker, to come over for a prolonged stay each summer, and to bring Mrs. Baker with him. But Baker preferred grouse hunting on the Scottish moors and was a bit puritanical about work in preference to play. Thus his visits were relatively few over the years, while his letters suggest a detectable note of disapproval at his American partner's prolonged summer vacations.

Looking down toward Smith Cove and the lagoon at Presdeleau. The yacht *Hauoli II* lies off the dock at left. The bridge at center right was later replaced by a Japanese bridge. (F. M. Smith collection.)

The Japanese bridge, just outside of the weirs for the lagoon at Presdeleau, about 1900. (F. M. Smith collection.)

Borax Smith taking his customary morning ride. The fence in the background bordered the east side of South Ferry Road. Presdeleau, about 1903. (F. M. Smith collection.)

The barn at Presdeleau, about 1903. Note golden eagle weather vane over pediment at center. (F. M. Smith collection.)

Yachting

With the superb seascapes, bays, and harbors available around the Shelter Island region, it was probably inevitable that Borax Smith would rapidly develop an interest in yachting. He began with a 17-foot cat boat, the *Surprise*, which he followed by chartering a small steam yacht, the *Ariadne*. About 1900, he bought a larger steam yacht, the *Trophy*, the overall length of which was 99 feet.[30] He started serious sailing by acquiring a medium sloop, 37 feet in overall length, which he named the *Marion*. This was followed by *Effort I*, also a sloop, a Nat Herreshoff boat built in 1901 at Bristol, R.I. She was of wood construction, 58 feet in overall length and 36 feet, 5 inches at waterline.

But Smith was looking for speed. To get it, he made a typically unorthodox move. In 1903 he gave Henry J. Gielow, a naval architect, his first commission, which was to build *Effort II* carte blanche. Gielow decided in favor of a relatively small boat—a single sticker with sloop rig, 62 feet in length at the waterline and 93 feet, 3 inches overall. Her hull was bronze, reinforced within by steel ribs. *Effort II* was a superb craft, both in appearance and in performance, proving herself by taking the Astor Cup races in 1903. Her greatest day was yet to come, however. King Edward VII had donated an impressive silver cup to the New York Yacht Club for an annual race to be sponsored by the club, with the winners' names to be inscribed each year. August 8, 1906, was chosen for the first race, and Smith entered *Effort II*. This put her up against some very formidable competition, such as J. Rogers Maxwell's speedy *Queen*, his son Harry Maxwell's *Yankee*, Richard Mansfield's *Amorita*, Cornelius Vanderbilt's *Rainbow*, and several others.[31] The chosen course began at Brenton Reef Light, headed straight east off Newport for 16 miles, turning south at Hen and Chicken Light for 4.5 miles, then turning again at Vineyard Sound Light for the 17-mile return run to Brenton Reef—a total of 37.5 miles.

The New York Sun described it as a race that "will long be remembered," while *The New York Herald* termed it "sensational." *Yankee* and *Queen* got off to their usual fast starts, clearly overshadowing the comparatively small *Effort II*, which held her own in a middle position by "tacking close under the beach all the way to the first mark," but actually gaining time by this shrewd tactic of her captain, S. B. Howell.[32] *Queen* was first to cross the finish line and thus seemed assured of victory. But not quite, for as *The Herald* account remarked about the last lap,

Four boats from her [Queen], far, far astern, was the sloop Effort, new and of bronze. She had made one of the grandest fights on record over an ocean course of tumbling waters and fresh easterly breezes, and long before the finish the conclusion was reached that the sloop had shown marvelous weatherly qualities and much speed, showing it unmistakably in beating to windward, in reaching and in running. But the most imaginative veteran yachtsman on the course could not have concluded that she had the ghost of a chance to be placed at the head of the column at the finish and be awarded the victory and the royal prize.

But such was the end of it and was the official verdict. Nine seconds on corrected time, though beaten in elapsed time by 20 minutes 33 seconds, which means a stretch of ocean, at the pace made, of miles. The figures did not tell a story, though there were heartbreaks on the result. The Effort was allowed 20 minutes 42 seconds, and the difference may be calculated by a single mental click. Nine seconds! It brought joy to the soul of Mr. F. M. Smith, the Effort's owner; to Mr. Henry J. Gielow, her designer, and to Captain Howell, her skipper, who sailed her with such judgment as to merit universal commendation. [33]

Probably the key to *Effort's* outstanding success was her wonderful ability to gain speed rapidly when sailing into the wind. But there was another factor, too: Evelyn Ellis and Marion Smith Oliver were aboard, and throughout the remainder of their lifetimes it was their firm contention that they actually had won the race "with our feet." They had been sent aft and told to dangle their feet in the water to help balance the craft before the wind. By doing so they were sure they had aided her progress. [34]

In fact, on the basis of *elapsed* time, *Effort II* had actually come in fourth. But because yachts differ in total sail areas and other factors, formulas are employed to equalize these differences, by converting elapsed time to "adjusted" or corrected time. It was through this adjustment that *Effort II* emerged the winner by nine seconds. In any case, her victory in this great race and in some lesser ones caused her to be designated "Boat of the Year" for 1906. Henry J. Gielow, *Effort II's* architect, noted at the end of 1906 that during that season her owner had entered her in 27 races, in which she took 23 prizes. The King Edward Cup is still on display at the New York Yacht Club, and a facsimile was presented to F. M. Smith. No more competitions were ever held for this unusual trophy.

F. M. Smith's 90-foot racing sloop *Effort II* heels over under full sail. She won the King Edward VII cup off Newport in 1906. (F. M. Smith collection.)

Effort II's owner takes his turn at the wheel. About 1906. (F. M. Smith collection.)

Hauoli II off Smith Cove. Presdeleau, about 1904. (F. M. Smith collection.)

F. M. Smith reading the morning paper on board *Hauoli II*, about 1904. (F. M. Smith collection.)

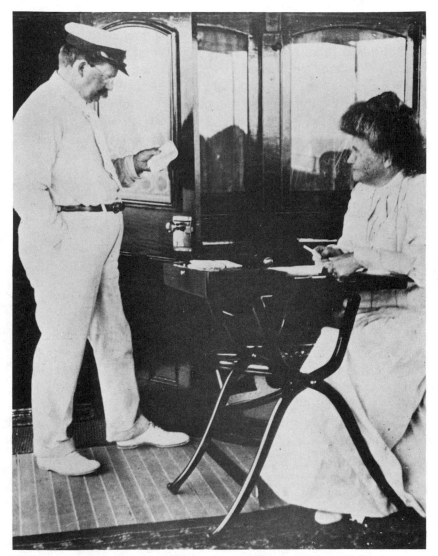

F. M. Smith dictating a letter aboard the *Hauoli II*, about 1904. (F. M. Smith collection.)

As a sportsman, F. M. Smith did not limit himself to sailing. Beginning with *Ariadne* and *Trophy*, he got into steam yachting by 1900. Then came *Hauoli I*, a vessel of Gielow design that entered service in the spring of 1903, but which lacked the speed that he was seeking. She was a participant but not a winner in the International Yacht races in August 1903. So Smith again turned to Gielow, commissioning him to build *Hauoli II*, which entered the water in the spring of 1904. She was a short-range vessel, moderate in size, built of steel, of handsomely rakish lines, and driven by a single screw. Her overall length was 211.2 feet, as against 166 feet at the waterline, while her rated speed was 18.5 knots. When pressed, she could easily exceed this by an extra three knots or more.

On June 18, 1904, Smith challenged H. H. Rogers' famous *Kanawha* for the Lysistrata Cup. *Kanawha* was the winner by 3 minutes and 29 seconds. This was not surprising, for she was a large vessel, noted for her exceptional speed. *Hauoli II* averaged 19.5 knots, so she was "beaten but not disgraced," Smith declared. She won more than her share of competitions, gaining the reputation for being one of the fastest vessels along the Atlantic Coast.

Mary R. Smith's Trusts for Orphan Children

When the press reported on August 9, 1906, that *Effort II* had won the big race of the day before, it was noted also in one account that F. M. Smith deeply loved children. His principal way of showing this feeling was to take them in large numbers on the *Hauoli* for rides around Gardiner's Bay, Great Peconic Bay, Dering Harbor, and other choice spots in this magnificent area.

Mary R. Smith fully shared her husband's affection for children and his joy in giving them pleasure. It was their common misfortune not to have had any of their own. Indeed, this unhappy fact was never far from prominence in her thoughts. In 1872, the year that F. M. Smith discovered Teel's Marsh, a young English writer by the name of Benjamin L. Farjeon had published a book called *Blade-o'-Grass*. *Blade-o'-Grass* is the story of two orphan children, one of which had the good fortune to be raised by a kind family, while the other did not. As the writer's daughter Eleanor told the story, as a young wife Mary Smith chanced upon a copy, which immediately captured her interest:

> *She had lately lost a child, and her heart was moved by the tale of the waif who grew up in misery, without a chance, and the waif's twin-sister, who, adopted by gentle people, had her chance and grew up in happiness. If ever she was rich enough to do as she pleased, young Mrs. Smith determined to save from misery as many little Blades-o'-Grass as she could. Her husband, Frank Smith, became the Borax King of America.* [35]

Benjamin Farjeon's book had confirmed Mary's conviction that character is formed by environment and not by inheritance. Nurture, not nature, makes the difference, she believed.

By the end of the century, Frank and Mary R. Smith had accumulated a fortune, which made it possible to carry out her unceasing desire to provide a family life for children who had none. Her program was to be financed entirely by the Smiths' own resources, with no tax support whatever. The central organizing concept was to be a system of detached cottages, each with a house "mother" and between five and 10 young girls, of ages from babyhood to a maximum of 14 years. Each cottage would provide for regular duties, training in the practical arts of homemaking, medical care, public schooling, and opportunities for play and recreation. Much emphasis was placed upon sharing, with the older girls helping and guiding the smaller ones. At the center of each "family" was a carefully selected woman possessed of the diverse skills required, but above all, governed by a love for and understanding of children. All of the old-fashioned notions of "orphan asylums," welfare "institutions" and the like were to be completely avoided, on the principle that small separate groups with kindly and affectionate leadership would provide the element most lacking in the larger public institutions of that time: the family as the unifying principle.[36]

The project came into being February 14, 1901, when a single little girl came under the care of the Mary R. Smith's Trusts. By April 22, 1901, the first permanent cottage, the Marion, designed by Bernard Maybeck, was completed. Two more soon followed, the Florence, designed by Walter Mathews, and the Josephine, designed by George W. Flick. Then—on February 11, 1902—F. M. Smith turned over 34 acres on the north side of Park Boulevard (then Fourth Avenue), opposite the grounds of Arbor Villa. Two days later, Mrs. Smith set up a trust consisting of $25,000 for each of the first five cottages, plus $25,000 for an emergency fund, together with the cottages and their furnishings—for a total conveyance to the two trusts of approximately $300,000.[37] As of that time, five cottage mothers were caring for 37 children, all of whom were then attending the public schools.

By 1913, there were nine cottages. Mae and Evelyn Cottages were outstanding for their architecture, both products of the superb craftsmanship of Julia Morgan. Grace, Initial, and Lila were then added, along with The Lodge, which was beautifully designed by George Flick to serve as a secretarial office. It still remains. Initial was

Four of the "Solid Six" of the first Smith family, probably at Presdeleau in 1893. In clockwise order from left: Sarah Winifred Burdge, Anna Mae Burdge, Marion Smith, and Evelyn Ellis. (Courtesy of Mrs. Elizabeth Scott, daughter of Mae Burdge.)

the first point of reception, while Auxiliary, located in Alameda, provided reserve facilities. By 1913, 79 children were residing in the cottages.[38]

"It should be noted that five of the cottages drew their names from the "Solid Six"—Winifred Burdge was left out. Lila Cottage was named for Mrs. Frank C. Havens and donated by her husband. Josephine was named for a niece of Mrs. Smith's."

The cottages continued to flourish for many more years, so that even today their "graduates" are still found occasionally in the Bay Region. However, the increasing complexity of state and federal welfare laws ultimately made it necessary for the Board of Trustees to seek the permission of the court to abandon the original system, and to allow the income from the trusts to be distributed to poor children in medical need or for related benefactions. So the nine cottages that had so thoroughly borne out Mary Smith's faith disappeared from the scene, either to be torn down or converted to private use.

Eleanor Farjeon learned about Mary R. Smith's dream and its

realization when she received Mary's request at the turn of the century that Benjamin L. Farjeon sign her copy of *Blade-o'-Grass*. As Eleanor put it: "I think Ben Farjeon's heart was bursting as he signed the book, for Mrs. Smith in America. He lived to receive her letter of thanks and tidings."[39]

Although this very remarkable experiment in private philanthropy had to be brought to an end, it gave enormous satisfaction to the unusual Englishman who originally conceived it. No less important, the experiment was an outstanding success; indeed, the only reasons for its termination involved social changes that reduced the number of cottage children and new welfare regulations that made the system impracticable.

Note should also be taken of a related institution also established by Frank and Mary Smith: the "Home Club." It was their idea that a neighborhood should actually be a community with strong social ties, and that such a community would be particularly beneficial to the cottage girls. Accordingly, a large piece of land on a high knoll on the northeast portion of the cottage property was set aside for a large building in the Palladian style, with columns and pediment, to serve as a social hall, ballroom, and club house, a handsome structure for which the architect was Walter Mathews. Later a gymnasium and art gallery were added. The club itself was then organized, with Mr. and Mrs. Smith providing leadership and funds to bring in speakers and musical groups and to pay for parties and dances. The Home Club proved successful and lasted until the decline of the cottage system in the 1920s.

The trusts attest to Mary R. Smith's generous nature and the strength of her convictions. One might wonder how two such strongly independent personalities as Frank and Mollie Smith could make so successful a marriage. They were emotionally well-suited to each other, and each had such keen personal interests—borax in the one case, and the cottages in the other—that this factor brought them close together. Around 1901 Marion Smith Oliver recalls riding with her foster parents when Frank declared, "I have my projects and you have your trusts. We will work together for the betterment of Oakland."[40]

As a personality, Frank was inclined to be impulsive and trusting, brimming over with energy and enthusiasm for all of his ventures, and invariably optimistic about their outcome. Mary was more cautious, and Frank instinctively came to rely upon her cool judgment. When visiting businessmen in pursuit of investment capital

Cottage Hill as seen from Arbor Villa in 1912. At middle left are Mae Cottage and, just above, Initial. In lower center is Marion Cottage, with Florence, Grace, and Lila above. Lower right shows The Lodge, with Josephine Cottage above and Evelyn to right. Large white buildings are the Home Club. (Warren E. Miller collection.)

Looking northwest at the Home Club on Cottage Hill, 1912. Front building at left had the ballroom and auditorium. Those at right were the gymnasium and art gallery. (Warren E. Miller collection.)

El Campanil of Mills College, for which the architect was Julia Morgan. Gift of Mr. and Mrs. F. M. Smith, 1904. (F. M. Smith collection.)

dined with the Smiths, it was Frank's habit to defer discussions of business matters until after dinner, and then to have Mary quietly join the group, busily engaging herself in knitting but saying nothing. Then, after the guests had departed, he would seek her opinion. In one instance, Mae Burdge Miller recalled, she gave him a strong negative, adding, "Frank, never forget that borax gave you your wealth. Never allow other interests to jeopardize it."[41]

Mary R. Smith was a good judge of character and was not easily taken in. And despite her impulsive generosity toward friends, acquaintances, and children, she could be firm, even tough. For example, she had planned an open house on New Year's Day, 1900, to revive an old custom. Somehow the question of a punch bowl laced with alcohol arose in the newspaper publicity. This brought most of the local prohibitionists together in an attack against what they considered her dangerous idea. When inquiry was made by the press, she avoided a direct confrontation, saying simply, "On my list there is no one who does not respect the standard which a hostess chooses to set for her home. You will pardon me if I say that any further discussion of my home or guests seems to me unnecessary and a trifle ridiculous."[42] Alcoholic punch was served to those who wanted it.

It is also of contemporary interest that Mary Smith was an active suffragette. She often invited the local women's suffrage group to have its meetings at Arbor Villa, and at one time headed the organization herself. Those who were close to Aunt Mollie typically describe her as warm and generous, a great organizer of social affairs, and a superb hostess. But she was also strong in will, and capable of being tart and critical in disagreements. Invariably, though, she eventually would relent, apologize for any sharp words, and quickly restore good relations.

F. M. Smith had a different social temperament. He loved to entertain and he drew his greatest pleasure from making people happy. To supplement these characteristics, he became an unstinting spender as well as a generous contributor to good causes. No doubt his warm relationship with Mollie was aided by his willingness to let her proceed freely with the building of Arbor Villa and Presdeleau, tasks that she performed magnificently. Although Frank, too, was both strong-willed and stubborn, these qualities seem to have provoked very little conflict between the two of them. Probably Frank could have done just as well without the theatrical productions and the great parties, but this was no problem because he could always remain quietly in the background or join a few close friends. In speech and manners, Smith was a warm and friendly man, although in business affairs he could be very tough. But he was no braggart, he usually kept his voice moderate, and he sought to dominate no one at these gatherings. Normally, even his laughter was on the subdued side.

In 1905, the Smiths celebrated their 30th wedding anniversary. Early the following January they had a trip all planned for Cairo and the Nile. But late in the afternoon of December 31, 1905, following several days of intensive shopping, Mary complained of not feeling well, and retired to her room for a rest. She did not reappear, and by 9:30 that night was gone, following a massive stroke from which she never regained consciousness. When the doctors gave Frank the verdict, he shut himself up in his quarters, spending the next 24 hours alone.[43]

On January 3, private services were conducted at Arbor Villa, after which Mary R. Smith's remains were placed in the family vault in Mountain View Cemetery. The eulogies were many, and all of them stressed one theme: her many charitable interests and benefactions over her quarter-century residence in Oakland.

Suddenly, Arbor Villa had become a vast and empty place. Frank had lost his partner of 30 years, four of the Solid Six were gone, and only Grace Sperry and Evelyn Ellis were left. The grand social life was over, and Borax Smith immersed himself in business affairs.

The Second Marriage and Second Family

Evelyn Kate Ellis was an English girl, born on December 11, 1877, at Eastington Hall, near Kidderminster, Worcestershire. Her mother, Kate Grainger Ellis, was a member of the well-known Grainger family, which had been highly successful in the pottery business for nearly a century. Eventually they became a subsidiary company of the Royal Worcester works, though they continued to produce their own line until 1902. In 1884, Felix D. Ellis brought Kate and her children to the United States, where they settled in Oakland. During her brief tenure as a schoolteacher, Evelyn had met Mary R. Smith. Their acquaintance soon became a friendship, partly because Evelyn was not only highly intelligent but also was endowed with a natural aptitude for business affairs. In addition, she was handsome and gracious, and perhaps a bit self-effacing—all qualities that had caused Mary to take to her strongly.

Frank had known Evelyn for at least 10 years while she had lived at Arbor Villa serving as Mary's financial officer and then as her secretary. At times during this period, she had also written business letters for Frank. Indeed, by 1905 the Smith and Ellis families were so close that Mary had arranged for Evelyn's parents to occupy the "old red house" at Eighth Avenue and East 24th Street. Then (in March 1906) Borax Smith took both Grace and Evelyn on the trip to Nevada and Death Valley.

Gradually, Frank and Evelyn found themselves increasingly attracted to each other, and their intimate friends were beginning to be aware that an understanding had been reached between them. In this respect they were beginning to fulfill a prophecy made by Mary R. Smith to Mae Miller, more than a year before her death, while she was recovering from a heart attack. Her words were: "If anything happens to me, Frank is certain to marry again, and I hope it is Evelyn Ellis."[44]

Late in the afternoon of January 21, 1907, F. M. Smith had obtained a marriage license. He had a surprise dinner already planned to announce his engagement to Evelyn, but premature publicity had spoiled his plans. The wedding trip was to provide one more opportunity for F. M. Smith to spring one of his surprises—in this instance an invitation to his niece, Grace Sperry, to come along, which she did.[45]

On the evening of January 23, Evelyn and Frank were married at the home of the bride's parents (in the Smiths' "old red house"). Earlier that evening, Frank could not find the marriage license. It happened to have been left in the pocket of one of his suits, which, along with a great load of other impedimenta, he had asked Grace to find room for in her trunk. He insisted that the trunk be brought into the house at once. As soon as it was unlocked, he began flinging around drawer and contents in a frantic effort to find the missing document. With calm intervention, Grace quietly recovered it and then had to pack all over again. The following morning this unusual trio boarded the private car *Hauoli* for the wedding trip. The first stop was Los Angeles, where they stayed a few days at the Hotel Alexandria. On leaving Los Angeles, the *Hauoli* was attached to a local on the Sunset Route. Arriving three hours late at Bowie, Arizona, the junction for Globe, the car was detached and added to the waiting branch-line train. The party was able to have a brief visit with friends at Safford, and then had to return to Bowie. This time the *Hauoli* was added to the *Sunset Limited*, and was cut in just behind the baggage car. This damaged the car's running gear. After a rough ride to El Paso, they were delayed all day for repairs.

The rail trip proceeded from El Paso to New Orleans, and then on to Miami, Florida, where Borax Smith's steam yacht, *Hauoli II*, was waiting. Biscayne Bay was too shallow to dock the yacht, so a launch had to be used for boarding. There followed a rough crossing of the Gulf Stream, a stopover at Nassau in the Bahamas, and afterward a run to Havana. At this point the party left the yacht and after a few days in Havana ventured forth by railroad to Santiago—a rough ride with some less-than-satisfactory hotels thrown in. From Santiago they crossed to Jamaica. Their trunks were delayed, and this required the ladies to get new clothes made up in a hurry. Frank outdid them by buying five linen suits, thereby causing a parade of tailors rushing in at all hours for fittings.

From Kingston the party returned to Havana, then boarded the *Hauoli II* for Miami. There, the other *Hauoli*, the railroad car, was waiting. Soon they were under way to Memphis and Kansas City, where the car was transferred to the Santa Fe for the run to Williams and then up the branch line to the Grand Canyon. Evelyn and Grace bravely traveled the Bright Angel Trail by donkey. Then back to Williams and a run to Ludlow, where Frank had ordered a special train to be waiting to take the *Hauoli* and its occupants over his new railroad, the Tonopah and Tidewater, all the way to the end of the track, somewhere near Death Valley Junction.[46] Then came the return trip to Crucero, where *Hauoli* was transferred to the road of his old adversary, Senator Clark, for the run to Daggett.

By this time Smith was eager to get back to business, and so a stopover at Borate was in order. It was accomplished by rigging up an umbrella and some chairs on a flatcar for the run over the Borate and Daggett. This was probably Evelyn's first view of this great property, and very likely her last, for within a couple of months the Lila C would be operating and Borate closed. On March 29, 1907, the three travelers were back in Oakland after a trip of 65 days.

Although it was a December-May marriage, Evelyn's partner was anything but a doddering old man. At the age of 61 he was a multi-millionaire, controlled the biggest borax company in the world, and at the same time was well-embarked upon his develop-

Evelyn Ellis Smith in 1913, when she was 36 years old. (Courtesy of Dorothy Smith Bayley.)

Francis Marion Smith, about the time of his marriage to Evelyn Ellis in 1907, when he was at the peak of his career. (Scharz photo, Oakland.)

ment of the Key Route, the Oakland Transit, and the Realty Syndicate, not to mention the building of the Key Route Inn and the
Claremont Hotel, ownership of three banks, a local chemical company, and the operation of a half-dozen mining ventures in California and Nevada.[47] Smith's marvelous reserves of energy enabled
him to keep a firm hand upon all of these diverse enterprises, while
setting a fast pace for all of his younger associates when it came to
getting things done.

From the outset, the new marital partners proved to be ideally
matched for each other. Evelyn had long admired Frank's strength,
leadership, and generosity, while he fully appreciated her good
looks, intelligence, and business ability. Indeed, the time was to
come 24 years later when Evelyn had to take over the management
of her husband's companies. When it did, she proved to be entirely
equal to the task.

There was but one negative factor in the second marriage, fortunately a transitory one. It was that Frank and Mollie's foster daughter, Marion Smith Oliver, initially opposed it adamantly. In fact, it
has been said, she did so with harsh and bitter language to her
father.[48] It was entirely uncharacteristic of Marion Oliver to react in
this way, and all those who knew her recognized her for the kind
and loving woman she actually was. Fortunately, Marion soon
perceived her mistake, after which she and Evelyn resumed their
long-time friendship. Over the years the bonds between them, if
anything, grew stronger than before.

Evelyn was now the new mistress of Arbor Villa. She was equal to
it, for she knew the great house inside and out, had the warm
respect of the staff, and possessed the necessary common sense of a
good manager. She had her own ideas, and they did not call for a
sterile copying of Mary R. Smith's way of life.[49] She continued to
have the now-famous charity fetes, and she enjoyed giving intimate
dinner parties for their close friends. But the great parties were over,
for they were not to her taste. For the same reason, one surmises
that if she could have built her own Arbor Villa, it would have been
smaller and perhaps of a different style, much as she fully admired
its grandeur and the magnificence of its interiors.

When Frank Smith married Evelyn Ellis, he longed to have
children. Fortune smiled upon their mutual wish, and between late
1907 and early 1913 they had four. The first three were girls.
Naturally their father began to hope for a boy as well—so much so
that even before the third child, Mildred, was born, the prospective

Mr. and Mrs. F. M. Smith and their young family, 1915. In front, from left: Evelyn, Dorothy, Mildred, and Frank, Jr. (The Bancroft Library.)

father began calling her "Jack," a custom he continued for some time after her arrival. Finally, in February 1913, Francis Marion Smith, Junior, made his appearance, and the family was complete. Arbor Villa now had a nursery on the second floor of the rear wing. About this time Frank Smith bought a wicker pony cart, driven by Evelyn or the French governess, to give the youngsters rides around the neighborhood.

Inevitably, social life at the big house changed rather radically under the direction of its new mistress. Raising four youngsters within an age span of only six years denied her opportunity for the social splash—which would not have interested her anyway. She did keep up the May Fetes at Arbor Villa and the Harvest Festivals at Presdeleau. She had her sister, Marian Ellis, and Grace Sperry as permanent guests, and her children recall that close friends and other relatives were usually also present at dinner. The children themselves had their dinners in the third-floor dining room, or on special occasions at a separate table in the big dining room.

As a parent, F. M. Smith was warm, generous, and affectionate—but also firm. He had clear expectations regarding good behavior, and when anyone got out of line, a warning glance or a single word of admonition was all that was needed. Both parents always kept their tempers well-controlled. Even after they had encountered their very difficult financial problems after 1913, they kept them from the children.

Undoubtedly, F. M. Smith guided his young family along the lines of his own upbringing. Sundays were reserved for Sunday School, church, dinner, a ride and a social call, and a quiet evening in the big sitting room. Little orange and white cards had a way of appearing on the children's bureaus, bearing injunctions such as "Do your best," "Be prompt," and other simple rules. At mealtimes, a clean plate was the prerequisite for dessert. On Sundays, the youngsters were not allowed to use the tennis court. On other evenings, the mother and father often played billiards or dominoes, while 500 rummy was popular when guests were present.

It would be misleading to suggest that F. M. Smith was strongly puritanical toward his young family. Quite the opposite. He regularly took them on picnics to such beauty spots as Trestle Glen and Shepherd's Canyon, where all the family would ride in the big horse-drawn carryall. He provided the youngsters with plenty of dogs, cats, canaries, goldfish, sheep, a goat, and even a parrot. On one occasion, when one of the daughters was at summer camp, her favorite horse, Midget, had sustained an injury to its leg. Father was summoned in panic by telegram because the owner had decided that Midget would have to be destroyed. On arrival, F. M. Smith pulled out his well-worn checkbook and bought the horse on the spot, so that it could be taken back to Arbor Villa to recuperate.

Christmas, of course, was always a major event. The octagonal opening in the ceiling of the large central hall permitted a "two story" Christmas tree. Decorating the huge tree was a great activity. All of the cottage children would come over for a visit, and on Christmas Day all available relatives would be on hand. Gus Carlson would blow a horn outside, and Walter Cole, husband of Winifred Burdge, would magically appear from behind the big fireplace to distribute the gifts.

At Arbor Villa the children's lives were enriched by a plenitude of places to play—the observation tower, the spiral staircase to the small dining room on the third floor, Lilac Cottage, the billiard room, music room, and bowling alley. As the girls grew older, each day their mother would lead the two older ones on horseback up through Trestle Glen to Miss Ransome's School in Piedmont. Frank, Jr., the youngest child, was initially educated by a French governess—so much so that he spoke French before he learned English.

At Presdeleau, the family had an opportunity to relax undisturbed, although intimate friends were frequent visitors. Because it was summertime, the children had plenty of chances to play. Here the favorite spots were the old Cartwright wing of the house—which was firmly believed to be haunted—and, of course, the woods and deer park. The barn and stables were also an attraction, along with the horses. There was also the magnificent beach on Smith Cove, and the punts for clamming, crabbing, and eeling in the lagoon. A long narrow concrete walk ran down from the house to the little Japanese bridge by the weirs from the lagoon. Each child had his or her initials and footprint embedded in the cement (at Arbor Villa, each child planted a special Norfolk pine on the grounds). Every morning Evelyn would take her three little girls down to the dock for their morning bath. When the dressmaker made them new dresses, their mother would have them swim in them first, to shrink the clothes to size.

Gus Carlson was always on hand at Presdeleau to drive the family around the island. In addition, there were the Chinese houseboys—now probably in late middle-age—to take care of the cooking and serving, and to teach young Frank the mysteries of Chinese kites. Ah Fun—just "Fun" to the family—was the leader and favorite among the children.

Upon the family's return to Arbor Villa each September, F. M. Smith resumed his daily regimen. As an early riser, he began with his usual horseback ride, then inspected his gardens, especially the roses, and fed the quail. After breakfast he would set out on his regular walk around the lower end of Lake Merritt and up 14th Street to Broadway and then to the Syndicate Building. In the 1920s, storekeepers used to say that they could set their watches by the time when he passed their doors.

On weekends or just on impulse during hunting season, Smith would rise at 3 A.M., have Gus Carlson meet him with the

Locomobile at the big *porte cochère,* and then set out for Gustine, in the upper San Joaquin Valley, below Tracy. The usual route was out East 14th Street. Before many blocks had been passed, Smith would begin urging Gus to go faster. With this powerful car 60 miles an hour was readily attainable as well as a constant temptation at that early hour. Soon the needle would reach this point. More often than not, a motorcycle policeman would roar up, make them stop, and write out a ticket. Gus would then put the big car into gear and off they would go, while Borax Smith simply tossed the ticket into the back seat. At Gustine he would put on his boots, load up his gun, and wade out into the marsh in hopes of getting some ducks. He was an excellent shot. Perhaps because of his rural origins and many years of frontier life, Smith was always a keen sportsman, whether it was fishing in Lake Tahoe in the early 1880s, or moose hunting with Chris Zabriskie and Ernest Ransome in New Brunswick, or duck shooting at his hunting lodge in the Coyote Hills near Alvarado, California.

F. M. Smith was very fond of classical music, even learning how to play the flute. He favored chamber music and frequently brought in small groups of artists to perform in the drawing room at Arbor Villa. It had been his hope that his four children could learn enough to make up an acceptable ensemble, with young Evelyn at the piano, Mildred with the violin, Dorothy with cello, and young Frank with the flute. The children would gather at the second-floor music room, with their fond parents before them, and the concert would begin. Frank Junior soon dropped out for lack of interest, but the girls hung on, to their father's great pleasure.

Financial problems from 1913 onward were not allowed to intrude upon family life. Thus the children grew up knowing very little of the tragedy their parents had had to endure for so many years. Instead, their recollections all involve a warm and close family life, filled with interests and diversions.

Some Physical and Personal Characteristics of F. M. Smith

Physically, F. M. Smith was not a large man, although his carriage and dignity nonetheless made him an imposing figure. In stature he was about five feet seven inches in height, and inclined to be stout by his middle years. By all odds his two most distinguishing features were what Evelyn used to refer to as his "great mop of hair" and his carefully-trimmed handlebar mustache. His hair was so thick and bushy that the only way that he could keep it controlled was to wear it in pompadour style, which he did throughout his adult life. In youth its color was brown. Gradually it became flecked with gray, and ultimately took on a silvery hue, which lasted until his death.

Smith had blue eyes and wore gold-rimmed glasses until they went out of style in the 1920s, during his old age. His mode of dress was impeccable. He always bought the best, and he had the appearance and bearing of the classical American mining magnate, once he had left the dusty camp of Marietta, Nevada, in 1881. In the early part of his urban phase, he favored frock coats, silk hats, and wing collars with a stick pin in his tie. After 1900, he adopted more modern but still conservatively-cut three-piece business suits, with three-button jackets. Dark blues and grays, on occasion with fine striping, were his favorites, while he preferred hats in the Homburg style, except when the weather and the social setting permitted a Panama. He also owned an ample stock of sporting clothes for riding and hunting. For many years he carried a thin gold pocket watch and a special wallet for carrying gold pieces.

With his personal appearance and careful mode of dress, F. M. Smith quickly became a well-recognized figure wherever he went. However, there was nothing pompous or stuffy about him. He was simply typical of the prosperous Americans of his time, with elegance of appearance reflecting pride in himself as a successful man of business. In that day, this was nothing to be ashamed of.

It is not easy to interpret Smith's personality because he has been gone for half a century and there remain no contemporaries today. One must rely upon letters, newspaper accounts, legal testimony, and the recollections of those who knew him from among the generations that followed his own. The key to F. M. Smith is likely to be found in his unceasing determination to become independent, a quality helped greatly by a lively imagination, an inclination to take large chances, and a very strong will. In his youth in the mid-nineteenth century, young men with these qualities were most likely to grow up on farms, and to develop early an insatiable desire to make their own way. In those times, the means to accomplish this was to go westward, to the open frontier, where opportunity was most easily found. In short, Borax Smith was a product of the open society and the open lands of the America of his youth. It made him an individualist in all of his relationships with others, and incidentally a sportsman and outdoorsman.

These qualities sustained him over a dreary five-year search for wealth. After he had found it, his soaring imagination drove him quickly onward to the development of a major mining industry, despite a very difficult environment. This same imagination later unfolded to him the vision of developing a great city on the east shore of San Francisco Bay.

The evidence indicates very strongly that Borax Smith sought to achieve and to hold the final authority in all of his business ventures. True, he wanted associates of the best quality around him, but in the end he wanted to make the big decisions. This, of course, is consistent with the individualism central to his character. His colleagues for the most part were extremely capable. They were not "yes men," because he gave them much scope for their tasks. But it is significant that the common trait of the best of them was loyalty and devotion to their chief.

However, Smith's drive for independence was not easy to detect, for his outward demeanor was temperate, friendly, and kind. He rarely showed anger, and when he did it was of the cold and restrained variety. Most of the time he was a person of good humor, who loved a good joke, told interesting stories, and was wholly contented to be with his wife and family, at home, on a trip, or at a picnic. His children meant everything to him. When they recall him today, it is with warm pleasure at the remembered twinkle in his eyes and countless little gestures to make them happy. At Presdeleau he would sit at his desk with a small telescope at hand, so that he could keep an eye on them at play. He also derived an old-fashioned pleasure at having "company" stay for days or even weeks at a time at Presdeleau or Arbor Villa, in the same spirit as country people everywhere used to do in nineteenth-century America. He liked to have guests, and he liked to please them with the many diversions available on the two estates.

Both of his marriages were unequivocally successful. In both instances, his wives were of handsome appearance, a very perceptive intelligence, and an aptitude for business affairs. Given that both had these qualities and that their husband was so strongly inner-directed, one would have predicted trouble for both unions. But it never happened. In Mary R. Smith's case, probably the basic reason was her husband's willingness to let her manage family and social affairs. With Evelyn Smith, there was less social ambition, but a deep understanding of and admiration for Frank Smith's complex personality. Both women, too, understood business in a sophisticated way, and helped him immeasurably with the "details" he detested. Finally, both gave him unstinting devotion and affection.

In the end, unfortunately, ambition was to destroy Frank Smith's first fortune. But it also was to drive him relentlessly, in old age, to the accumulation of a second one. Thus it seems that will and imagination, and the search for independence, are the qualities that made him the unusual man that he was.

7

The Oakland Ventures:

The Tractions, the Realty Syndicate, and the Key Route

With the formation of the Pacific Coast Borax Company in 1890, F. M. Smith had made himself the undisputed mogul of the industry, both within the United States and abroad. An official government report for the fiscal year 1891–92 shows that PCB accounted for 5,000 tons of borax in that period, or almost exactly three-quarters of total American production.[1] With prices averaging seven cents a pound at the time, the gross receipts of the company would have been about $700,000.[2] With imports insignificant and soon to be limited further by a new tariff, and with domestic competition limited to a few small producers, PCB had the advantages both of size and of the control of the great reserves assembled from the old Coleman and Smith properties. Small wonder that PCB began producing an ever-increasing stream of dividends for its principal owner. By 1893 his monthly income was quoted publicly at $20,000 a month. Obviously it was this impressive inflow of cash that made it possible for Smith to buy the Presdeleau lands, to build Arbor Villa, and to begin to think about branching out into "other lines."

Until the early 1890s, he had been simply a borax magnate, engaged in a relatively obscure industry with sources of supply that were remote and almost inaccessible. He enjoyed a certain prominence because he was known as the man who had opened up Death Valley, the man who had wrested a fortune from a forbidding region that few had ever seen. Now he was about to display boundless energy, fertile imagination, and an impatient desire to build in an entirely different field—metropolitan development.

152

In moving in this new direction, Borax Smith had undoubtedly been influenced by having settled in Oakland in 1881, after nearly 10 years of regular visits to the San Francisco Bay region on behalf of his growing business at Teel's Marsh. As the years went by after he had become a permanent resident, Smith gradually began to implement the great dream of his life: the development of the continental side of San Francisco Bay for industry, shipping, and settlement.[3]

A glance at the map will readily show that the city of San Francisco lies at the head of a peninsula that affords land access only from the south. Much of that peninsula is narrow and mountainous, while to the east lie five miles of water that separate the city from the continental shore. At that time, rail access required either a long and indirect route around the south of the bay or expensive lighterage and car float operations.

The East Bay side is a rather different proposition. Essentially it consists of a narrow strip of relatively flat land about 30 miles long, five miles in width to the foot of the Oakland and Contra Costa hills, and with a broad V-shaped point which lies in West Oakland. This strip fronts along the tidelands of the bay, which makes it ideal for rail terminals, docks, warehouses and factories. All this F. M. Smith foresaw in 1890, when Oakland and Berkeley were comparatively undeveloped, with large areas of open land, and relatively little industry or ship-to-shore trade. Within the continental area, furthermore, public transportation was limited in scope and obsolete in character. Dominating the scene were the ancient steam trains of the Southern Pacific (until 1885 the Central Pacific), augmented by the "narrow gauge" steam service (until 1887 owned by the South Pacific Coast) to Alameda Pier and San Francisco, and a gaggle of rickety and independent horse car, cable car, and electric railroads with four different gauges. The Southern Pacific operated the only lines into East Oakland and Berkeley.

Thus, despite its superb natural endowment, the East Bay area was a kind of backwater—a "bedroom town" for San Francisco and little else. As F. M. Smith made his daily trip on the "narrow gauge" and its ferry back and forth between his San Francisco office at 230 Montgomery Street[4] and his home in Oakland, he began to do a lot of serious thinking about the poor quality of transbay passenger service, the high expense and inconvenience of San Francisco for factory sites or as a transfer point for freight, and the largely unexploited potential of the Oakland side.

Borax Smith's Metropolitan Development Plan for the East Bay

Smith's reflections gradually led to the formation of a well-conceived plan in his mind, all aimed at conquering these problems. It gradually began to absorb him so much that it could be thought of almost as an obsession. Impatient for creative action, he soon embarked upon a 20-year project to carry through the entire scheme, even at the risk of his entire fortune.

Smith's great vision embraced four main elements. First, the diverse collection of rattletrap street-railway companies was to be acquired and then consolidated into a single unified and modernized system. Second, a new transbay train and ferry service to link the East Bay with San Francisco would be introduced and would be conducted as a company separate from the contemplated local traction system. Initially, Smith had envisaged steam trains serving a ferry terminal to be built on the shoreline, at the foot of Yerba Buena Avenue, in Emeryville. Well before 1900, he had been won over to the interurban electric railway because of its speed, cleanliness, and efficiency of operation. He now contemplated placing the terminal on Yerba Buena Island (then called Goat Island), to be approached by an underwater tube about a mile and a half long, starting from a trestle extending from the shore to what was called the "pier head line." The stretch from the island to San Francisco would be traversed by ferry.[5]

Third, a land syndicate was to be formed to merge the holdings of several large owners, and to acquire much more property, all for purposes of subdivision and settlement. Smith reasoned that extensions of the traction system into newly subdivided areas would encourage building and settlement, while increasing the revenues of the carrier. By 1900, Henry Edwards Huntington, nephew of Collis P. Huntington of the Central and Southern Pacific, was already beginning to apply the same principles with marked success. His Los Angeles Railway was serving local subdivisions of his lands, and what was about to become the Pacific Electric Railway would promote suburban land development and interurban traffic.

The fourth element involved some 340 acres of tidelands (acquired by Smith as part of his overall plan) lying between the Oakland Pier of the Southern Pacific on the south and the proposed transbay line on the north. It was his idea that this area could be filled in for warehouses and factory sites, with conveniently located docks at which freight and passengers could be exchanged between rail and ships.

There was an undeniable scope and magnificence to Borax Smith's scheme—in fact, it was a private enterprise version of city planning. In the language of the economist, it was a practical form of "growth model" in several respects. It was well adapted to a specific physical and urban setting, and did not rely upon tax money. Because its parts were interlocking and mutually reinforcing, it took full advantage of the principle of synergism, but within a context in which markets could operate freely. In other words, it was a form of framework and infrastructure planning, to be of general utility to the business community and to the urban area as a whole.

To illustrate, the unified street-railway system would open up lands for subdivision and settlement, producing traffic for the system as a direct result. Moreover, the new transbay service would induce many San Franciscans to transfer their places of residence to the East Bay—where land was much cheaper—and also encourage travel to San Francisco for reasons of commerce as well as for shopping and entertainment. At the same time, the new interurban system would provide a convenient terminal and switching service for overland freight. The availability of cheap land for factories and warehouses would create jobs on the continental side, which in turn would encourage construction, settlement, and local passenger traffic. Finally, because the entire project would be located on the eastern shore of the bay, it would become a natural target for any transcontinental or mainline railroad, because ready access to the wharves and factory areas would make a reality of the Oakland slogan, "where rail and water meet."

By 1890, the Southern Pacific was already well entrenched in the East Bay, with its transcontinental and Portland line occupying the northern portion of the continental shore; its Los Angeles route in the southern portion; and its local passenger services in possession of Shattuck Avenue into the center of Berkeley, and of Seventh Street toward East Oakland, both from Oakland Pier. All of this complex represented a very substantial investment, with the advantages of monopoly fully available to it, except for Smith's vitally important tidelands, which somehow had been overlooked by the usually cautious Huntington. In any case, if Huntington, who died in August 1900, and E. H. Harriman, who took over after him, shared any of Borax Smith's enthusiasm for his great plan, they managed to keep it well concealed. After all, there was competition latent within it. In 1900 the Santa Fe arrived, establishing an extensive terminal in Richmond, and, aided by F. M. Smith, gaining access to Oakland as well. By 1910, George Gould's Western Pacific had opened its new line from Oakland to the east. By then, everything seemed to be in place for Smith's plan to work. Unfortunately this was not to be, at least for several decades to come.

Unification and Modernization of the Traction Companies

It is by no means certain exactly when Frank Smith entered the traction business, but it was probably on February 4, 1890, when he acquired a minority interest in the California Railway. On that date the California Railway Company was organized to operate a line that extended northeast from East 14th Street in Oakland, past Mills College, and ending in two short branch lines. One went east to Columbia Park, where a large quarry was situated that later provided tons of riprap for the future transbay mole; the other, in a switchback trestle, first turned northward, then reversed eastward. This segment was to serve Smith's Leona Chemical Company, by hauling iron pyrites southwest across East 14th Street to a sulfuric acid plant on San Leandro Bay.[6]

The basis for the inference that Borax Smith made his debut into street railways with this small property is that William H. Chickering, his personal attorney at the time, was on the board of directors that effected the incorporation. Smith often preferred to operate in secret when executing his numerous complex deals, assigning others to act for him and terming such persons "dummies" to make sure that those whom he wished to know would grasp clearly where the real power lay, while the public would be left in ignorance of the fact. On occasion, Smith's dummies would hold his shares in their names. Another advantage to Smith in gaining control of this concern was that he wanted to develop his pyrites holdings, and to have a reduction plant built in the marshes along the bay, where the fumes would not arouse local residents—as had occurred with PCB's West Alameda plant.

Although it will not be possible to follow in detail Smith's career in street railroads, we need to review its outlines in order to gain an appreciation of his accomplishments in this field, along with a better understanding of his master plan.

In May 1893, it was disclosed that F. M. Smith had gained control of a bankrupt and decrepit narrow gauge steam road bearing the grand title of the California and Nevada Railroad. This company owned or controlled under lease a considerable acreage west of San Pablo Avenue, extending to its ferry terminal on the shoreline. Part of the land was in Oakland and part in Emeryville. The line ran east toward 40th Street, then turned north, proceeding to Berkeley and Richmond, after which it headed east into the San Pablo Valley, terminating at a station called Bryant (now the site of the public school in the community of Orinda). The road provided irregular service over "two streaks of rust" for a total distance of 22 miles. It was one of those cases of starting somewhere but ending nowhere.[7]

But Borax Smith saw possibilities in the road. Supposedly a new ferry terminal would be built immediately, while vague suggestions were put out about a circular network of electric railways in the East Bay hills that would link up with the new terminal. The road was to be double-tracked and converted to broad gauge, and would run down the center of a boulevard 100 feet wide.[8] None of these undertakings was to come to pass for several more years. Nonetheless, the land and right of way of the California and Nevada Railroad were to become the eventual site of the Key Route shops, powerhouse and storage yard, along with the Key's main line to San Francisco, the Oakland terminal, and the Santa Fe's right of way to Richmond.[9]

Of added importance for dating Smith's progress in the street railway field was the news published on April 29, 1893, that he had made his second payment for acquisition of a controlling block of stock in the Oakland Consolidated Street Railway. By July he was in full possession.[10] By the end of the year, he had also acquired control of the Central Avenue Railway (now West 12th Street), as well as publicly acknowledged minority interests in the California Railway and the Alameda, Oakland, and Piedmont Electric Railway.[11]

Early in 1894 there appeared a curious announcement that F. M. Smith had made an agreement with a delegation of businessmen to build his "ferry line" and to extend the C&N to Walnut Creek if investors would subscribe $250,000. On the following day, the figure was cut to $225,000. It was to be a guaranteed amount, to be invested in the stock of the Oakland and San Francisco Terminal Company, a Smith venture with $1.5 million in authorized capital stock. Smith was to get $698,000 worth, at par, by contributing $1,334,000 (par value) in stocks of the four street railways in which he held an interest, plus the terminal lands and facilities owned or leased by the California and Nevada Railroad.[12]

Here, in fact, was the actual nucleus of the original Key Route, although hardly anyone except Frank Smith was aware of it at the time. In any event, on February 6, 1894, Smith suddenly canceled his offer, and refused to allow his attorney to negotiate a settlement of differences.[13] Nine days later, Smith announced that he would carry out the ferry scheme himself, on his own terms and in his own time. However, the report also said that he was trying to raise $150,000, which would allow construction of an extension of the C&N from Bryant to Walnut Creek and construction of the "proposed ferry system" as well.[14] Clearly, the idea for the Key Route was very much alive in Smith's mind even at this early date. Evidently, though, the capital was lacking for moving forward at that time.

In 1895, Smith joined with Frank Colton Havens to form the Realty Syndicate, which was to carry out one of the four key elements in the former's plan.[15] The Syndicate quickly became a means of raising cash, and its two promoters used its funds to improve the railways under its control as well as to extend them. In this way, their four companies became known as the "Syndicate" railways. Indeed, the Syndicate became the unifying agent for aiding Frank in ultimately assembling a single consolidated system.[16]

The process gathered speed early in 1898 by interline agreements covering track and equipment. On March 21, Smith and Havens formed the Oakland Transit Company from the predecessor concerns. During the remainder of this same year, three more properties were taken over by Oakland Transit. This left but two independent companies in the field. One, the Oakland Railroad Company, had the Central Pacific as its real (but not apparent) owner. In April 1901, following some complicated financial transactions, it joined the Syndicate system. The other was the lengthy Oakland, Alameda and Haywards Electric Railway, which was added to the system through a three-way negotiation in which Smith and his associate, William G. Henshaw, advanced the cash to Oakland Transit; Oakland Transit bought the Haywards stock, but then turned it over to the Syndicate for cash and Syndicate debentures.[17] Then the Syndicate effected a consolidation of Oakland

Transit and its new Hayward line, to form Oakland Transit Consolidated as the successor company, on March 29, 1902.[18]

From an operating point of view, this lengthy series of acquisitions by Smith continued important advantages both for the public and the companies themselves. It is a truism that the street railway business is a "natural" monopoly, essentially because as consolidation increases the scale of operations, the scale of the fixed investment in plant, equipment, and other fixed facilities enlarges in lesser degree, which reduces the average fixed cost per passenger mile in operations. Duplicate facilities can be eliminated, routes and policies can be merged and standardized, and a smaller single management can replace several separate ones.

Frank Smith had intuitively placed himself on the right track with his persistent efforts to put together a unified system. Costs were reduced and capital was more easily attracted. And although he was not without autocratic tendencies, or at least strongly preferred to be free to make the final decisions, his policy always was to select the best possible executives, and to give them ample discretionary authority to produce results. His history in borax fully attests to this. In the case at hand, he brought in Wickson F. Kelley of New York City to manage the system, beginning in September 1899.[19] Kelley was an experienced traction man and very capable at managing operations as well as planning future development. Later, he was severely criticized for an alleged hard-boiled attitude toward the public, but to the extent that there is truth in this it should be borne in mind that in those days, when a ride cost a nickel, Kelley's chief preoccupation was with gathering enough capital to finance a large and growing consolidated system. This was difficult to do to the satisfaction of F. M. Smith, who had high standards but was often pinched for cash, and of politicians who knew little about the business but could readily find votes by beating the drums for projects appealing to various interest groups among the company's passengers. The modern tactics of public relations were just coming into being and had not yet reached Oakland Transit Consolidated. Given their monopoly position in those days, the old traction men tended to adopt a "take it or leave it" attitude.

From the formation of Oakland Transit Consolidated in March 1902, to the last Smith reorganization, the San Francisco–Oakland Terminal Railways Company, in March 1912, the main theatre of action involved the long-deferred transbay interurban and ferry system. Nevertheless, Oakland Transit continued to play a prominent role in the story. In September 1904, Smith and Havens turned aside the threat of a new competing company by consolidating it with OTC to form the Oakland Traction Consolidated. In September 1906, some Berkeley real estate men formed the Berkeley Traction Company. Eight days later, Oakland Traction Consolidated absorbed the firm, consolidating with it to bring into being the Oakland Traction Company.[20] This company was to have a corporate life of about five and a half years. Then, on March 21, 1912, Smith abandoned his established principle of two separate companies—the Key Route, which had started operations in 1903 for the transbay services, and the OTC for local streetcar service. In 1912, he combined both under the title of San Francisco–Oakland Terminal Railways Company—which also included the California Railway and the East Shore and Suburban.

In his 1937 history of street railways in the East Bay area, Dallas W. Smythe made some severe criticisms of Smith and Havens. One was the charge that they had engaged in repeated "stock inflations," by which Smythe apparently meant over-capitalization and "watered" stock. Another of his complaints was that they had "milked" the railways to enrich the land syndicate, by means of excessively low fares and the unprofitable extension of lines into unsettled areas. Lastly, Smythe contended that the railway companies failed to charge for depreciation of fixed plant and equipment in calculating their earnings.

To take the charge of stock inflation first, two examples may be cited, both of which involved calculations that rest upon par values for the stocks involved.[21] In March 1898, the Oakland Transit Company was organized to take over three other Smith roads, by consolidation. OTC was authorized by its charter to issue $5 million in capital stock at par value. Of this sum, $3.15 million was used to buy $1.915 million in stocks of the three former companies (all values expressed at par). The effect was to ascribe a total value at par for OTC stock that was, Smythe claimed, 64.6 percent above the nominal value of the stocks of the predecessor companies—that is, $1.915 million of the original stocks became $3.15 million in new stock. However, on the basis of par values, the holders of the original stocks wound up having contributed less than even 22 percent in cash or other property for the new stock they had received. In fact, Smythe pointed out, the total stock issued by OTC brought in exchange a contribution of cash and other property of only 19.3 percent. (Smythe was calculating on a basis of $5 million at par for his total.)

In the second case, Smith and Havens took the OTC of 1898 through a later reorganization of forming the Oakland Traction Company (hereafter also called OTC) in November 1906. The new OTC was authorized to issue $7.05 million in preferred stock, and $10.925 million in common, for a total of $17.925 million *based upon par values*. Smith and Havens used the $7.05 million in preferred for exchange, share for share at par, for an equivalent amount of Oakland Traction Consolidated stock. In addition, they added a bonus in the new OTC common of 1.5 shares for each full share of the predecessor company. The balance of the new common—$300,000—was paid to the Berkeley group for $200,000 in its stock, all at par values.

Putting these figures together on a par value basis throughout, Smythe concluded that the equity account of the new OTC had been inflated by $10.875 million. To balance the books, the asset called "Cost of Road and Plant" therein was written up by an equal amount. Then, taking both classes of new stock together at par— $17.925 million—it turned out that the actual cost contribution of the stockholders in the new OTC in cash or equivalent property was only $1,753,864, or 9.8 percent of the aggregate for both issues.

Several observations may now be made, all of which involve the principle, "things are not always as simple as they seem." First, in those days many states required that capital stock be assigned a par value, and that all book transactions involving issue or exchange of stock be conducted at par values, regardless of their market price. More frequently than not, stocks of new or reorganized companies simply could not be issued for initial sale or exchange at par values. Particularly was this true for street railways and interurban companies, which were risky ventures from the start, and, with subsequent consolidations, often had a history of losses or poor earnings to depress the market value of their securities. In consequence, securities of newly consolidated companies frequently had to be sold at an actual discount from par. If the law forbade this, however, then the issue was distributed at par, and both the proprietorship and cost-of-road accounts would be so written as to sustain the fictitious par value. Of course, this involves some accounting legerdemain, but what really matters here is whether the business

ultimately builds up its earnings to sustain the upward recapitalization of assets involved. These events took place decades before
today's strict regulations had been imposed.

The same problem is found in the old and extensive practice of
taking promoters' profits in stock. In both cases, we are dealing with
the capitalization of future prospects. Accordingly, the observation
of Dr. Samuel Johnson in opening the bidding at the auctioning of
Mrs. Thrale's brewery sheds a bit of light and humor on what was
actually going on:

> We are not here to dispose of a parcel of boilers and vats, but the
> potentiality of growing rich beyond the dreams of avarice.[22]

With promoters' profits as well, the old practice was to capitalize
the assets of the new enterprise highly enough to support an issue of
common stock. The stock would go to the promoters as their reward
for undertaking a risk, granted that it would be worth little or nothing
at the outset on the market. Then, if they assembled a good
management—and if fortune smiled upon the new company—
earnings would begin to grow, dividends would eventually be paid,
and gradually the stock would appreciate on the market, occasionally "beyond the dreams of avarice." In point of fact, the great J.
Pierpont Morgan himself employed this very device in forming the
United States Steel combination in 1901, taking most of his com-
pensation in common shares of little or no market value. Over the
following decade, he deliberately built up the value of the stock by
"making a market" for it, and ultimately the stock began to "float"
on the company's own earnings, and J. P. Morgan could begin to
cash in on his holdings. In this whole exercise, he was neither a
pioneer nor an exception. It was simply standard practice to create
common stock for this purpose.

This was the primary motive of F. M. Smith as well. He used the
consolidation device repeatedly in both borax and his public
utilities, and in some cases emerged with a profit, while in others he
did not. It may be said that the upward recapitalizations of his
companies were the direct reflection of his unquenchable optimism
about his Oakland projects, and a concomitant growing need for
capital. Because capital was not easy to raise in the early years of
this century, Smith did much of his financing through personal
short-term borrowing, which was amply secured by company stocks
and bonds, typically on a 2:1 basis. As time passed, he resorted
more and more to this practice. But because the growth of the

railways' traffic was slower than he had expected, over-capitalization began to grow instead of disappearing as earnings increased. As capitalization became top-heavy, his credit gradually became exhausted, beginning about 1910. It should be emphasized that the "stock inflation" attributed to Smith was not unusual or illegal at the time. It is fallacious reasoning to attempt to carry back current legal and philosophical standards in making judgments about earlier times. Nor was it to the physical damage of the companies he was working hard to build up. On the contrary, the system he created gradually came to be recognized as one of the best in the country.

Before leaving the tractions, we must say a few words about the charge that Smith and Havens supposedly "milked" the railways for the benefit of their land company, the Realty Syndicate. The basis of this charge was that fares on the railways were kept excessively low to encourage traffic on lines built into open lands being subdivided for settlement, while the lines had been built at a loss to encourage sales of land. In short, the claim was that Smith and Havens had their real interests in the Syndicate, while their rail system was hardly more than a tool for the Syndicate's purposes.

Smythe's allegation was based upon testimony given in 1917 by George K. Weeks, who had by then replaced F. M. Smith as head of San Francisco–Oakland Terminal Railways. Testifying on behalf of an increase in fares, Weeks sought to convey the idea that because Smith dominated both the railways and the Syndicate in a relationship "very similar to the relation between the two pockets of the same man's trousers," it was of little concern to him if the profits came from land or from the railway. In short, what he lost in low fares he made up in sales of land at enhanced values.[23]

Naturally, Weeks wanted to make as strong a case as he could for increased fares, as any transit executive would. Furthermore, his trousers analogy was essentially correct—except that Smith had invested millions in the railways to carry out the four parts of his great vision for metropolitan development. In addition, he had done an impressive job in unifying and modernizing the tractions, while the Key Route had wrought a revolution in transbay transportation after 1903. Borax Smith was immensely proud of these achievements. Thus the allegation that he sacrificed the railways in favor of raising land values quite misses the point. His scheme had always had four components, not one. He wanted desperately to put the railways on a paying basis. His failure to accomplish this fully had its sources elsewhere. But a willingness to defer higher fares at a given

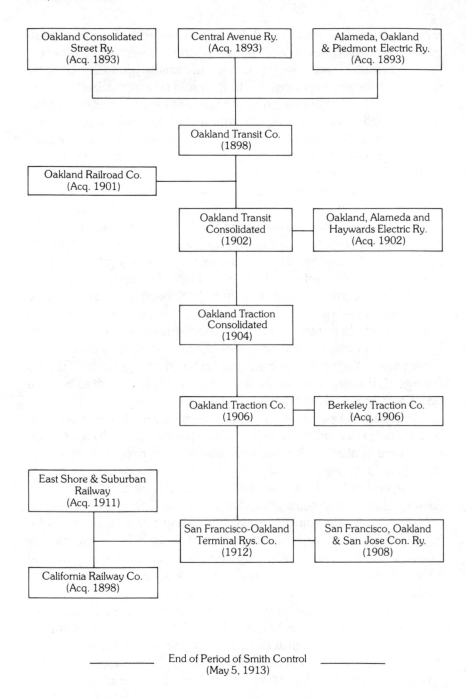

End of Period of Smith Control
(May 5, 1913)

**Fig. 2. Corporate History of F. M. Smith's Major Street Railways in the East
Bay Area, 1893–1913.**

time to build up traffic potential for the future is not much different from selling loss leaders in a supermarket to expand total patronage at the store. To provide a better grasp of F. M. Smith's entire achievement, one must consider the full story, which also involves the histories of the Realty Syndicate and the Key Route.

The Realty Syndicate

Around 1895, F. M. Smith had become friendly with Frank C. Havens. Havens was about the same age, had been around Oakland since 1866, was an engaging extrovert with a personality of much appeal to some,[24] and was a born promoter. Havens' specialty was buying up undeveloped lands and subdividing them. He was much impressed by Smith's already large holdings of acreage, and more so by his seemingly limitless wealth. Here was a partner worth having. Frank Smith could bring money and vision into the combination, while Havens knew how to develop raw land. At the same time, Havens controlled the People's Water Company, which could profit from increased development.

The interests of F. M. Smith and F. C. Havens thus were running in tandem at that time. As a result, on September 23, 1895, it was announced in the press that "a huge real estate syndicate" had been formed, with an authorized capitalization of $5 million,[25] although the actual initial assets were only about $1 million. In addition to Smith and Havens, the names of some of the other directors are also of interest: they included William G. Henshaw, who was close to Havens; Hiram Tubbs, a hotel and land owner; William J. Dingee, Havens' associate in water and land; W. H. Chickering, a Smith attorney; Victor H. Metcalf, then a Congressman and later a member of the cabinet of President Theodore Roosevelt; H. C. Miner of New York City, a theater man and a relative of Mary R. Smith's; and Alton Clough (of PCB) and E. A. Heron, both Smith associates.

One definition of a "syndicate" is "a group of persons or concerns who combine under a usually temporary agreement to carry out a particular transaction."[26] This description is appropriate for investment houses who join to market a new security, but it does not fit our case, because the Realty Syndicate was neither temporary nor was it directed toward a particular transaction. On the contrary, it sold stock in itself, dealt in land and investments, and contemplated a permanent existence. With its inception, its principal assets were land and electric railway stocks, and short-term loans due principally from Smith and Havens. Its principal liabilities were its investment certificates, which were a kind of unsecured debenture paying six percent and soon to become locally famous as "Syndicate Sixes." By sale of the "Sixes," the Syndicate raised large amounts of money which it used to fund its projects, which in turn were steadily growing in diversity. For example, within a year of its formation, Smith turned over his holdings in the Oakland Consolidated and the California and Nevada Railroad.[27] A year later the Syndicate obtained the East Oakland Street Railroad under foreclosure, and added two other companies within the next 60 days.[28] Furthermore, the Syndicate also acquired some stock in Borax Consolidated, Limited. In essence, Smith had begun using the Syndicate as an investment company, which enlarged the capital at his disposal.

In the fall of 1898 the Syndicate was rumored to be preparing to develop the long-discussed transbay rail and ferry system. The story was promptly denied, and four more years were to elapse before this project actually got under way.[29] By November 1901, the *Oakland Tribune* was referring to what it chose to call a "queer project" of the Syndicate to build an electric railroad from Oakland to San Jose, with branches to Los Gatos and Santa Clara.[30] The new line would be known as the Oakland and San Jose Railroad Company, and its purpose, said the *Tribune*, was to head off a similar project involving Baltimore capital. F. M. Smith and F. C. Havens were to be directors; Smith subscribed for $40,000 in stock, and Havens $20,000.

Three weeks later, the project was given a new twist when Smith and Havens incorporated the San Francisco and Piedmont Railway in preparation for building the long-awaited transbay system.[31] The plan called for a trestle to run from the east shoreline of San Francisco Bay straight west to the pier-head line (where the Key Route ultimately built its ferry terminal). At that point, the road would descend into a steel single-track underwater tube for the run to Yerba Buena (or Goat) Island, at which point a train terminal that would connect for San Francisco would be built for transfer of passengers. According to a lengthy statement by Havens, "Work will begin immediately." Within the East Bay area, the line would run on 40th Street eastward to Piedmont, and then onward to Leona Heights in East Oakland, for a total distance of 17 miles. The Realty Syndicate was credited with organizing the project.[32]

On December 16, 1901, F. M. Smith wrote his associate in London, R. C. Baker,

> You may be interested to know that the Realty Syndicate is reaching out for a ferry from Oakland to San Francisco. I might rather say that they are reaching out for a block of land on Goat Island and a tube from Pier Head line to same. The tube will be a single one, a double tube not being required at the present time to handle the traffic. The tube will be one and one-half miles long. The single tube only is necessary as we would only be going part way to San Francisco and trains could be run both ways on a single track.
>
> I believe the cost of this tube in London is $1 million a mile. We could have no trouble about financing this proposition. The only difficulty would be to get the location on Goat Island which would answer the purpose of a switching place, should we a few years later wish to come on to San Francisco with a continuous tube.[33]

This was the kind of foresight that made Borax Smith extraordinary. It was a bold undertaking, for all of this was to be accomplished through capital stock of $2.5 million at par, of which Smith would subscribe for $60,000, and Havens $20,000.

Until this point, one could infer with good reason that the Realty Syndicate was actually what today would be called a conglomerate holding company, so diverse were its plans and activities. Still, its primary concern was land and its development. In this respect, the Syndicate was a pioneering version of a savings and loan association. It raised money mostly by sale of its long-term "Sixes." It bought great tracts of land along the waterfront, in strategic sections of the East Bay flatlands, and all over the Contra Costa and Oakland hills, from Richmond to Hayward. At its peak, the Syndicate owned 13,000 acres. Its initial policy was to finance subdividers and builders, as well as settlers wishing to obtain mortgage money. Later it moved into tract development on its own. Smith and Havens also made a fine contribution to the aesthetics of the Oakland and Berkeley hills by planting thousands of pine and eucalyptus trees all over the Syndicate's vast land holdings in this area.

Some idea of the Syndicate's growth can be had by comparing its initial (1895) capitalization of $5 million, and assets of $1 million, with its balance sheet as determined by Klink, Bean and Company for April 26, 1913.[34] As of that latter date, the Syndicate had an *unadjusted* net worth of $5,987,080.77, deriving from *unadjusted* total assets of $16,168,241.77, less *unadjusted* total liabilities of $8,095,707.78 plus surplus of $8,972,533.99.[35] After the special adjustments made by the accountants, net worth became only $2,912,975.50; even with this drastic write-down, a share of Syndicate stock had a value of $65.00.

On an adjusted basis, the Syndicate by 1913 had acquired tracts and acreage conservatively valued at just under $7 million, plus an additional $1.7 million in land contracts and buildings. It also held stocks and bonds in affiliated companies with an adjusted value of $4.4 million (almost entirely composed of the borax companies, the Oakland Traction, and the Key Route). In addition, F. M. Smith, who controlled the Syndicate after Havens' departure in 1910, owed it approximately $300,000 for notes and advances in 1913.

The appraisals of 1913 were occasioned by F. M. Smith's grave financial problems at that time. The Syndicate had grown rapidly in less than 20 years, by means of its triple role as a land developer, an owner and financing agent for the Smith railways, and a banker for financing Borax Smith's increasingly complex and extensive business interests.

The Realty Syndicate figured in Oakland history in yet another way. It made possible the building of the Claremont Hotel in the Berkeley foothills, and the Key Route Inn in Oakland at the terminus (at that time) of the 22nd Street Key Route line.[36] Both structures were in Elizabethan style, and the Inn was a particularly charming example, designed by Edward Foulkes. The Claremont, which still exists and has recently undergone extensive renovation, has a magnificent view and location. According to the Havens papers, its original cost was about $880,000. Smith and Havens built these hotels by means of a type of partnership arrangement they had established between them. When they broke up in 1910, Smith took the Syndicate and Havens apparently got both hotels, plus a bundle of Smith's personal notes and some bonds in the People's Water Company.

In 1903 the Realty Syndicate built a three-story office building in Oakland at 1440 Broadway, next to the Central National Bank on the 14th Street corner. During 1911–12, the structure was raised to 10 stories, with offices on the top floor for F. M. Smith and his associates. Smith had his own office paneled in Circassian walnut, with the upper walls painted to reproduce scenes of Death Valley. The artist, Charles Dickman, did a superb job in capturing the strangely radiant light that the Valley so often displays. The office also had a large fireplace with a mantel supported by exquisitely carved buffalo heads. F. M. Smith's desk was made of highly pol-

Original emblem showing how the San Francisco, Oakland & San Jose
Railway received its famous nickname. About 1904. (Louis L. Stein
collection, courtesy of Robert Stein.)

ished quartz, embellished by a ribbon of quartz and onyx blocks.
Adjoining his private office was a complete personal barber shop.

When the Syndicate building was sold in 1979, its new owner
declared that it was still in excellent condition because Borax Smith
had built it with only the finest of materials. Hence the building has a
permanent place in Oakland.

The Key Route

F. M. Smith owed his international fame, of course, to his
achievements in the borax industry. One might say that this was the
macrocosmic side of his career. But, displaying the same talents and
character traits, he began developing a parallel career on the micro-
cosmic side. It, too, made him famous, primarily around San Francisco Bay. In its full dimension, this second career embodied the
great dream of his life: development of the continental side of San
Francisco Bay as a metropolitan area of its own. The element that
brought him renown in this endeavor was his Key Route system for
transbay passenger transportation.

The evidence suggests that transbay service began to fascinate
Smith as early as 1893, when he had brought the California and
Nevada Railroad under his control. Over the next eight years three
false starts were made, all defeated by lack of capital. Nonetheless,
Smith controlled the California and Nevada terminal, as well as its
substantial terminal lands and right of way. Also, he had formed the

Oakland and San Jose, and the San Francisco and Piedmont railways in 1901. With these three companies, a beginning for the long-delayed transbay system was by then imminent. The corporate phase was completed with the fusion of these concerns on June 9, 1902, when the San Francisco, Oakland and San Jose Railway came into being.[37] This was the original Key Route, although that popular sobriquet only came into use about a year later. In its initial form, the new transbay line possessed a pattern similar to a traditional long-stem inside door key. The ferry terminal that Smith was compelled to build (when he was denied the use of Yerba Buena Island by Congress) represented the prongs of the key that turn the tumblers after its insertion into a lock, and the ferry slips served as the actual "prongs." The long straight stem reflected the trestle, mole, and inland tracks of the company, while the three circular holes forming the handle end represented, in clockwise order, the branches to Berkeley, Piedmont, and Oakland—the first three communities served by the company.

After further efforts early in 1902 to obtain operating privileges to Yerba Buena Island—all to no avail—Smith decided to erect a large ferry terminal, which would stand in the waters of the bay and connect to a trestle that would extend from the continental shoreline. At this latter point, the double-track line would enter a subway under the five SP tracks, and then emerge on the continental side—where yards, shops, and a power station were to be built. In this area, the first branch later turned off to the south at Interlocking Tower No. 2 to serve both 22nd Street and 12th Street in Oakland. The main stem continued east along Yerba Buena Avenue, crossing San Pablo Avenue, and shortly thereafter dividing into the Piedmont branch along 40th Street to Piedmont Avenue, and the Berkeley branch up Adeline Street to Shattuck Avenue, terminating at University Avenue.

On three occasions, Borax Smith stubbornly sought to gain federal permission to place the Key terminal on Yerba Buena Island. In March 1902, it was reported in local newspapers that he had raised $10 million in Boston for his subway project, but to no avail.[38] One day later, the Realty Syndicate was credited by the press with planning to use the $10 million for both the transbay and Oakland–San Jose projects. It was explained that F. M. Smith had just discussed his plans in confidence with the California delegation in Washington (where he was urging approval of his subway project), evidently taking care to point out that a pier terminal on the Oakland side of the island could be used.[39]

Engineer Howard Holmes' sketch of F. M. Smith's initial plan for a tube to Yerba Buena Island (Goat Island), with a ferry terminal on the western side. The signature is Smith's. (F. M. Smith collection, courtesy of Mildred Smith Nicholls.)

At this early stage, Smith was hoping to induce the Santa Fe to join with the Key Route by using its projected new terminal and ferry system. But the Santa Fe had no such interest because it already had its own terminal and ferry in Richmond. However, its president, E. P. Ripley, was prepared to make a deal with Smith to use the old C&N right of way to gain access to Oakland, and this eventually came to pass.[40]

Within a few weeks, Smith decided to proceed on his own, and to abandon the tube in favor of a terminal in the bay. Bids were also let for two new ferry steamers, propeller driven and of the latest type. They were to be named the *San Jose* and the *Yerba Buena*.[41] On May 29, contracts were let for the trestle and its terminal. The project called for slightly over 16,000 feet of track from the shoreline to the pier, all to be erected on piles.[42] From the pier terminal to San Francisco, the distance was only 14,500 feet. By comparison, the SP's Oakland pier had a distance of 18,000 feet, and its Alameda narrow gauge pier, 16,500 feet. With the Key's fast new boats and electric trains, the Southern Pacific would be out of the running.[43]

The ferry terminal was a splendid achievement in difficult engineering, and the credit primarily belongs to two men: Howard C.

Holmes, the chief engineer; and Walter J. Mathews, the architect for the superstructure. To protect the passengers from rain, Mathews devised a *porte cochère* arrangement that completely sheltered the bow (or stern) of the steamer when tied up at the terminal. To make access to or departure from the trains convenient, the ferry slips were placed at right angles to the tracks, of which there were five, all diverging at a common point about 600 feet east of the outer end of the terminal. The trains were spaced from each other so that passengers could pass easily to the proper track and board the cars with little walking.[44]

Smith had hoped to get the Berkeley line into operation by New Year's Day of 1903. But the St. Louis Car Company was slow in delivering the rolling stock, which had to be assembled in the open air until the shops were completed. As with the elegant ferries, the Key Route cars were fresh and clean in design, and beautifully finished. On the outside they were painted an attractive "Key Route" (or "traction") orange, and were embellished with silver striping and numbering along the sides of the car below the sash. The name of the company and the title "Key Route," were rendered in silver, with the latter above on the letter board and the former on the side of the car. Later the corporate name was raised to the letter board and the sides were left unmarked. Brown was used for the window sash, and a light gray for the roofs. All side windows were topped by a handsome gothic-arch section, in stained glass, while the clerestory roof had elegant stained glass and curved transom windows. At each end of the clerestory deck the top was brought down in a graceful curve to the roof line, in early interurban style. Inside, the ceilings were in empire design, with gold striping on light green, accompanied by a handsome interior clerestory ceiling, with the central panels beautifully fitted to the transom windows through graceful openings composed of compound curves. Mahogany was used for all wall panels.

These were the cars that made up the handsome new train standing at Shattuck and University Avenues in Berkeley on the morning of October 26, 1903, opening day for the new line. F. M. Smith's own paper, *The Oakland Herald*, told the story.

> At 9:28 o'clock this morning the train of five cars left Berkeley. Superintendent J. P. Potter gave the word that sent the big train down the long straight track. Assistant Superintendent Clark Yerrick was at the motor and in the first car sat Mr. F. M. Smith, accompanied

View of the Key Route pier about 1904, showing the early Lehigh cars at far left, and the first series of the St. Louis cars center and right. (Author's collection.)

A Key Route train at the pier terminal on opening day, October 26, 1903. Note potted palms and the little fire car on track at extreme left. The pier burned in March 1933. (Vernon J. Sappers collection.)

by Mrs. F. M. Smith, Miss Marion Smith, Miss Florence Nightingale, Miss [Evelyn] Ellis and others.

W. H. Kimmell was the conductor in charge. K. A. Morrison, M. C. Mitchell, J. Fitzsimmons, and H. C. McAtee acted as collectors. [45]

Borax Smith had looked very far ahead when he committed his fortune to this great project. He had revolutionized transbay transportation at one stroke. To do it, he had brought together the best in human talent and technology. The new Key Route immediately won great popularity, enlivening the local scene while opening up the area to greatly accelerated development. For 55 years the Key continued to provide safe and reliable service, certainly a record for an interurban line and proof of its utility to the community. [46]

As the founder of the Key Route, Smith won much good will with the public. But as his frustrated effort to build a tube to the desired island terminal readily illustrates, becoming a founder is not without its troubles. Although it eventually consumed his wealth, in its own way it was a most appropriate monument to the man who did so much for his adopted city.

In 1903 George C. Pardee was Governor of California. The Governor was caught in a conflict between the Key Route and the

An unusual aerial view of the original Key Route pier. Probably about 1920. (Louis L. Stein collection, courtesy of Robert Stein.)

A Key Route trailer coach, built by the St. Louis Car Company. About 1909.
(Louis Stein collection, courtesy of Robert Stein.)

Southern Pacific, which were about to become competitors for the
transbay traffic. Pardee was an Oakland man, an eye doctor who
treated Smith, and a friend of his. Fortunately, there survives some
correspondence between the two that reflects well the ancient ten-
sions between politician and businessman.[47]

At the outset of 1903, Smith had written Pardee complaining that
the Key had been trying for nearly a year to get a convenient San
Francisco slip for its boats, yet was told that this slip would be on the
extreme north side beyond the Ferry Building, which the State
controlled. Smith rightly pointed to the dangers in requiring the Key
boats to cross the paths of both the Marin and Santa Fe ferries. He
went on to observe that the SP rented four slips, of which three
were used while the fourth was occupied by steamers on lay-up.
Smith rightly believed that SP boats should be tied up at SP's own
Oakland pier. "The logic of the case is, our slips should be in the
center, for the reason that in such case we would not cross the lines
of any existing ferry."[48]

Pardee replied on January 22, promising to investigate. On
January 28, Smith wrote the Governor, arguing his case with his
usual vigor. If the SP can operate in and out of Oakland Pier from

Piedmont train on the Key Route, at Yerba Buena and San Pablo avenues, about 1908. In the early years the motor cars sported two pantographs. (Vernon J. Sappers collection.)

The *Fernwood* passing Yerba Buena Island, about 1908. She was one of the second series of Key Route ferries. (Louis Stein collection, courtesy of Robert Stein.)

The first Key Route ferry, the *Yerba Buena*, enters the slip Borax Smith fought so hard to get at the San Francisco Ferry Building. (Vernon J. Sappers collection.)

one slip, why does it need more than one slip for each of its services to San Francisco when it could tie up its idle ferries at its two piers on the Oakland and Alameda side? After reiterating the obvious desirability of a slip that would enable the Key to avoid crossing the paths of any other ferry lines, Borax Smith assailed a Mr. Kirkpatrick, a member of the State Board of Harbor Commissioners, who had proposed that the Key circle Yerba Buena from the north side. Smith, who as an experienced yachtsman understood nautical charts, fired back this missive:

> I am quite surprised at the suggestion of Mr. Kirkpatrick, that he supposed we were going to the north side of the island. A Harbor Commissioner is supposed to know something about the Harbor. He either shows gross ignorance, or he is an imposter, for any navigator knows that it is impracticable for us to go to the north side of the island, that the shoal shown on the map is so close to the north side that it would be impossible to go between it and the island, and that it would be a long detour to the north to avoid the shoal otherwise.[49]

Protesting that the Key proposed to offer a passenger service, ". . . not hauling trucks, chicken coops, and the bad odors that accompany them," Smith insisted, "We must have an upper landing and we must be centrally located." When F. M. Smith wanted something, he was not easily turned aside.

Pardee evidently ducked the issue, for it went undecided for another eight months, to the eve of the beginning of transbay service. Referring to a Commission hearing, Smith wrote to Governor Pardee that the SP representative opposed the Key Route's request, adding, "I did not only see the force or wisdom of the position that he took, but somehow I felt my helplessness in this situation. . . . I doubt not that the SP are pulling very hard to have us assigned to the most inferior position. While they are very good people in a way, they have never done me any favors." Smith went on to add, "I must not forget to say that I hope to see you [Pardee] on board one of our ferry-boats next Saturday. Mrs. Smith tells me that she has sent an invitation to yourself and your good wife. I would like very much to show you what we have in the way of boats, wharf, and so forth. I think you would be amply repaid for your trip if you could run down and meet us at 40th Street at 11 o'clock on Saturday next."[50] Here Smith must have been referring to a special trial run for Saturday, October 3, for his letter was dated September 30, a Wednesday, and he speaks of "next" Saturday.

The first train to carry passengers ran on that day, starting from 40th and San Pablo and carrying Smith and his friends. It was drawn by a flatbed electric motor with a cab in center, and consisted of two open-ended coaches built in San Francisco by the W. L. Holman Company. After arrival at the pier, the party boarded the *Yerba Buena* and then sat down to luncheon, orchestra music, and a trip around the bay.

Regular ferry service did not begin until Monday, October 26, 1903. In the meantime, the Key Route finally had obtained the slip it had been fighting to get for nearly two years. For the next eight years, expansion ruled the day. By 1912 the company had 32 miles of track, had bought many larger cars of the same original design, and had added three new ferries: the *San Francisco* (1905), the *Claremont* (1907), and the *Fernwood* (1908). In fact, the Key and the street railways together now comprised a system of about 245 miles.

But the Southern Pacific had not forgotten its quarrels and its loss of business to the energetic new company. In 1910 it had struck

A train emerging from the subway under the Southern Pacific tracks, and heading out on the original Key Route mole, about 1904. (Author's collection.)

The first Piedmont Avenue station of the Key Route, about 1904. (Author's collection.)

The Key Route Inn, Edward Foulkes's little gem in the Tudor style, about 1907, before the Key trains ran out Grand Avenue. President Taft stayed here in 1911. (Author's collection.)

back by beginning the electrification of its East Bay steam lines, also adding much new service to Berkeley and East Oakland. Not by coincidence, four of the new SP lines ran to Berkeley, diverting much Key traffic. The bigger road's deliberate aim was to slow up the growth of the Key's profits, which it succeeded in doing in good measure beginning in August 1911.[51]

On June 1, 1904, the Piedmont line was opened, from 40th Street and San Pablo Avenue to Piedmont Avenue. In May 1906, the 22nd Street line began service, taking off from the main stem at Interlocking Tower No. 2 in Emeryville, and running to the Key Route Inn at 22nd Street and Broadway in Oakland. Either in the fall of 1907 or spring of 1908 (the date is not certain), the new company opened its Claremont line, initially as a shuttle service provided by street cars operating from the Claremont Hotel to 40th and San Pablo for a San Francisco connection. In 1909, through service from the pier was introduced as far as College Avenue, and in 1912 it was extended to the hotel terminus.[52] Next, on April 1, 1909, the company initiated its central Oakland line, with through

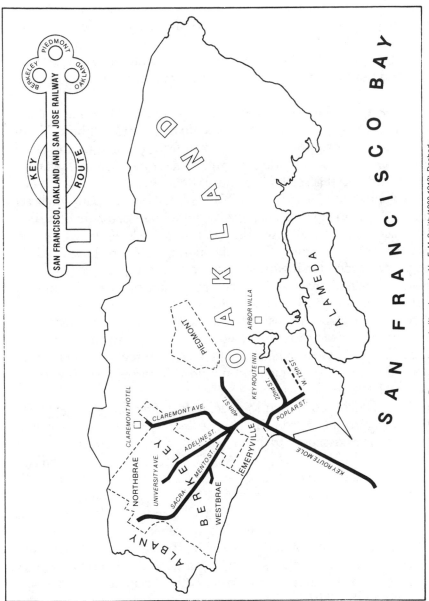

MAP 6. The Key Route system as built and operated by F. M. Smith (1903-1913). Dashed line indicates connecting street car service from Poplar Junction to downtown Oakland.

service from the pier via Tower No. 2 to Poplar Junction (Poplar and West 12th Streets), where transfer was made to special connecting streetcars to 12th and Broadway. This needless transfer was imposed by the Oakland City Council, which would not allow the company to operate its large interurban cars in the central city. Either in 1914 or 1917—the evidence is conflicting—through trains from the pier were finally allowed to operate through to East Oakland, terminating at the old Central Car House just east of Lake Merritt.

The last Key line was introduced in June 1911, operating along the old C&N right of way on Sacramento Street to Northbrae, North Berkeley. A short branch was also built from this line northwest to Westbrae. It was intended to run this branch all the way to Richmond, but this section was never built.

Altogether, under F. M. Smith's control, the company built six through lines in eight years. It also acquired part of a right of way to San Jose, known as the Key Route Country Railway. However, the San Jose Line was never built, although in 1924 track was laid on an unused section in Piedmont, permitting through service from the pier to Oakland Avenue. The company had purchased a private parallel right-of-way between 40th and 41st Streets to accommodate the projected San Jose line. However, no track was ever laid in this section. In fact, the last major expansion involving new track was the Trestle Glen extension of the 22nd Street line, which was opened in 1917, but which did not provide through service to the pier until 1925.

Borax Smith had hoped to effect a deal, first with the Santa Fe, and then with the Western Pacific, so that these companies would operate their passenger trains in and out of the Key Route pier. He was unsuccessful. However, on April 7, 1913, a new interurban line known as the Oakland, Antioch and Eastern did begin using the pier and also the Piedmont line as far as 40th Street and Shafter Avenue, for service to Bay Point (now Port Chicago). On September 3, 1913, this company introduced through service to Sacramento.[53]

Because the Key offered 20-minute service until the late night hours, augmented by a large fleet of "tripper trains" during the peak morning and evening hours, along with about 20 OA&E trains throughout the day, the density of operations between Tower 2 and the pier reached approximately 600 trains daily on weekdays, over a two-track line. With such close headways, the company decided in 1912 to introduce a unique system of automatic block signalling along the mole and trestle. On every fourth pole between the two tracks, an electric signal was installed with a short red semaphore that could take three "aspects" (positions): vertical, for clear; 45 degrees, for caution; and horizontal, for immediate stop. The position was determined by the location of the train ahead: if it were in the second block ahead, the semaphore would be at caution, and the following train would either be stopped by its engineer before reaching the signal or a connected metal arm extending outward from the semaphore would engage a tripper apparatus on the left front side of the roof of the head car. When tripped, this would mean that the following train had overrun its block, and the car mechanism would throw on the train brakes in emergency position. In short, the system provided for a minimum of one open block between all pairs of trains moving in the same direction.[54]

When Borax Smith built the Key Route he had the advantage of controlling the local streetcar system, known in early 1902 as Oakland Transit Consolidated. The advantage was that he could use some of his streetcar trackage for his Key trains as well. At the same time, the extensive traction system undoubtedly helped the new company to build up its passenger business by affording convenient connections for access to additional residential areas, particularly new ones developed by the Realty Syndicate. To illustrate: With the opening of the 12th Street line to central Oakland, the traction cars picked up incoming Key passengers at Poplar Junction, taking them into town and as far beyond as 41st Avenue and Leona Heights in East Oakland. When the company was finally allowed to operate its trains through town, it used street railway trackage all the way to Central Car House. It did the same thing from the Key Route Inn out Grand and Lakeshore Avenues to Trestle Glen. Summed up, the Key was able to increase its route and track mileage substantially without laying more track.

There was another feature to these arrangements that was rather less advantageous. This was the Key's so-called "Traction Division," which operated streetcar service over Key Route trackage from Piedmont Avenue to 40th and San Pablo, and from the latter point to Adeline and Ward Streets, in South Berkeley. Apparently this service was exacted by the city fathers, as the price of allowing the Key trains to refuse accepting local passengers.

There was also the Alcatraz Avenue line, so familiar to students in San Francisco attending the University of California at Berkeley. Built in 1893 as a single-track line from Adeline Street to Telegraph

Avenue, it was bought by Smith's Oakland Transit Consolidated in 1904. With his usual vigor, he installed double tracks, extended the line to College Avenue, provided direct connections with the Berkeley line, and by 1912 had introduced service through to Telegraph Avenue and Bancroft Way, giving direct access to the university.[55]

Was the Key Route a financial success from its beginning in late 1903 until the big merger of March 21, 1912, when it became part of San Francisco–Oakland Terminal Railways Company? The answer is not easy to determine because of the several mergers and consolidations effected over the years. However, data for the Key Route alone indicate that the company did return a modest profit during the calendar years 1904 through 1911.

Table 3
Gross and Net Revenues from
Operations, Key Route System, 1904–1911a/

Year	Gross Income	Gross Operating Expenses	Net Earnings from Operations
1904	$ 419,350	$193,267	$226,083
1905	535,134	267,757	267,377
1906	668,832	297,812	371,020
1907	812,868	447,223	365,645
1908	901,110	476,246	424,864
1909	1,001,802	532,917	468,885
1910	1,120,278	647,727	472,551
1911	1,266,900	779,242	487,658

Source: San Francisco Call (July 26, 1912).

a/ Figures published with an offer of $1.5 million new five percent general mortgage bonds of San Francisco–Oakland Terminal Railways Company. Contractual interest on all Key bond issues was disclosed to be $304,350 as of 1911.

It can be seen that for 1911, deduction of interest of $304,350 on the Key's bond issues does not include interest on the company's floating debt. If we assume that the latter amount of interest was counted as part of gross operating expenses, then we have an operating ratio of gross expenses to gross income of 61.5 percent—a very favorable figure under conventional standards of railroad finance. If we then deduct $304,350 in bond interest from net revenue in 1911, the road had $183,308 for a return on its equity in that year—not so favorable relative to $2,750,000 in common and $5,000,000 in preferred stock issued and outstand-

Collage displaying initial Key Route tickets, hat checks, and commute book signed by F. M. Smith. (F. M. Smith collection.)

ing. In other words, the rate of return on equity was very low, barely 2.4 percent in fact. Clearly, the Key Route segment of the Terminal Railways had by 1911 proved to be no bonanza, although it had shown substantial growth, some ability to pay its own way, and an apparently bright future. At that time, the basic financial problem of the transbay company was an excessive ratio of debt to equity. In short, the concern was overloaded with debt, much of which was owed to F. M. Smith himself in exchange for advances for construction and betterments.

As for the SF–OT itself, the report for 11 months during 1911–1912 disclosed an operating ratio of 63.81 percent, and a net revenue, after all expenses plus bond interest and miscellaneous

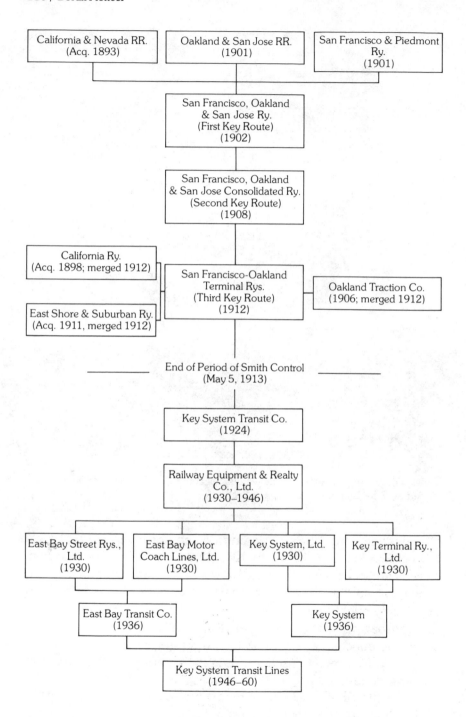

Fig. 3. Corporate History of the Key Route.

F. M. Smith's private car, the *Hauoli*, at the Emeryville Shops of the Key
Route, about 1907. Hauoli is a Hawaiian word, meaning "delight." (Louis
Stein collection, courtesy of Robert Stein.)

charges, of $702,855. This figure represents the return on equity.
However, no dividends were paid because of lenders' restrictions
for short-term financing. As of May 1912, Bradstreet's had quoted a
valuation for all of the company's assets of $30,546,000, as against
$17,483,000 in bonded indebtedness outstanding.[56] In addition,
during the 10 months preceding January 31, 1913, the new company had carried 82 million passengers, which implies an annual
rate of roughly 98 million persons.[57] Of these, approximately 14
million could be estimated as contributed by the Key Route transbay operations, and 84 million for the local traction lines.

To sum up, in the 20 years dating from 1893 to early 1913, F. M.
Smith had brought into being a unified system that by the latter year
was carrying almost 100 million passengers annually. Roughly 85
percent of these were carried locally within the East Bay area, while
15 percent traveled on the Key transbay lines. The system was not

yet highly profitable, but it was modern and well-managed. Even more, it had brought enormous benefits to the region it served. In a sense, Borax Smith had repeated in another field the triumph he had achieved in borax.

The Port Terminal Project

It will be recalled that the fourth element in Frank Smith's grand design was a system of docks, switching tracks, and factory sites. Under the Key's franchise it had the right to use 1,000 feet of fairway (a wider strip with outer boundaries) on each side of its bay trestle. In addition, Smith had bought about 340 acres lying between the SP's "broad gauge" mole and the Key Route trestle, and bounded to the east by the shore line. In July 1902, he sold the tidelands and adjacent property to the Key Route for $2.9 million in stock plus the company's assumption of construction liens in the amount of $315,000 in bonds and $166,230 in cash. Smith and Havens divided the stock on a 2:1 ratio, reflecting their personal arrangement.

Little more need be said about the terminal project. No wharves were built and no tidelands were filled in throughout Smith's remaining tenure, because he was unable to raise the capital. In 1916, three years after he had lost his fortune, Smith tried again to carry out the port project. Working with a financier named Rufus Jennings, he sought to induce the Oakland city government to grant him a long-term lease on the tidelands, in exchange for which he would guarantee investment of five million dollars to bring the port project into being. The Davie Administration was opposed to the plan, but disliked entering into an open fight with Smith. The latter thereupon proposed a popular vote on the issue, offering to pay the costs of the election himself. His offer was accepted. The election cost him $30,000, but he carried the vote. At this point the politicians began a clandestine obstruction. Smith and Jennings took public note of the fact, declaring that now that the politicians were in opposition, they had lost interest in the scheme. "Therefore we quit," they announced bluntly.

And so the great dream failed at its most vital point, not for lack of foresight or of soundness. Indeed, a look at Oakland Harbor today will prove beyond question how correct Borax Smith's vision was. Starting with the Oakland Army Base in 1942, the Port of Oakland has added its Outer Harbor on the very location of the old Key

A later version of Smith's port terminal project, drawn about 1911. (F. M. Smith collection.)

Route tidelands, and today is the largest general cargo port on the West Coast. Furthermore, four years after the Key Route was abandoned in 1958, the people of the three most populous Bay counties voted to create and finance the Bay Area Rapid Transit District. By 1972, BART trains were operating between Oakland and San Francisco through an underwater tube, like the one this remarkable man had sought to build seventy years before.

8

The United Properties Company and Its Failure

By 1913, the unadjusted value of the assets of the San Francisco–Oakland Terminal Railways Company was approximately $30 million. The SF–OT was Borax Smith's last consolidation, undertaken in March 1912, to combine the Key Route and the Oakland Traction Company in one company, under the direct management of William R. ("Billy") Alberger. It is useful, at this point, to review the development of Smith's financing of the Key Route in the intervening years since 1902.

Early Financing of the Key Route
All facilities westward from 41st and Linden Streets, all the way to the pier terminal, including the first two ferries and the first cars along with the fixed plant and power house, were financed by F. M. Smith himself, at a cost of $1,514,405.47. In return, the company issued to him $1.5 million in first mortgage five percent bonds, at par, to reimburse him for these advances.[1]

This transaction is the key to much of the capital financing undertaken by Smith during much of his business career. His procedure essentially was as follows: (1) use the substantial cash inflow from borax dividends to initiate projects—both personal and commercial; (2) take back new securities in return for cash advances so made; (3) use these securities as collateral for short-term notes, issued to increase liquidity and investable cash; (4) augment such short-term borrowing by using prime securities—for example, the borax stocks—for further short-term financing through advances to companies owned; and (5) from time to time sell "free" securities, such as would be obtained as promoter's profits, to increase liquidity and to control the scale of the floating debt.

In all of this, Smith's primary difficulty was that his reach tended to exceed his grasp. In financial terms, his practice was to borrow short to invest long—through demand notes, call notes, and fixed term notes, usually in magnitudes running between $5,000 and $20,000, although much more on later occasions. Truly F. M. Smith was a "borrowing capitalist," willing to take big risks because of the unconquerable optimism inherent in his temperament and his times.

According to Smythe, the Key's $3 million in first mortgage bonds financed the original construction plus the Piedmont line. A second issue, secured by a second mortgage for $1.5 million, came out in 1906. This permitted the 22nd Street and Claremont lines to be built. But with this issue, Smith and Havens had virtually exhausted their credit.[2] Accordingly, in 1908 they recapitalized the Key by forming a second company, the San Francisco, Oakland and San Jose Consolidated Railway. The $5 million in par common of the first Key company was exchanged for $5 million in Consolidated preferred stock, the authorized common of which was fixed at $2.5 million at par, plus an additional $250,000 in common arising from the earlier sale by Smith and Havens to an intermediary company of an empty right-of-way of the same value. In the end, the second Key company raised its account for cost of road and plant by $2.5 million, to balance the increase of $2.5 million in the common stock at par value. A new bond issue was contemplated, but no buyers were available.[3] As a result, the company had to finance itself by allowing its floating debt to rise slowly. It had failed to allow adequately for depreciation and replacement charges, and had continued to issue bonds and preferred stock to F. M. Smith in exchange for cash advances. He, in turn, partially financed this process by using the additional stock and bonds as collateral for his own slowly growing floating debt.

At some undisclosed date before 1910, Smith and Havens came into conflict, for reasons unknown. One explanation was that Smith had decided to join William S. Tevis and Robert G. Hanford in a merger that would bring additional water to the Bay Region, in competition with Havens' People's Water Company. Another was that as an "insider" in the Syndicate, the Key Route, and the traction companies, Havens was in a position to know where rights-of-way were to be acquired and new lines were to be built. It was claimed that he took advantage of this foreknowledge to tip off his family and friends, at Smith's expense, since the lands would advance in value when Smith's companies began to purchase them or to open new lines into such areas.

On December 9, 1910, it was made public that Smith and Havens had divided their interests. According to the press, Havens transferred a $3 million interest in the Key, the Oakland Traction and the Syndicate to Smith in exchange for all of Smith's securities in the People's Water Company, plus $2 million in cash. One extensive account described the two men as "the closest of social and business friends for many years . . . [who] came to a parting of the ways some three or four years ago and the actual cause of their quarrel has never been disclosed." A slow but methodical separation of their properties followed, and, "it is said, the two principals have never met or spoken together since."[4]

The impetus for this dissolution had begun in the spring of the year.

The Yacht Agreement

In May 1910, F. M. Smith was in London for a BCL directors' meeting.[5] Either at that time or shortly afterward in New York City, C. B. Zabriskie introduced him to William S. Tevis and Robert G. Hanford. The meeting was neither purely social nor accidental.[6] As of that time, Smith's personal short-term debt stood at least at $5.5 million, largely through advances to the Key Route that he had obtained by personal notes secured by bonds and preferred stock of that company.[7] To proceed with his Oakland project, it was vital that he obtain adequate long-term financing, so that he could bring his short-term borrowing under control. Accordingly, he had his resourceful chief lieutenant in New York on the lookout for fresh sources of capital.

At the same time, Tevis and Hanford were also on the prowl for new financing. Their reason was different in some respects. Starting in 1902, they had joined forces to create a series of light, water, and power companies: Bay Cities Water Company, Union Water Company, Sierra Water Supply Company, United Light and Power Company, Union Land Development Company, and Santa Clara Land and Water Company. In 1911, after Tevis and Hanford had joined with Smith to form the United Properties Company, they set up two more corporations for inclusion in the merger. These were the Pacific Terminal Company and the Consolidated California Land Company. They also controlled an independent business known as the Occidental Land Company. Tevis and Hanford then announced their intention to build two electric interurban lines, the Sacramento and the San Jose Short Lines. The pair just happened to do their financing through a firm called the Hanford Investment Company.

Two observations became immediately clear. First, with one exception, these public utilities were not actual going concerns. Rather, they were mostly "scenery," that is, projects, some of which had been partially completed, while others were awaiting development. None of them produced significant profits. Second, Hanford in particular had aroused the interest of F. M. Smith by unfolding to him a dream of "magnificent scope" that just by chance embraced many of the objectives of Smith's own impressive project—a huge land syndicate of 45,000 acres; a Sacramento railway as well as one to San Jose; and water and power utilities that would fit nicely into Borax Smith's own scheme. All that was needed was capital. Hanford had worked out a way to raise it in his own fertile brain: combine the Tevis-Hanford companies with Smith's local railways to form a gigantic holding company with plenty of access to capital.[8]

The next step in this affair has its beginning in the notes recorded by Mrs. Evelyn Smith in her diary for October 1910:

Sunday. [October 16.] A beautiful day, so I decide to go to New York [from Shelter Island] with Frank, C. B. Z., and Mr. Alberger on the yacht to pick up Mr. Tevis and Mr. Hanford. Leave 2 P.M. and I have a delightful trip, arriving 23rd Street 10:30 P.M. Most glorious moonlight evening.[9]

Sunday. [October 23] Mr. Tevis, Mr. Hanford, C. B. Z., and Mr. Alberger return on board Hauoli. *Windy and cold. I still do not go downstairs.*

Tuesday. [October 25] Leave on board Hauoli *at 10 A.M. for New York where Mr. Tevis and Mr. Hanford leave us, also C.B.Z.*

What were the gentlemen doing during those nine days? Clearly, it was more than viewing those beautiful waters from the *Hauoli*, much as Borax Smith loved to give his guests pleasures of this kind.

The real objective of the visit was not pleasure, but a business deal, as the names of those present will readily reveal: W. S. Tevis, a former San Francisco banker, member of a leading family in that city, dealer in lands in Bakersfield, California, and lately a public utilities operator; Robert G. Hanford, a promoter and financier originally from Montana, a developer of mines and lands, and lately a partner of Tevis; C. B. Zabriskie, Smith's close associate for a quarter of a century, now head of PCB's New York office and a financial agent for Smith; W. R. Alberger, head of the Key Route and soon to become vice president and general manager of all Smith's railroads, including the Tonopah and Tidewater; and F. M. Smith himself.

The basic purpose of these men was to formulate a memorandum of agreement under which they would combine certain of their extensive properties to form the United Properties Company of California. The UPC was to be a public utility holding company that would manage and finance the operating companies, although the latter would retain their separate identities. This memorandum became known as the Yacht Agreement, because it was formulated aboard the *Hauoli* on October 25, 1910, en route to New York City. It never became a formal contract, but rather, was only an agreement to make a future contract. There were five principal elements.

First, Tevis was to purchase 1,550 Key Route bonds of $1,000 par value each, at $900 each, for a total of $1,395,000 in cash, to be paid in installments.

Second, Tevis and Smith agreed to sell to the UPC "at least" 75 percent of the various capital stocks of the nine companies under their control, of which two were then controlled by F. M. Smith, directly or through the Realty Syndicate. In this sale, the UPC was to be authorized to issue $200 million in capital stock, of which $100 million would be common, $50 million in non-voting 5 percent preferred, $50 million in non-voting shares convertible into 5 percent bonds at par, and $200 million in 5 percent 50-year bonds. Of these latter bonds, $23,207,000 worth were to be issued in exchange for the outstanding existing bonds of the nine constituent companies. Seventy-seven million dollars were to be held in treasury for future development financing; $50 million were to be held in treasury for ultimate exchange for UPC's $50 million non-voting convertible shares; and $49,793,000 were also to be held in treasury. In total, therefore, the nominal or projected capitalization of the company was fixed at $400 million. However, no bonds were ever issued for sale. Thus the only securities ever issued consisted of common stock, the non-voting preferred stock, and the convertible preferred stock, which together came to $200 million.[10]

Third, the stocks of the Key plus the OTC were to be exchanged for 64.8 percent of their par value in UPC common; 62.9 percent in UPC preferred; and 30 percent in UPC convertible stock. The Tevis–Hanford companies got 80 percent in UPC common for their stocks; plus 29 percent in UPC preferred; and 42.8 percent in UPC convertible stock. In effect, using par values, UPC paid a 57.6 percent total premium for the securities of the two Smith companies, and 51.8 percent for the Tevis group. Thus $90,675,000 in operating company stocks at par were traded for $139,157,000 in UPC stocks at par. Put another way, the UPC securities were to be exchanged at a substantial discount.

As part of these exchanges, it was also agreed that a partnership fund would be established, to be distributed after the formation of UPC and the exchanges had been completed. "At least" 75 percent of the original stocks were to be placed in the fund, in exchange for the new UPC securities. Upon distribution, Smith would get 60 percent of each class of holding, and Tevis and Hanford 40 percent.[11]

Fourth, the partners agreed to pool the $51,740,130 million of total UPC common for 15 years in a voting trust to be controlled solely by F. M. Smith.[12]

Lastly, it was agreed to allot to Tevis $1 million at par in UPC convertible stock to reimburse him for $700,000 in cash advances to Sierra Water Supply Company, and $1.2 million convertible stock for advances to Bay Cities Water Company. Tevis was also to get not more than $2 million, one-half in UPC preferred and one-half in convertible stock as an underwriter's bonus for certain other acts of financing for his companies.[13]

According to Smythe, the three partners also agreed verbally that Smith would assume 60 percent of UPC expenses, and his associates 40 percent.[14] Smith later denied that he had made this agreement, and eventually ceased making payments.

At this juncture, it is appropriate to ask: What did the parties hope to gain through this highly inflated new holding company? For F. M. Smith, the immediate advantage was the sale of $1,395,000 in Key Route bonds, which would afford him some relief from the enormous load of personal debt he was carrying. Alternatively, this would be a means of rebuilding the Key Route's approach to its pier terminal by moving the mole route north, which made it necessary to introduce an S-curve to turn the line south again for entry to the pier terminal. In turn, much of the trestle would be replaced by a rock-filled mole. Because of tidal problems as well as wear and tear, this improvement was rapidly becoming essential, although the Key Route simply was not earning enough money to carry it out. Borax Smith had already stretched his credit to the limit. Thus, if the United Properties Company could be financed, the liquid capital would become available at last to carry through his entire metropolitan plan.

As for Tevis and Hanford, they believed that Smith's two companies were already highly profitable and possessed of large liquid surpluses. His enterprises were going concerns with promising records of growth, while those of his partners were so largely undeveloped that their prospects had yet to be established. If Smith could be induced to enter a merger, there should be plenty of cash to carry to completion the several largely uncompleted companies they controlled. For this reason, a Smith associate later described the merger as one in which F. M. Smith was contributing gold, and his partners iron washers. This was not strictly accurate, but the imbalance *was* apparent.

On December 30, 1910, the United Properties Company of California was incorporated under the advantageous laws of Delaware. The proposed common issue was cut by $75 million, while the convertible stocks were increased by the same amount.

Difficulties in Financing the New Company

The Yacht Agreement had required both parties to turn in "at least" 75 percent of the capital stocks of the subsidiary companies. When these amounts had been reached, then Smith would get 60 percent and Tevis and Hanford 40 percent of the partnership fund so created, in securities of UPC at the ratios fixed for each of the nine existing companies. As part of the agreement, the principals included their existing holdings, either owned or controlled, of the common and preferred stocks of the nine companies. F. M. Smith's position was as follows:

Table 4

Railway Stocks Owned or Controlled by F. M. Smith, by Class of Stock (in percent)

Company		Common	Preferred
Oakland Traction			
Owned		31.24	13.28
Controlled		47.65	32.30
	Total	78.89	45.48
Key Route			
Owned		40.90	48.10
Controlled		36.20	29.10
	Total	77.10	77.20

Source: L. Baar, v. F.M. Smith, p. 218. Plaintiff's Exhibit No. 9

It is not worthwhile performing similar calculations for the holdings of Tevis and Hanford, because five of their companies were owned outright or almost entirely so.

Smith had more than enough stocks, taken at their face values, to meet his 75 percent minimum for Oakland Traction common, Key Route common, and Key preferred, respectively. But these figures are misleading in two critical respects. First, the Traction Company was a highly profitable concern, while the Key made scarcely any money.[15] But the Traction preferred was Smith's main source of dividends, and this was the weak spot in his vast array of holdings. Second, large amounts of all of his holdings had long since been pledged as collateral for his short-term notes, which then exceeded $5 million. Smith had created and expanded both companies largely by short-term financing because he had found it virtually impossible to float bonds, except to the Realty Syndicate. It is also possible that the real problem was not lack of available financing but rather Frank Smith's reluctance to share control with investment bankers.

The principal method by which Smith could meet the 75 percent requirement was by paying off his notes and recovering his collateral for deposit with the UPC. Still, there seemed to be another way. If he could persuade the banks to accept his new UPC securities as substitute collateral, this would free his preferred stock, which he then could turn in to the UPC to meet his quota. However, the new holding company was as yet untried, had no record of earnings to gain the confidence of investors, and through its projects represented a serious threat to powerful local interests. Evidently Smith had not foreseen these obstacles when he entered into the venture. They blocked the progress of the exchange of securities and, at the same time, hindered the new company's opportunity to issue bonds. As the attendant delays wore on, the company lost standing on the market at the very time that it most needed credit.

The three promoters of the United Properties Company had large ambitions, and these goals represented serious direct threats to established interests in and around San Francisco. There was Smith's old adversary, the Southern Pacific, which had now "got even" with the Key Route, but wanted no elaborate port terminal facilities to encroach upon its own very profitable freight business. Then, Tevis' water projects for the Bay Region were a threat to the Spring Valley Water Company in San Francisco and to Havens' People's Water Company in the East Bay. Also, Tevis' plans for bringing electric power into the region were not viewed warmly by either Pacific Gas and Electric or the new Great Western Power Company.[16]

Since the heads of the leading banks—men such as Frank B. Anderson, I. W. Hellman, John S. Drum, and Mortimer and Herbert Fleishhacker—sat on the boards of these companies and had a stake in them, they could hardly be expected to extend cordial financial assistance to an untried holding company that had already commenced a series of extravagant announcements of its intentions,[17] in Hanford's usual flamboyant style.

At the beginning of 1911, Hanford assumed the role of administrator for the exchange of stocks. In brief, in what was termed Hanford Offer No. 1, the UPC would issue $141.7 million in securities at par, and in return would get $69.3 million par value in securities turned in by the Tevis group of companies.[18] Hanford Offer No. 2, for the two Smith companies, was complicated by Frank Smith's inability to meet his exchange quotas. If he could have done so, the UPC would have received $94.99 million in stocks at par, for which it would have exchanged $187.1 million in its own securities at par. As a temporary expedient, the actual exchanges were reduced to the levels of Smith's unpledged shares, to which the earlier agreed-upon percentages would be applied.[19]

Both offers were accepted by UPC. However, the exchanges of securities involving Tevis and Hanford allowed some stock to fall into the hands of some of their stockholders, since "controlled" stock was included in Offer No. 1—that is, stock in friendly hands but not actually owned by Tevis and Hanford. According to Smythe, the explanation lay in "efforts of Tevis and Hanford to fulfill the terms of the Yacht Agreement." This maneuver allowed UPC securities to escape from the partnership fund, which violated another part of that agreement; this leakage also included the bond "certificates" for the first mortgage issue to come. In contrast, Smith's controlled stocks were owned by the Realty Syndicate, which he also controlled. While he kept his promise not to sell any of his UPC securities, his partners did not. This certainly contributed to Smith's suspicion of and eventual estrangement from his two associates.

Increased Problems of Financing the United Properties Company

F. M. Smith's continuing inability to produce his 75 percent share in company stocks to be turned in to UPC for exchange precluded following up with the original financing plan. In turn, the weak and undeveloped financial condition of Tevis' companies underscored the skepticism within the financial community regarding UPC securities. Because they could not be marketed, Hanford, in particular, began a search for financing.

Smith's problem was met by a series of extension agreements, allowing him additional time to add unpledged stocks for exchange. By strenuous efforts, he managed to get the total of his shares subject to pledge up to 75 percent, but of this, only 33.2 percent of the common and 27.7 percent of the preferred stocks in his companies were free of pledges as collateral for his notes.[20] By March 25, 1911, he had managed to turn over 59.3 percent of his unpledged stock. As of August 18, 1911, he had brought the figure up to 62.4 percent of all of his stocks.[21]

In this same month, Hanford approached the important and venerable financial house of E. H. Rollins and Sons, where he managed by use of UPC's holdings in the two Smith railway companies to raise $2.5 million in four-year notes, to be followed later by $18–20 million in long-term bonds. This short-term money was to be used to pay off floating debt, provide extensions and improvements, develop the terminal facilities, and build the new lines to San Jose and Sacramento.[22] But Rollins extracted very severe conditions. It refused to make the loan to the United Properties Company; and it obtained F. M. Smith's agreement to deposit two-thirds of the stocks of his two railroads as collateral within one year, starting with 51 percent immediately and ending at 75 percent by March 1, 1913.

These were very onerous requirements, but not the only interesting aspect of the loan. Only the Smith companies were deemed worthy of such credit. Rollins refused to touch the Tevis concerns, and this fact supports Smith's testimony a decade and a half later that he had been deceived by Tevis and Hanford regarding the value of their properties. For this same reason, Smith said that he repudiated the arrangement to deposit additional stock to reach the level of 75 percent.[23] Rollins also insisted upon and obtained the formation (in August 1911) of a new holding company, Oakland Railways, to issue the notes which both the Key and the OTC would guarantee. As a result, UPC exchanged its railway stocks for 100 percent of the common and 59 percent of the preferred of the new concern.

E. H. Rollins exacted still other conditions: that the firm have a representative on the boards of the two F. M. Smith companies; that the companies pay no dividends while the notes were outstanding; and that the stock of the Pacific Terminal Company, which Hanford had set up in January 1911 to buy the very valuable tidelands acreage from the Key by paying out $1.56 million in UPC bonds, was to be turned over to Oakland Railways as collateral for the loan. The loan was to be used specifically to pay off the floating debts of the two Smith companies, and to provide a half million to finance the Key mole and trestle improvements.[24]

In February 1912, Hanford was proceeding with negotiations for the long-term Rollins loan when quite abruptly F. M. Smith exercised his powers under the voting trust to remove him from these negotiations. Smythe believes, without providing evidence, that "vanity" was a factor; also that Rollins might impose unsatisfactory and even embarrassing terms.[25] But there was more to this matter. By this time, F. M. Smith had come to distrust his two associates, partly because he had discovered some irregularities in their transactions with UPC,[26] and partly owing to disappointment at the poor quality of most of the assets they had brought into the merger. Beyond this, Borax Smith was too independent by nature to enjoy the presence of a Rollins man on his boards, or the tight restrictions under which the short-term loan was granted. Most importantly, he doubted his ability to raise his contribution of stocks to 75 percent by March 1913, because his floating debt stood in the way.

Smith, by early 1912, had evidently begun to think of getting out of the UPC entirely. At any rate, he took a step in that direction by having the Key Route repurchase the tidelands from the Pacific Terminal Company, following this by effecting a consolidation (on March 21, 1912) of the Key, the OTC, the East Shore and Suburban, and the California Railway, to form the San Francisco–Oakland Terminal Railways. Now Smith had his railroads and tidelands in his own hands. So far as he was concerned, the UPC episode was over.

The Partnership Breaks Up

Smith now took the offensive, proposing that the principals divide up the stocks of the operating companies; dissolve the UPC; and turn over to Smith the SF–OT stock, and 40 percent each of the SF–O Terminal Power Company and the United Light and Power Company. Tevis rejected these proposals as "absolutely impracticable," but did offer to negotiate.[27]

Smith's next move was to inform Rollins that the $2.5 million in notes were going to be paid off on September 1, 1912. He proceeded to raise the funds by executing a ten-months' loan for the same sum from N. W. Halsey and Company. In taking this step, he did not even bother to inform his associates. Then, acting in secrecy, he executed a complicated series of agreements by which the Key sold the tidelands for one million dollars, successively through two new companies, with Oakland Railways as a guarantor. His two partners were further embittered by these actions. What conceivable advantage, they asked, could there be in substituting a 10-months' note for one that still had three years to run? The answer was that they did not understand their colleague very well. He had decided to get out of the UPC and no longer cared what they thought. And he wanted to set the stage for getting his railways back with no more interference from Rollins and no more obligation to increase his deposit of collateral stock.

Apparently, Smith was hoping to get some badly needed long-term financing from Halsey, before the short-term note fell due in June 1913. He failed in this effort. Little time was left before Halsey could foreclose—and then the UPC would collapse.

Meanwhile, the redoubtable Hanford decided to try to raise the money himself. In spring 1912, he claimed to have turned up $15 million on offer from Europe. There is a possibility that this originated with George Gordon Moore and Elliott G. Stevenson, both of Detroit. Both were financiers, and Stevenson was also a lawyer, with banking connections in Toronto and London. In any event, Tevis could not even get a hearing from Smith on Hanford's proposal, doubtless because Smith had already made up his mind to try for a complete separation of interests.[29]

In September 1912, Hanford brought in the first Moore-Stevenson proposal: (1) Raise $10 million through bonds to be issued by the railways and the Union Water Company; (2) use $7.5 million to pay off Halsey, the tidelands note, and all floating debt; (3) have Moore and Stevenson appoint a majority of SF–OT directors, with Smith to remain president; (4) retire the UPC "bond certificates"; and (5) have Smith, Tevis, and Hanford pay Moore and Stevenson one half of their UPC holdings. Smith rejected the deal outright, hoping for help from Halsey; in any case, he was determined to free himself somehow from associates whom he now completely distrusted.

Why would Smith have rejected this opportunity? A brief look at the terms will supply most of the answer. Borax Smith was simply not the sort of entrepreneur to submit himself to anyone else's control, and this is what the loss of a majority vote meant. In addition, Smith had invested about $5 million in the UPC. He was not about to see half of it go down the drain to two outside financiers, while also contributing to pay off bond certificates emanating mainly from Tevis and Hanford's sale of part of their shares in the partnership fund, in violation of the partners' understanding in 1910.[29a]

In desperation, Tevis wrote Smith begging him to go along with the Moore-Stevenson proposition, ending his letter on a note of hopelessness:

> *I have gone into this detail, Mr. Smith, not with the idea that I can persuade you to do this thing, but in order that I may go down on record as having at least warned you of the impending danger. You apparently are not able to see it. I cannot only see it, but I know that it is practically at hand, and I see no possible way to avert it.*[30]

But Smith was a stubborn man. His mind had long since been made up, and he did not deign to reply to Tevis' letter.

With the UPC rapidly running out of funds, and with the former partners hopelessly split, Moore came forward with a letter to Hanford, dated December 2, 1912, unreservedly endorsing Tevis and Hanford against Smith, and implying rather strongly that they should take the latter to court, and that if they did, they could look to Moore and Stevenson for help.[31] In short, Smith's suspicions had justification.

Tevis and Hanford chose to take the route of arbitration, rather than go to court. On January 25, 1913, an agreement was made between Smith, Tevis, Hanford, and the Hanford Investment Company, under which the parties would turn over to a Board of Trustees all of their securities issued by the UPC; and "all claims, demands, and causes of action of each and all of the parties against the UPC and its subsidiary companies, except for claims, demands, or causes for action relative to funds loaned or paid out since January 1, 1911."

The Board of Trustees was to consist of Herbert Fleishhacker, chairman; Joseph F. Carlston of the Central Bank of Oakland, nominee of F. M. Smith; and William S. Rheem, of the Standard Oil Company of California, as nominee of Tevis, Hanford, and the Hanford Investment Company. The Board was given absolute power to act for and to bind the principals, and in this connection to work out an agreement with George G. Moore and Elliott G. Stevenson for financing the United Properties Company. The Board was to serve two years, and was empowered to appoint three impartial arbitrators to determine and resolve all issues arising since the Yacht Agreement, through decisions binding upon all of the principals. The authority of the arbitrators was to include claims against Smith relative to deposit of stocks for exchange with UPC securities; and the obligations of Tevis, Hanford, and the Hanford Investment Company either to transfer or to account for certain UPC securities "now in the hands of others."[32] There seems to be no evidence that the arbitrators were ever appointed, but in any case it is certain that the Board itself accomplished nothing.

The operation of this first Board of Trustees had a labyrinthine quality about it that makes its actions, and inaction, hard to understand. Two of the Trustees refused to sign a confirmation of acceptance of the renewed Moore-Stevenson offer, although one of the primary purposes of the Board was to find a means of permanently financing the United Properties Company.[33] When E. H. Rollins entered the picture through the actions of another Trustee, Moore withdrew his offer, charging the Board with bad faith. Meanwhile, it turned out that Rollins had no intention of making an offer. In short, the Trustees had failed completely in their first obligation, which was to obtain adequate permanent financing.

About March 1913, while this Board was still functioning, certain ominous developments began to occur that gravely affected the financial position of F. M. Smith. His assistant, Dennis Searles, brought him the news that, for the first time, the banks were refusing to renew his notes or to accept new ones from him. There was no realistic chance that Smith could raise at least $5 million virtually overnight, yet that was rapidly becoming his predicament. He was caught in what turned out to be "The Rich Man's Panic," and he was extremely vulnerable to actions to place him and his estate in involuntary bankruptcy, despite his massive total assets and substantial net worth. Liquidity, not assets, was his real problem.

The prelude to this approaching financial disaster went back to late 1911, when W. R. Williams, then State Superintendent of Banks, began to find a great deal of "Smith paper" accumulating in the banks under his jurisdiction. During an examination that extended from the latter part of 1911 through 1912, as Williams later testified, ". . . I required the—requested—the banks to dispose of the paper, to take it out or get it out from among their assets." In explanation, Williams said, "I did not consider that the paper was such that the banks should continue to hold."[34] However, Williams admitted that he had made no examination of F. M. Smith's assets before taking this drastic step.[35] On severe cross-examination by James F. Peck, attorney for Mrs. Smith in this much later legal proceeding, Williams conceded that Smith's paper had effectively been "frozen" because his large floating indebtedness was simply revolving without being reduced over the preceding few years. Yet he also admitted that he had no reason to think that F. M. Smith was insolvent at the time.[36]

Now that the squeeze was on, Smith called in an old and close friend, Mark L. Requa. Requa was a prominent mining engineer soon to be closely associated with Herbert Hoover in European food relief. Smith disclosed his problem and asked Requa to intercede with the banks in hopes of arranging some sort of standstill agreement to surmount the crisis. Requa's first act was to meet with the principal bankers in the San Francisco Bay region, to lay before them F. M. Smith's basic difficulty—a lack of liquidity sufficient to pay off his short-term debt within a period so brief that it could be described as "immediate." The response of the bankers was to insist, first, that Smith make a full disclosure of his assets and liabilities; and, second, that a reputable firm of accountants promptly audit his financial condition. After the audit had been completed, a plan of action would then be formulated.

Meanwhile, the first UPC Board of Trustees had resigned and withdrawn from the picture.

F. M. Smith's Assignment of May 5, 1913

Almost exactly 25 years following the collapse of William T. Coleman and Company, Borax Smith found himself in a similar predicament. By sending Requa as his emissary, he was admitting that his net cash flow was now negative. Hence he could not cover his maturing notes, renew them, or replace them. Undoubtedly, State Superintendent Williams' directive to throw out his "paper" had precipitated the crisis. However, there is one thing we shall probably never know: whether the crisis was engineered by hostile hands, or whether it was simply the cumulative impact of a national credit squeeze upon Smith, who had made himself vulnerable by years of excessive reliance upon short-term borrowing.

In any event, on May 6, 1913, Klink, Bean and Company, an accounting firm, submitted to the bankers their report on Smith's finances.[37] Table 5 provides a summary tabulation of the results, particularly with regards to floating indebtedness.

Table 5

Partial Data Concerning Finances of F. M. Smith on May 6, 1913

1. F. M. Smith, Accounts Payable:

To outside companies or persons	$ 264,262.93
To affiliated companies	294,981.87
Loans payable to outside companies or persons	5,131,025.00
The Pacific Coast Borax Company	400,000.00
Total	$6,090,269.80

2. The Realty Syndicate, Current Liabilities: a/

Accounts payable	32,885.63
Loans and notes payable	1,358,866.71
Demand and call notes	887,375.00
Investment certificates	515,801.61
Total	$2,794,928.95

3. Total Short-term Indebtedness: $8,885,198.75

Because F. M. Smith became sole owner of the Realty Syndicate in December 1910, it is assumed herewith that its short-term indebtedness and other maturing obligations in the near term can be considered part of F. M. Smith's personal debt.

Source: Baar v. Smith, Plaintiff's Exhibit No. 7, pp. 1367ff.

After drastic write-downs in the values of Smith's long-term assets—for example, valuation of $0 per share for SF–OT common, and sharp reductions in the appraised value of the Syndicate lands—Klink, Bean concluded that

F. M. Smith owned	$8,945,275.09
F. M. Smith owed	6,090,269.80[38]
Net worth	$2,855,001.29

Clearly, F. M. Smith was not only solvent, he was still a wealthy man.

However, he was also still tied to the United Properties Company. Accordingly, the auditors declared that his net position in that company must be "taken into consideration in order to arrive at a final determination of the net worth of Mr. Smith."[39] Thus they reckoned that Smith's undelivered preferred stock had a value of $1,544,400. Deducting this from his net worth because it was considered an obligation, reduced his net position to $1,310,601.29. Against this, Smith's properties contributed to the UPC were valued at $3,450,000. If the Tevis-Hanford share was estimated at $3,000,000, then the total becomes $6,450,000 (allowing no value to either of the common stocks contributed by Smith). Thus F. M. Smith's 60 percent share would yield $3,870,000 as the value of his UPC holdings. Adding this figure to $1,310,610.29, which was Smith's net worth after adjustment for undelivered stocks, his net worth estimate became $5,180,000. It might be even more, the auditors conceded, if their write-downs proved to be excessive.

And so, even on this drastically conservative audit, we have a man with virtually $9 million in assets and a potential net worth of perhaps $5,180,000, confronted with the urgent need to go hat-in-hand to the bankers for help. How did the bankers respond to his plea for assistance?

On May 5, 1913, a trust agreement was laid before F. M. Smith, party of the first part, and the Mercantile Trust Company of San Francisco, trustee and party of the second part. The third parties were designated as the F. M. Smith Advisory Committee. This committee consisted of Frank B. Anderson of the Bank of California, chairman; John S. Drum of the Mercantile Trust; C.O.G. Miller of the Pacific Lighting Corporation; Mortimer Fleishhacker of the Anglo-California Trust Company; and W. W. Garthwaite of the Oakland Bank of Savings.

In executing this trust agreement, F. M. Smith transferred to the Mercantile Trust Company (acting as trustee) all collateral securities,

> "shares of stock, bonds, certificates for bonds, notes, debentures, evidences of debt, contractual rights, choses in action and other claims, demands and causes of action, or all of the right, title and interest of the first party therein, thereto or thereunder . . . for the purpose of having the same administered for the benefit of all the creditors of the first party . . . and for the benefit of the first party, under the advice and by the direction of the said Advisory Committee. . ."[40]

The trustee and the Advisory Committee were granted full power to act in the administration of Smith's assets, first for the benefit of his creditors, and secondarily for his benefit.

In executing this agreement, Francis Marion Smith stripped himself of every cent he had in the world, despite the underlying strength of his basic wealth. His only hope was that some of his equity could be salvaged. In any case, the agreement provided with less than compassionate consideration the following:

> The said Trustee shall, from time to time, as part of the administrative expenses of this trust, pay to the first party [Mr. Smith] from money coming into its hands under these trusts for the support and maintenance of the first party and his family, such sums as may, by said Advisory Committee be deemed reasonable for that purpose. . . .

When asked on direct examination in the case of *Baar v. Smith* some 12 years later, "Did they ever pay you anything?" Smith replied bluntly, "Not a cent."[41] Indeed, if such offer had even been made, it would have been flatly turned down.

Fortunately, over the years from 1907, the year of their marriage, F. M. Smith had given his second wife, Evelyn, full title to both Arbor Villa and Presdeleau, as he had done for Mary R. Smith earlier; sound securities of various sorts; and the Sorosis Fruit Company, which owned two parcels of valuable California farm land. In this way, the family could be maintained economically intact, although at a sharply reduced level of expenditure. Frank Smith deeply loved his young wife, whose business acumen had helped him with numerous problems. In return, he had provided for her generously, knowing that she would inevitably survive him by many years.

When Borax Smith executed this deed of trust, he thought that he was bringing into being an advisory committee that would be just that: a body to help him to reorganize his finances and renew his hitherto highly successful business career. In his own homely way, Smith told R. P. Henshall, counsel for Baar in the case of *Baar v. Smith*, ". . . when I named the . . . advisory board . . . I expected them to act in an advisory way with me and act in a cooperative way with me. . . . It was not true that I was broke and you know that. I made [the assignment] because I expected to get the cooperation of the five bankers that I turned my property over to." Then Henshall asked him whether he had failed to get the proper cooperation, and Smith replied, "I did not get the cooperation I expected to, no. I have not had a look in since, really. I turned over all that I had, yes.

My lead pencil tells me that I had quite an asset when I did that. I mean there was an equity there."[42] He might have added that with time and prudence, the Committee could have helped him extricate himself.

Actually, Smith's position was not an unreasonable one, for it involves a solution that has been used innumerable times during credit stringencies. Smith believed in the earning power of his borax interests, and he was confident that urban growth would put the Key Route in a strong position and also raise substantially the value of the Syndicate lands. His urgent need was for working capital based upon permanent financing, and it was his belief that the bankers would help him to work this out. More vaguely, he also hoped that means would be found to disentangle his affairs from those of Tevis, Hanford, and the United Properties Company.

When he said in his quiet way, "I have not had a look in since, really," his declaration rings true. For the primary objective of the Advisory Committee turned out to be as rapid a liquidation of Smith's obligations as possible. It was in no way interested in Borax Smith's continued management of the companies he had created. So, with mounting impatience and frustration, he became a helpless witness to the rapid dissolution of his business interests.

Further Steps in Liquidation and Disentanglement

On the same day as F. M. Smith's transfer of all of his assets, Smith, Tevis, Hanford, and the Hanford Investment Company reinstated their trusteeship of January 25, 1913, to carry out the assignment that their first Board of Trustees had hardly even begun. This time they named five prominent businessmen, bankers, and lawyers to carry out the originally intended separation of interests in the United Properties Company.

The next step was for the new Board of Trustees and the F. M. Smith Advisory Committee to address the urgent need for financing maturing obligations of the San Francisco–Oakland Terminal Railways. This company had the Halsey note falling due on June 12, 1913, for $2.5 million, plus a floating debt of $800,000. Actually, this note had been given to Oakland Railways, along with collateral which it employed to borrow the money. In addition, the Oakland Terminal Company had $1.1 million in notes, secured by the tidelands, and these obligations would fall due on August 20, 1913.

Oakland Railways also had guaranteed principal and interest on these notes.

To meet these urgent problems, the two committees first attempted to form a concern called New Corporation to work out a plan of financing. However, this was blocked by certain creditors of Smith.

Meanwhile, the Advisory Committee moved to organize Smith's secured creditors (to prevent a rash of bankruptcy suits) while it urgently attempted to work out a plan of long-term financing. What it did was to incorporate the F. M. Smith Securities Company. Then, each noteholder was urged to deposit his note with its collateral, to receive in return a new note, with accumulated interest, from the Securities Company. As part of this arrangement, Mrs. F. M. Smith guaranteed payment from her liquid assets on these new notes for one year. This arrangement proved successful, affording the Advisory Committee time to rearrange their permanent financing.

Meanwhile, Hanford had injected himself into the situation by asking for an option to buy Smith's interest in the United Properties Company. But the Advisory Committee was not disposed to cooperate with him. Later still, Hanford would attempt to force F. M. Smith into involuntary bankruptcy. By this means, Hanford believed that the court could redistribute Smith's assets, and the Advisory Committee would be rendered a nullity.[43]

A group of suits followed. In the meantime, Hanford sought and obtained an option from the new UPC Trustees, with the help of Gavin McNab, allowing him to buy all of Smith's UPC securities and claims for $1.5 million (their par value totaled $107,517,000). At the same time, Hanford bound himself to buy all the SF–OT common at $1 per share, and preferred at $50 a share, that Smith, the Syndicate, or the Advisory Committee might offer within 18 months after he chose to exercise the option. Hanford bitterly protested this "burden," but nonetheless accepted it so that he could proceed with his search for financing.[44] At this time, the imputed value of the preferred, after deducting $17 million for funded debt, was approximately $108 per share. In other words, Hanford was looking for a bargain. At this point, the two boards succeeded in obtaining an extension on the Halsey loan, subject to actions by the Terminal Railways to straighten out its own affairs, with additional money from Halsey. Meanwhile, Hanford failed in his attempt to throw Smith into bankruptcy, although he did gain some assurances of outside financing.

Beyond the efforts to take the railways out of the UPC, there was a more basic question: To what extent were the United Properties Company and its few security holders creditors of F. M. Smith, as distinct from those creditors—mainly banks—represented by the Smith Advisory Committee and its administrative agent, the F. M. Smith Securities Company? The answer of Tevis and Hanford was consistently that he owed both groups, and that the Advisory Committee was engaged in a pretense that it spoke for all of Smith's creditors when, in fact, it did not. In their view, he owed the UPC for the value of his undelivered stocks, and he owed the UPC's outside security holders for the depressing effect on the value of their holdings of his failure to go through with the merger.

Smith and his spokesmen contended, in turn, that the Yacht Agreement was nothing more than a memorandum of agreement. It was never executed and therefore was not presumed to be a binding instrument. They also argued that Smith had put more money into the company than his associates, that Tevis and Hanford had sold part of their securities to outsiders despite their promise not to do so, that they had borrowed from their own companies to finance their stock contributions, and that they had lent UPC funds to companies not part of the UPC, but controlled independently by Tevis and Hanford.

Obviously, the only way out of this maze of claims was to effect a complete separation of interests, as the first UPC Board of Trustees had been instructed to do in January 1913.

During October and November 1913, Hanford made two proposals to induce F. M. Smith and his Advisory Committee to sign off their interests in the United Properties Company. In one, Hanford would pay Smith one million dollars for his UPC securities (which Klink, Bean, it will be remembered, had very conservatively valued at $3,870,000 before deduction for uncontributed stocks). Also, Hanford would pay off the Halsey and Tidelands notes. In return, he would get full control of San Francisco–Oakland Terminal Railways, and Smith would have no equity whatever. Alternatively, Smith would turn in his UPC securities, and would receive the tidelands, while Hanford would obtain financing for the Halsey notes and the floating debt of the railways. Again, Smith's equity in the company he had built would vanish.[46] However, either way Smith need deliver no more stock to the UPC.

Both sets of trustees showed an interest in Hanford's proposals. It soon came to light that he was dealing with George Moore, and that

Moore wanted some changes in Hanford's proposed options. Within a few days the Advisory Committee opened discussions with Moore—without Hanford's participation. The Committee was impressed with the apparent financial strength of Moore and Stevenson, and one of its members, William I. Brobeck, a leading attorney in San Francisco, frankly wanted Hanford out because the latter had proposed to take possession of Smith's UPC holdings for a bare million dollars, which Brobeck considered outrageous.[46] Hanford naturally saw danger to himself in his possible exclusion from the negotiations.

On November 19, 1913, *both* boards rejected Hanford's option. In response, he sought to get the UPC Trustees to act independently of the Advisory Committee. But this body employed evasive tactics, leaving the initiative to the Smith Advisory Committee. By this time, Moore preferred to get the SF–OT out of the UPC entirely, as a prelude for his own financing plans. In mid-January of 1914, a separation of Smith's interests from the UPC was finally accomplished, by means of seven interlocking agreements. In the basic agreement of January 16, 1914, Smith relinquished his claim for over $600,000 against the UPC. He was released from his obligation to deliver $3,357,430 in stocks to the UPC and also from all other demands of the UPC against him.[47] Directly related were two other provisions: (1) Securities with a par value of approximately $25 million (issued by SF–OT) were removed from the UPC and Oakland Railways, and were turned over to the Realty Syndicate, and (2) Smith turned over his UPC holdings to its subsidiary, Oakland Railways, and to Tevis and Hanford. Separation at last was complete.[48]

Mention must also be made of the agreement of January 17, 1914, involving Moore, the Realty Syndicate, and the Mercantile Trust Company. By its provisions Moore agreed to buy $2,250,000 of SF–OT preferred A (par value was $6.5 million), in four lots over four years, subject to the Halsey and Tidelands debts. He was to provide $4.1 million to pay off the latter debts at maturity, and $1 million was to be paid to the stockholders of the East Shore and Suburban Railway. In addition, Moore was to get a bonus of $12 million in SF–OT common for his financing services, and a four-year voting trust was to be established under the control of Moore, Anderson, and Brobeck. Finally, Moore was to appoint the top management of SF–OT.[49] F. M. Smith, of course, was out.

Moore lost no time in taking control of the railways. On January 20, 1914, it was announced that Andrew W. M'Limont would take over as general manager, replacing Billy Alberger. Frank Frost, former secretary-treasurer, was also replaced, and a new vice president was appointed. The new team was a strong one, although M'Limont had had a questionable previous link to Tevis and Hanford.[50] In any case, the new group was fated not to have much chance to demonstrate its talents.

On August 31, 1914, the *San Francisco Call* revealed that Moore had defaulted on his July 15 payment because the intervening outbreak of World War I had cut off his British sources of financing. If Moore lost control of the Key Route, the *Call* said, all of his new Key Route management would step down. By September 2, 1914, this was indeed the outcome. Alberger took over again as general manager, and the old Smith men were back in charge.[51] Once more the Smith Advisory Committee was in control of a large traction property with many difficulties. This control was to continue for another 12 years.

One final matter requires mention. It concerns the Advisory Committee's disposition of F. M. Smith's assets. Clearly, the crown jewels were his great majority holding of borax stock. Most of it was sold before the war began, through a specially organized British syndicate.[52] Sale of the borax stock yielded the Committee $4 million, of which Smith got nothing. He protested against the Committee's haste in selling; later he always claimed, convincingly, that they had let the stock go for too little.

Borax Smith's other big asset was what he had now become accustomed to calling "the poor old Key Route." The Advisory Committee thought it had made a good deal with Moore and Stevenson. Yet only six months were to pass before the promised financing was defaulted, well before the European war had erupted. Neither Smith nor his Committee could be called lucky in this instance. Wartime inflation of operating costs plus the frozen nickel fare steadily eroded any equity Smith had had. After 1920, mass ownership of automobiles was a reality, carrying with it two fatal disadvantages for Smith and his "advisors." First, the rise of the motor car cut even more deeply into the traffic of the company. Second, the officials of the communities it served went on a paving binge, reasoning initially that the street railway should pay the entire cost of the surface between its tracks and to the outer ends of its ties, even though the only beneficiaries would be the already highly subsidized motorists. Oakland politicians added to the already over-burdened company's anguish by warmly encouraging the postwar "jitney" movement, while Mayor John L. Davie even purchased a bus called "Rosalie" to flit around town—also skimming off the company's passengers.

So, by numerous cruel twists of economic and financial fate, San Francisco–Oakland Terminal Railways and its successors passed through two postwar bankruptcies, and Smith's equity was entirely wiped out. But F. M. Smith, for all his faults, was a man of character. He saw most of those troubles coming when he signed the separation agreements of January 1914. He knew he was giving away his shirt, and he fought for two hours against signing the agreement at a luncheon in the Palace Hotel with his trusted and trustworthy attorneys, William I. Brobeck and James F. Peck. Brobeck finally said, "It is all right for you, so far as your personal properties, and your personal affairs are concerned, to determine that you will or will not sign this document. But there is more involved here than your personal affairs. There are the affairs of your creditors involved in this transaction."

At this point Smith turned to him and said, "Mr. Brobeck, give me 25 cents to go back to Oakland, and pay my creditors, and I will be content." And then, Borax Smith signed the document.

Brobeck concluded, "I thought it was a very high-minded position for him to take."[53] All the more so, it might be added, in view of the uniformly shabby treatment he had received from those same arrogant bankers.

𝒪

After the Crash

The financial collapse of F. M. Smith's interests was an extremely complex affair, followed by nearly 20 years of litigation that, if anything, was even more complex. Because our concern here is with the life story of a very unusual man, we cannot turn it into a corporate history or a series of legal opinions. Yet a large part of Smith's later life was involved in such affairs, and they cannot be excluded entirely. Moreover, in the welter of claims and counterclaims surrounding all of these issues there exists an obligation to give an adequate account of what actually happened to F. M. Smith, as well as of his own part in the principal events.

The Underlying Nature of Borax Smith's Financial Difficulties

Borax Smith joined the Tevis–Hanford combination because he saw in the United Properties Company a means for raising the large amounts of capital he required for the fulfillment of his great vision of metropolitan development on the Oakland side of the bay. In this connection, it must be said that he was a novice in finance and not always a good judge of men when it came to such matters. In borax, oddly enough, he had acquired a superlative group of colleagues and subordinates, probably because production and organization, rather than finance, were the dominant considerations.

F. M. Smith was primarily an entrepreneur and a builder. Money was secondary—except as a means for carrying out his plans. As early as 1896, when Joseph Mather quit Smith's service as his New York representative, the unhappy ex-employee vindictively but accurately complained about Smith's financial methods. Mather owed a great deal to F. M. Smith—an excellent job in New York that he practically begged Smith to give him, and a second fine job in Chicago for his son, Stephen. Undoubtedly, a factor in the elder Mather's ungracious behavior was his resentment of what he called "foreigners," in this case the English partners who had joined with F. M. Smith in founding Pacific Borax and Redwood's Chemical Works. But Mather also disliked Smith's practice of using him to raise money on the former's short-term notes. Mather could do this because he had good New York connections. But it was distasteful for him, and he regarded such financial practices as imprudent. In Smith's view, they were a normal way of raising working capital for a firm—at least in its earlier stages. Unfortunately, as his wealth continued to grow, so did his short-term borrowing.

By the time Borax Smith began to build the Key Route in 1902, he had come to rely substantially upon short-term financing. The two basic problems that began to emerge were these: his personal account for notes payable finally became so large that it was out of control. In a word, it was frozen. By this point Smith had two note-brokers (Gerald C. Morgan and Lundborg-Morgan Company) constantly at work placing and renewing his notes, mainly with banks all over California. The second problem was that his commitment to the Key, the tractions, and the Syndicate forced him to go even further in borrowing on notes.

In consequence, then, by 1910 this very wealthy man had a growing inability to maintain adequate financial liquidity. He had become the prisoner of his own financial practices and of the companies that depended upon them.

How Smith Lost His Fortune

Borax Smith lost his personal wealth in three stages. By the UPC trusteeship agreement of January 25, 1913, Smith turned over to the three trustees his securities in the UPC acquired earlier when he deposited his stocks in his electric railways. This figure might well have reached $6 million.

As we already know, the first Board of Trustees accomplished virtually nothing. By March 1913, the banks began calling in or refusing to renew Smith's notes. Then occurred the second step: the assignment of May 5, 1913. By deed of trust, in favor of the Mercantile Trust Company of San Francisco, F. M. Smith turned over all of his remaining personal assets, which were to be managed—or liquidated—by the Advisory Committee. These assets fell into three classes: (1) the collateral attached to his secured notes, usually at a ratio of $2 for $1; (2) his free assets in the form of unpledged securities; and (3) his free assets in the form of physical property, such as his private car and his steam yacht.

The third stage involved the seven "unmerging" agreements of January 1914. The original UPC Trustees Committee had been replaced during the preceding May by a five-man group with the same powers and responsibilities, including possession of Smith's UPC securities as obtained by exchanges for the partnership fund. According to S. K. Ballard, the accountant who determined Smith's assets and liabilities, at year's end in 1911, Smith held UPC securities in the amount of $9,076,154.80.[1] In addition, UPC owed him short-term obligations of $171,450.00, while he owed the UPC $910,453.80, in what was called a "transfer" account.

In any case, Smith must have turned over enough railroad stocks by the end of 1911 to obtain $9,076,154.80 in UPC securities at their par values. Undoubtedly, their actual value on the market was far less—perhaps only half of this total—because of the inflated character of the new company's capitalization and the derivative conversion rates for securities turned in for the partnership fund.[2]

With the assignment in 1913, Smith agreed to turn over to the Mercantile Trust *all* of his remaining assets. Assuming that the valuations of Klink, Bean for April 26, 1913, are accurate, after their drastic write-offs for the value of the Realty Syndicate lands, railway stocks, and UPC bonds (a total reduction of $2,995,677); adding to that the assumption that the common stock of the SF–OT had no value whatever, while the preferred was worth, at most, only $50 per share; and deducting $1,544,400 for the undelivered portion of railway stocks due in the UPC for exchange, the conclusion is reached that Smith must have turned over $8,945,271.09 to the Advisory Committee.[3] If we count the first block of UPC securities (turned over in January 1913) as worth 50 percent of their face value, then Smith had by this stage yielded $12 million of his fortune.

The final stage in this tragic story of financial disintegration involved the unmerging agreements of January 1914. The purpose of these agreements was to effect a permanent separation of Smith's Terminal Railways from the United Properties Company. All that Smith could have hoped for was settlement of his debts on some distant day that would have left some surplus, however small, for himself. This never happened, both because of the way that the Advisory Committee went about its task—more as liquidators than as conservators—and because World War I, political rate-fixing, and the automobile destroyed his prospects so far as the Terminal Railways were concerned.

Borax Smith had suffered a huge loss from the entire episode. In assets alone, the range lies between Ballard's $24.9 million and Klink, Bean's $8.9 million. Given the drastic write downs imposed by Klink, Bean on Smith's equity in the potentially great value of the Realty Syndicate lands and on the Syndicate's holdings of Key Route securities, Smith's probable loss in the market values of his assets at that time had to be close to $12 million.

Furthermore, the Advisory Committee had put up Smith's huge block of 500,000 common shares in Borax Consolidated for almost immediate sale, giving R. C. Baker right of first refusal. If the Committee had been more patient, the borax shares alone would have provided enough to have paid off all of Smith's debts, for on BCL's reported profits for September 30, 1913, these shares were worth at least $8 million if reported earnings are conservatively capitalized at 10 per cent.[4] But all of this was not to be. Thus, the basic causes of the depletion of F. M. Smith's fortune were the bleak future of the Terminal Railways, the losses occasioned by the failure of that highly speculative venture, the United Properties Company, and the narrow and short-sighted outlook of the Smith Advisory Committee.

On contemplating the disaster that had befallen him, F. M. Smith and his associates were painfully aware of their grievances against Tevis and Hanford. Smith and his colleagues charged that Tevis had borrowed a substantial amount ($250,000) from one of his companies intended for inclusion in the merger, to complete the financing of Tevis' original purchase of Smith's Key Route bonds—in effect, diluting Smith's equity in the UPC.[5] They also charged that Tevis and Hanford had bought bonds in one of the constituent water companies at $59, and then resold them to the UPC at par— another dilution of Smith's equity. In addition, the Smith group claimed—and Tevis admitted—that Tevis and Hanford were selling part of their UPC securities (about $500,000) from the partnership fund, which depressed their market value as well as violated the principals' joint agreement.[6] Also, they were charged with diverting United Properties Company funds into an independent firm, the United Properties Realty Company. Smith and his associates likewise claimed that the Tevis companies, with one exception, were projects, not going concerns; that they were underfinanced and also overvalued.[7]

In making the assignment of May 5, 1913, apparently Smith felt safe in the beginning. He was comforted, no doubt, by Ballard's estimate of his net worth at over $15 million, and his total assets at $25 million, as of the end of 1911. For a brief period his usual optimism prevailed, and he saw the arrangement as a means for refinancing himself so that he could be relieved of an intolerable burden. His companies, particularly the railways, could be freed of pressing obligations and at the same time acquire permanent financing. On the surface, Smith bore the loss of his fortune with apparent good humor. But to his intimates he was "just busted, completely crushed."[8] The consistent opinion of those who knew him well was that F. M. Smith never was a highly demonstrative personality. He enjoyed a good joke but in large groups he usually preferred the background. It is not surprising that he kept his bitterness about the failure well-concealed, except when, with intimates, he would occasionally refer to "that damned bankers' committee." He had become convinced that it had little interest in helping him to save anything from the wreck.

A glimpse of F. M. Smith's inner feelings at that time can be had from two of his letters to his wife, written during this period. In one he refers to a new mining prospect saying that "I have been knocked down so many times of late that I don't like to be oversanguine" about anything. In another, he tells Evelyn that he had found the autumn rains in the east restful to him, adding sadly,

> . . . our life the last few years has been such a nervous strain that I cannot but look back with remorse if one could have but looked forward instead of backward. How much happier a life we could have planned, but all this is not given us poor mortals. Much has been given you and I and now if I succeed in recouping our fortune and we are able to come to our Shelter Island home it will only be for a short summer for the children will want to get back to school in California. Well we cannot have our life over again, we must be thankful for what we have. And God knows we have much to be thankful for.

Yet, even in these letters one senses a note of hope. Just as it was with those who had tried to steal his wood in Nevada so many years before, Smith was not a man to run away from a fight or to quit under pressure. Soon he was on his feet again, planning to protect his wife's estate from seizure by Tevis, Hanford, and their allies. Beyond this challenge, he was also beginning to think about how he could get back into the borax business.

How Tevis and Hanford Viewed the Issues

From the viewpoint of Hanford and Tevis, the assignment of May 1913 supposedly double-crossed them because it froze them out as possible claimants, although it took everything Smith had. In their reasoning, he still owed the UPC 18,663.3 preferred shares of Oakland Traction and 12,275 shares of Key Route preferred, valued at $2,500,000, for his undelivered portion to the partnership fund. They also held that he owed them $522,000 as his 60 percent share of $870,000 expended by them on their underlying companies; that he had a "moral" obligation to pay them $720,000 as his 60 percent of bonds purchased by them for $1,200,000.[9]

Hanford and Tevis saw Smith's assignment as a scheme to set up a class of preferred creditors, namely, those who held his notes. The greater proportion of these $9 million in notes was amply secured, with the participating banks as creditors. The collateral gave the Smith Advisory Committee practical control of the railways together with the very valuable borax stock, worth at least $4 million and probably much more. Thus Hanford and Tevis saw themselves shut out of any chance ever to finance the United Properties Company, or to get back what they claimed Smith owed to them. When they saw the second UPC Board of Trustees working closely with the Smith Committee, they felt confirmed in their suspicions.

At this point, Hanford decided upon two counter-moves: (1) to bring an action in involuntary bankruptcy against F. M. Smith, and (2) to try to persuade the new UPC Trustees to give him an opportunity to finance the UPC, now that Smith was out. The reason for the first move was to force the Advisory Committee to turn Smith's assets over to the court, where their own claims and those of UPC's outside security-holders could be included, and the assets parcelled out on a broader and different basis.

As a harassing maneuver, Hanford began his counter-attack by causing one J. C. Settle to file a complaint against Smith in the Superior Court of California on July 1, 1913.[10] This suit opened up the question of Smith's control of the West End Consolidated Mining Company of Tonopah, Nevada. The particular issue was the

charge that Smith sold a large block of stock in the Halifax–
Tonopah Mining Company to the West End. Settle argued that this
had damaged the West End, of which he was a stockholder.[11]
However, the real objective was to attack Smith as president of the
West End, with Settle as the instrument of Tevis and Hanford, and
to look for ways to enlarge his difficulties and also perhaps uncover
some hidden assets. Settle had bought his own 100 shares only as
recently as July 9, 1913, after filing suit. He demanded to see the
books of West End on that same day, and then returned several
times later.[12] Hanford cynically told the *Chronicle* that in selling the
Halifax stock to the West End, Smith had amply demonstrated what
he really meant "when he said he was devoting himself in every
possible way to saving his creditors."[13] In point of fact, however, the
Halifax deal turned out to be a very profitable one for the West End.

On July 12, 1913, Hanford struck a second blow at F. M. Smith,
through a complaint filed by Frederick G. Cartwright, a UPC stockholder, charging Smith with failure to complete the delivery of his
stocks to the UPC, to the damage of that concern and its investors.[14]
Apparently the Smith Advisory Committee was able to block or
postpone this relatively minor action.

The biggest threat to F. M. Smith and the Advisory Committee
was launched by Hanford at the end of July 1913, when he en-
deavored to throw Smith into involuntary bankruptcy.[15] Significantly, all of the persons involved as plaintiffs in what was called the
Dickey/Gilman/Hanford suit were connected intimately with Hanford and Tevis. Albert Hanford was Robert G. Hanford's brother;
Dickey was Tevis' private secretary; and Gilman was an engineer
and president of the Union Water Company, a UPC subsidiary
controlled by Tevis and Hanford. The petition claimed that Smith
gave or conveyed valuable holdings of stock in the West End Mining
Company to Mrs. Smith and to Ben F. Edwards at a time when he
was allegedly already insolvent, receiving no financial consideration
in return.[16] The Smith Advisory Committee managed to stall on
coming to trial on this matter for a long period of time, recognizing
that if the plaintiffs were to prevail, the Smith assignment would be
rendered invalid, whereupon the assets it controlled would pass to
the administration of the court for distribution.

For the F. M. Smiths, the threat implicit in this suit presaged a
complete financial disaster, because if the finding were that Smith
was insolvent some years before the assignment in 1913, then
much of Mrs. Smith's property could be seized as well, although

there was no basis whatever to infer that her finances were anything but entirely solvent. Nonetheless, financial ruin would then become a likely prospect for a young wife with four small children.

With the launching of the Settle suit on July 1, 1913, James F. Peck, attorney for Evelyn Smith, sensed immediately the impending danger to his client.[17] To protect her interests, he arranged for the transfer of those portions of her estate most vulnerable to suit to third parties not specifically known to her, and at a time and place also unknown to her. Peck then created a private corporation called Misposec (Miscellaneous Possessions and Securities Company) to assume ownership of these particular assets. He also devised a trust arrangement to be administered by intimates of the family, providing for future distribution of the assets in stipulated shares for the children and brothers of Mrs. Smith.[18]

Through this ingenious legal device, Evelyn Smith's estate was adequately protected. This preserved the Smith family's existence, which by this time was of critical importance now that F. M. Smith had surrendered all of his assets and therefore had very little remaining income. However, it should also be pointed out that while most of Evelyn Smith's property had been acquired through gifts from her husband, starting with Arbor Villa in 1907, not all of her holdings went into the trust. The reason was that Peck was certain that Hanford could not prove that F. M. Smith was insolvent, even as late as the end of 1912.

As *Webster's* says, the specific meaning of insolvency is a situation in which a person's liabilities exceed the *market value* of his assets (emphasis supplied). Both Ballard's audit for the end of 1911, and Klink, Bean's of May 6, 1913, demonstrated that Smith had a substantial worth. Accordingly, Peck was convinced that Borax Smith's gifts to the mother of his growing family were immune from attack by creditors of Smith himself. But just to make sure, he nailed down the Misposec assets very firmly.

Hanford and Tevis were unaware of Peck's remarkably astute strategy, although they were fully aware that Mrs. Smith had substantial property of her own. Unfortunately for them, standing in their way was their signed agreement of January 16, 1914, with the Terminal Railways, the Realty Syndicate and others, to hold harmless both F. M. Smith himself and the Mercantile Trust as his Trustee, and their successors and assigns "... of and from all claims, liens, demands and causes of action emanating from Tevis, Hanford, and Hanford Investment Company" ... "*or the holders of any of the certificates for bonds* heretofore issued by The United Properties Company of California" (emphasis supplied).[19] To all appearances, this language excluded Tevis and Hanford, along with their investment company, from any remaining claims against Smith. It also left out the claimants in the Dickey-Gilman suit, which Hanford had inspired the preceding July. It should be noted that Tevis and Hanford had voluntarily signed this agreement, and in so doing, had recovered their underlying properties and severed entirely their legal and business relationship with F. M. Smith. However, they continued to believe that they could get at Mrs. Smith's property for themselves. In 1925, when Smith was in his eightieth year, Tevis struck at him one more time, in a particularly insidious way.[20]

The L. Baar Suit

In December 1910, F. M. Smith had issued several unsecured notes in amounts of $20,000 and $50,000 in favor of Frank C. Havens, in settlement of their separation of interests agreed upon earlier that year. Havens later sold one of these notes to Nicholas Ohlandt, head of the National Ice and Cold Storage Company and the German Savings Society. Ohlandt later sold the note to John Buck of Vacaville, California.[21] At about this time, Smith defaulted on the note. Subsequently, the note was acquired by Miss Mary O'Connell, secretary for R. G. Hanford. Presumably the note was turned over to her in part payment of money owed to her by the Hanford Investment Company, which was dissolved in 1916.[22] On February 28, 1920, O'Connell obtained a judgment in execution against Smith for $7,548.54, asking levy against 819,632 shares of stock in the West End Consolidated Mining Company. On February 8, 1921, execution for this judgment was issued, and on the following day the sheriff of Alameda County served notice on F. M. Smith—as president of the mining company—of an attachment and levy upon his block of shares. Also on February 8, 1921, the shares were technically "sold" to O'Connell in satisfaction of her judgment.[23] On February 23, 1921, she was given a certificate of this "sale."

Following the sale, Miss O'Connell assigned her interest in the sale certificate to Robert R. Moody, an attorney formerly associated with Gavin McNab, counsel for W. S. Tevis; and later a partner in the firm of Moody, Henshall and Appel. These gentlemen, along with W. S. Tevis, all shared a suite in the Mechanics Institute Building in San Francisco.[24] On or about February 24, 1923, Moody assigned the certificate of sale to one L. Baar, who filed an amended complaint on the same date against a very large group of defendants that included among them: F. M. Smith, Evelyn Ellis Smith, B. F. Edwards, West End Consolidated Mining Company, Mercantile Trust Company, Frank B. Anderson, John S. Drum, Mortimer Fleishhacker, W. W. Garthwaite, P. B. Bowles, James K. Moffitt, Gavin McNab, William I. Brobeck, and other unnamed persons.[25] Legal counsel for the various defendants included two of the most distinguished firms in San Francisco: Brobeck, Phleger and Harrison, and Pillsbury, Madison and Sutro; along with James F. Peck and Louis W. Bennett. The reason for this formidable array of talent was the very great interest of the creditor banks in protecting the Smith Advisory Committee—which provided adequate inducement for them also to protect the interests of Mr. and Mrs. F. M. Smith. Indeed, they *had* to defend the Smiths to win their own case, since the central issue was the alleged insolvency of Smith on March 15, 1912—if not earlier.

The Baar case came to trial on June 22, 1925, and was litigated until November 9, 1926. One of its more interesting aspects was the Plaintiff, a ghostlike figure who was seeking West End Mining Company stock worth at least $400,000 in satisfaction of O'Connell's original judgment of $7,548.54—which probably had shrunk to a value of no more than $100.00 by the time of trial!

Baar gave no testimony and, so far as is known, never appeared, even as a spectator. The real instigator of the suit, William Sanders Tevis, professed not to know Baar, disclaimed all knowledge of him, conceding that he "may" have met him once, retaining at most only a vague recollection of him.[26] For reasons of his own, probably based upon the agreements in which he had joined in January 1914, Tevis elected not to undertake the plaintiff's role, but instead to resort to subterfuge. Yet Tevis shared offices with Robert P. Henshall, counsel for Baar, while it was Tevis who was Smith's enemy, and who in his reduced circumstances had the incentive to try to extract $400,000 from the former millionaire, now 80 years old.[27]

Another interesting feature of the case was the strategy adopted by Henshall in Baar's behalf. The key issue of the case was the plaintiff's attempt to get possession of the 819,632 shares of West

End Mining stock, largely given to Evelyn Smith by her husband on March 15, 1912, upon attempted proof that Smith had made a conveyance that was technically fraudulent, either because it was undertaken in contemplation of bankruptcy or as an act of bankruptcy. One of Henshall's two choices was to try to persuade the court to set the conveyance aside, and to order the property to be returned to F. M. Smith, whose creditors then could attack his possession directly. Alternatively, Henshall could adopt the principle of "constructive fraud," a legal term for proof of fraud by indirection or inference, whereupon any gifts to anyone by the donor complained against would automatically be deemed fraudulent and thus made subject to judgment, execution, and levy.

Henshall took the second course. He sought to prove that Smith was insolvent on October 10, 1910, when he entered into the Yacht Agreement, and that he remained insolvent right up to the time of his assignment of May 5, 1913. Henshall's method as well as substance of proof were loose and inconclusive. Indeed, he seemed more concerned with the history of the ill-fated United Properties Company than with the case at bar. In essence, Henshall's argument embraced the following contentions: that Smith had a very large amount of floating debt at all times between 1910 and 1913; that he failed and in fact refused to contribute his 75 percent share of stocks to the UPC partnership fund, and of necessity had to seek repeated extension agreements from his partners involving this obligation; that Smith's assignment was visible proof of his insolvency; and that Smith on various occasions allegedly admitted to Tevis that his financial condition was precarious and desperate.

Henshall managed to persuade the trial court, even with this type of indirect evidence, that Smith was indeed insolvent over the entire period. The court held that his gift of 750,000 shares of mining stock to Mrs. Smith, and her subsequent transfer of these shares, were invalid, because Smith's purpose was "to delay and defraud his prior, then existing and subsequent creditors." Collaterally, the trial court held that Smith continued to exert dominion and control over the affairs of the mining company. Accordingly, Judge Fitzpatrick found at law that L. Baar was "the owner of and entitled to the immediate possession of 819,632 shares of West End Mining capital stock."

Thus James F. Peck's intricate defense of this stock and other property of Evelyn Smith's seemingly was struck down. Yet nowhere in its opinion did the court demonstrate the basis for its finding of insolvency, nor was there even consideration of the equity of awarding Baar $400,000 worth of stock for $100.

Following this decision on November 9, 1926, the Smiths and their allied defendants launched an appeal. The initial basis was that Mrs. Smith did not have the stock, did not know where it was or who did have it, and therefore could not comply with the order of the trial court to make delivery of the shares. The Appellate Court upheld this argument, and granted a stay of execution. The matter then went to the Supreme Court of the State of California, where the Smiths won a reversal on the merits. They were able to show that both the Ballard and the Klink, Bean audits had demonstrated that Smith was a very wealthy man of substantial net worth. This had been so from the date of the Yacht Agreement in October 1910, until just a very few days before May 5, 1913, when the sudden calling of his notes, inspired by the Superintendent of Banks without prior examination of Smith's financial condition, suddenly destroyed his credit. More importantly, Baar had never managed— in fact, did not even try—to impeach the credibility of the Ballard and the Klink, Bean reports, whereupon the entire foundation of the finding of continuing insolvency was destroyed. It was determined that any and all of Smith's gifts to his wife up to the end of January 1913, were valid. Since the large block of West End Mining shares was conveyed to her on March 15, 1912, her right to this stock, plus additional shares given to her by her husband, or purchased by herself, before or after that date, was fully established. The same principle held for other gifts of property to her in this entire period—Arbor Villa, Presdeleau, the Ransome Concrete Machinery Company, and the Sorosis Fruit Company. In addition, any delays by Smith in delivery of all of his stocks to the UPC were the product of the agreement and consent of Tevis, Hanford, and the Hanford Investment Company. These acts, too, forestalled a finding of insolvency and also protected Mrs. Smith's right to her property.

Baar had sued for execution on November 12, 1926, and the appellants lodged their appeal on November 24, seeking a writ of restraint of any and all parts of the judgment of the trial court. In the end, the Supreme Court issued the writ as prayed for by the appellants. The incredible judgment of the lower court was struck down entirely, and the long case was over.

10

Smith Rebuilds His Fortune With Tonopah Silver

In the technical sense, Borax Smith did not go bankrupt in 1913. His assignment constituted an agreed-upon transfer of his assets for the benefit of his creditors. Within a year, this transfer destroyed his base in the borax industry. Toward mid-October, 1913, it was confirmed in London that his shares had been sold to "a British syndicate under the chairmanship of R. C. Baker" for an announced figure of $3 million, although the actual payment was "said to have been considerably more."[1] Since the stock had been paying dividends at 13¾ percent yearly, and had been a steady earner for years, a conservative basis of capitalization suggests that Smith's holdings were worth at least $8 million, and probably considerably more.

The Early History of Borax Smith's Involvement with the West End Company

In May 1900, James L. Butler, an impecunious lawyer and rancher from Monitor Valley, Nevada, near the old camp of Belmont, set out on a prospecting trip—supposedly to the "Southern Klondyke" region of southwest Nevada. He took along his favorite mule. By intent or otherwise, he detoured eastward into the San Antonio range, camping upon an elevated desert flat looking west over a broad and lengthy valley. On the east lay Mount Oddie, which received its name later from a future U.S. Senator; and on the southwest, Mount Butler (for the founder of Tonopah) and Mount Brougher (for Cal and Wils Brougher, both early prospectors). The campsite was then known as Warren Averill Springs, and later as Tonopah Springs.

As one version goes, the mule kicked at some rock and un-
covered a ledge apparently bearing ore.[2] Butler gathered samples,
obtained some highly encouraging results from an initial assay, but
took no further action at the time. On returning to Belmont, Butler
showed the samples to Tasker L. Oddie, a transplanted lawyer from
Brooklyn, New York, who practiced in Austin, Nevada. Oddie asked
a schoolteacher friend in Austin, Walter Gayheart, to make a second
assay. Gayheart found the samples fabulously rich in silver and
gold, with values as high as $300 per ton. Then and there the last
great mining camp in the Old West, Tonopah, was born.[3]

Typically, Butler, who seems to have been in no haste about
anything, put off making his locations until he had put his hay in the
barn and had taken care of some business matters. Late in August
1900, he staked out five claims on the Mizpah Ledge. Development
did not follow until mid-November. Because he had no capital,
Butler adopted the leasing method to develop the property. The
leases were strictly verbal: Butler would tell each lessee to step off
100 feet along the ledge, and would grant him 50 feet on each side.
In return, the lessee promised Butler a 25 percent royalty on net,
plus the right to process all the ore. Incredibly, no litigation ever
developed from these 120 leases. Instead, Butler himself would
arbitrate all disputes.[4]

The first lease is thought to have been granted to Louis Leidy and
Charlie Carr. By this time, the boom had begun. From the location
of Tonopah, Candelaria was the nearest railhead—about 70 miles
to the west in the Columbus-Belleville district. It so happened that
Ben Edwards, already an old friend of Borax Smith, operated a
mercantile store in Candelaria. The Tonopah rush soon became
reflected at the store, where the shelves were rapidly depleted of
supplies taken by 20-mule teams to the new camp. Before long,
Edwards himself travelled to Tonopah to look things over. His next
move was to establish a store there in partnership with Henry C.
Cutting, formerly a teacher in Candelaria. Thus the firm of Edwards
and Cutting opened its doors on Erie-Main Street, in Tonopah.[5]

This was not all that Ben Edwards accomplished on that trip in
early 1901. For in touring the camp, Ben encountered Louis Leidy
of Fish Lake Valley, at a lease on the lower slopes of Mount Oddie.
In the spirit of the traditional prospector, Leidy told Edwards that
the work was hard and the returns poor, but that Carr and he had
another claim "down below there at the west end," which he
offered to sell Edwards on lease for $2,000. The latter accepted the

offer, put the transfer before Jim Butler, and received verbal approval on the spot. Thus was born what was eventually to become the West End Consolidated Mining Company. Initially, however, its name was The Tonopah Extension Mining and Milling Company, formed November 4, 1901.[6]

Butler's verbal leases were for only one year's duration, after which the ground could be sold. Already, the Brock interests of Philadelphia had begun making acquisitions. This posed a real problem for Edwards, for he wanted to buy the Carr and Leidy lease, which was available from Butler for $50,000 if a draft for this amount could be cleared by the bank in San Francisco. Just to make sure, Ben Edwards naturally turned to his old friend Borax Smith, who promised to cover the option with his own money if necessary, and remained all day at his telephone ready to act.[7]

This incident has a double importance. It marked the initial identification of F. M. Smith with the West End property, although apparently he invested no money at that time. Furthermore, his willingness to back Edwards for up to $50,000 for a mining property he had never even seen reflects three characteristics of Borax Smith: trust, loyalty, and warm generosity. He always stood ready to help a friend, and he enjoyed nothing more than a chance to be generous toward friends and even strangers.

The Tonopah Extension started its corporate career with William J. (Billy) Douglass of Candelaria as president, C. B. Zabriskie as treasurer, and Ben Edwards as vice president. Capitalization was for $150,000. For the first five years, much developmental work was done, largely financed by advances from F. M. Smith.[8] Some years later, when the borax pioneer was engulfed by financial troubles, Ben Edwards told the press,

> . . . at times when we were unable to place any treasury stock, at any price, for the raising of funds for development purposes, and at a time when West End stock was quoted on the market at 25 cents a share, he [Smith] voluntarily offered to take treasury stock, sufficient to continue development work, at the rate of 50 cents a share, or double the market price. This was accepted and carried out by Mr. Smith.[9]

It must be emphasized that Smith *paid* double the market price for the shares to finance the new company. By February 1909, Smith had advanced $127,000 in total, Edwards told the press.

The Tonopah Extension company had found itself in ore in 1906, at an average value of $62 per ton. At this time, it was decided to reincorporate as the West End Consolidated Mining Company, with share capital of $10 million at $5 per share. Frank M. Smith became president of the new company, although he left most of the managerial tasks to Edwards and to the various general superintendents who came along. However, the company's main office was moved to 101 Sansome Street in San Francisco on March 1, 1906.[10] This was the head office of the Pacific Coast Borax Company, and, of course, of F. M. Smith himself. In other words, the West End from that time on was a Smith company, remaining such until 1926.

Zabriskie had written Edwards in 1903, telling him that Smith was willing to take up the entire balance of the company's treasury stock at fifty cents a share, paying for it through cash advances as needed for development of the mine. In Zabriskie's judgment "This is a very liberal proposition," which it certainly was. In another letter, written about the same time, Zabriskie also makes references to "the new certificate for Mr. Baker," which he offered to forward to him personally. A few weeks later, Zabriskie wrote Edwards again, this time regarding this certificate "in favor of Mr. Richard C. Baker for 10,000 shares." The fact that both men were involved in the West End with F. M. Smith in those more favorable times may help to explain some later events.[11]

In 1906, the West End acquired the Ohio claims for 200,000 shares of treasury stock (about $50,000 at market), and then went on to offer 150,000 for the ground of the McNamara Mining Company. However, the latter concern rejected the proposal. Two years later, when Fred Corkill was general superintendent at the West End, the two companies got into an "apex" dispute. In mining, the apex of a vein is the "end, edge, or crest" of a vein nearest the surface.[12] Legal tradition in American mining involves the doctrine of "extra-lateral" rights, which says that if two properties have a common side-line or boundary, then the owner of the ground in which the apex of the main vein (or "stalk" as it is often called) is located, has the right to follow the vein into the neighboring property. In this case, both companies had an apex—the West End on the north and the McNamara to the west.

At the instigation of either Edwards or Smith—one suspects the latter because he was usually ready to fight for what he believed to be his rights—the West End obtained an injunction to block the McNamara's intrusion. Fortunately, both sides compromised on the

Shaft headframe (left), trestle, and coarse ore bin, West End Consolidated
Mining Company, Tonopah, Nevada. (Fred Corkill collection.)

Hoisting works and head frame, West End silver mine, Tonopah. About
1906. (Fred Corkill collection.)

The Smith party goes below in the Ohio Tonopah Mine, 1906. Standing, from left: Fred Corkill, Chris Zabriskie, R. C. Baker, Ben Edwards, and F. M. Smith. Seated, from left: Margaret Zabriskie, Grace Sperry, and Evelyn Ellis. (Fred Corkill collection.)

eve of the suit, agreeing to respect their common side-line for both veins. The McNamara company may have secured the better of the deal.[13]

Starting in 1907 the West End began to make a little money, grossing nearly $600,000 by 1910. Late in 1909, Colonel S. H. Brady took over as general manager. In February 1911, with $90,000 advanced by Smith, the company bought the Midway mill, remodeling it to make it a slime plant in which the ore values were extracted by cyanide solution. Some $75,000 was expended for this work.[14]

From 1910 to 1913, the West End continued to progress both in production and in earnings. However, this was the time in which F. M. Smith's Oakland problems were becoming very difficult for him. Two related matters thus precipitated a crisis for Ben Edwards and the West End. First, some time just before June 1, 1913, Smith borrowed $50,000 at six percent from the mining company, secured by 1500 shares of the Realty Syndicate, then worth $65 each. Edwards stoutly defended Smith publicly, pointing out that the borax magnate had advanced the West End some $413,000 over the years from his private means. Edwards added that Smith had no other obligations, direct or indirect, to the company; also that the Smith stock was not to be thrown on the market or his control of the West End impaired.[15] A few weeks later, Zabriskie wrote Smith regarding the same loan, suggesting with conscious tact and a degree of unction that while "it is perfectly good and amply secured," there "is always room for criticism from outsiders" when corporate funds are loaned by directors to themselves or to institutions in which they are interested. Zabriskie's point was well taken, but Smith's financial position was extremely difficult at that time.[16]

Second, the J. C. Settle suit against Smith complained about the alleged irregularity involved between Smith and the West End in the purchase of Halifax–Tonopah stock for the West End Company. Again Ben Edwards stoutly defended his partner. He explained that the proposition originated early in 1911 from the Halifax–Tonopah side, and had been made to Zabriskie and himself, but they lacked the necessary capital. Accordingly, they submitted the proposal to F. M. Smith, who suggested that if it was so good the West End should buy the stock. But the West End was not in funds at the time. Smith thereupon offered to buy the Halifax stock himself for the West End, exchanging it for West End stock at its current market value of fifty cents a share. The West End obtained 692,180 shares of Halifax worth $865,225 in August 1913, at a cost of 395,027 West End shares worth $197,513 in early 1911, and worth $493,784 in August 1913. As of 1913, therefore, the West End stockholders received a profit, or more accurately an increase in net worth of $371,440 from this deal. Indeed, Edwards could have added that, to reimburse Smith for the advance of $196,160.86, the *accrued* profit to the company was actually $667,712. As it was, however, Edwards pointed out as strongly as he could that Smith received the current market price for the West End treasury shares, without a cent of profit from the transaction.[17]

Ben Edwards' statement, together with accounts in the general news, made it publicly clear that the Smith stock in the West End had been given to Mrs. Smith well before her husband's financial troubles had reached a crisis, and that the stock would remain in the Smith family, as in fact it did for many years.

Perhaps the strongest endorsement F. M. Smith could have hoped for came from Senator Thomas Kearns of Utah, the silver magnate and a vice president of the Halifax–Tonopah in August

1913. Kearns expressed himself with full vigor when he told *The Tonopah Miner,*

> *I believe the Halifax is going to develop into one of the greatest silver mines in Tonopah.*
>
> *Since my examination of the Halifax mine, I am amazed that anyone should have the hardihood to criticize the action of F. M. Smith in purchasing for the West End Mining Company the large block of this stock it now holds, and it is still more remarkable that anyone should be so ridiculous as to refer to this holding as 'a pile of junk.' If this impression is shared by any member of West End stockholders, I can only say that they fail to realize the immense value of their property. I have no hesitation in saying that I am willing to take this stock from the West End Mining Company at its actual cost plus $500,000 as a profit on the investment, and the money will be paid within 24 hours after my offer is accepted.* [18]

The Senator's flat declaration, backed by real money, must have provided badly needed comfort to Borax Smith in the midst of all of his troubles. His solace was further augmented by a warm editorial in the *Miner* that referred to the "indecent" attacks on him in the San Francisco and New York newspapers, noting, "In Tonopah a more generous appreciation is entertained of what F. M. Smith has done for the camp in the opening up of the West End and Halifax mines." [19]

The year 1913 was not all bad news for Smith. On November 7, the West End directors took account of the company's $40,000 average monthly profit and its reserve of $480,000 to vote its first dividend, of five cents a share ($89,424 in total). [20] The company was now beginning to take its place as one of the four largest in Tonopah.

Although of seemingly minor importance at the time, three men vital to the West End's future joined the company: J. A. Carpenter, mill superintendent and later Dean of the Mackay School of Mines at the University of Nevada; Herman D. Budelman, mining engineer and eventually general manager of the West End; and Fred C. Ninnis, who began in the mill under Carpenter, and in 1926 became president of the company. Two years later (1915), the company acquired John W. Sherwin as its general manager. Sherwin was a capable and highly regarded mining man who served Borax Smith first in Tonopah and later in Oakland, as a member of a small but very loyal group whom Smith kept around him until he died in

1931, and who then took over the continued management of his remaining interests, serving with much distinction.[21]

The West End-Jim Butler Apex Suit

On June 26, 1913, Colonel S. H. Brady, general manager of the West End, wrote a very optimistic letter to Ben Edwards, telling him that in the mine an ore body had been blocked out at the 600-foot level, yielding evidence of values at $20 per ton, or a gross valuation of $2,250,000 for the 112,500 tons believed to be present.[22] The West End was beginning to look like a potentially great mine after 12 years of gradual development. Within but a few years, it would reach the 1700-foot level. However, its best ore lay well above that depth.

Unfortunately, soon after this important strike the company entered into a serious dispute with the Jim Butler Tonopah Mining Company over its claim to extralateral rights involving veins descending into the Butler company's ground. Initially, efforts were made to settle the issue through arbitration. Accordingly, a meeting was held at the Palace Hotel in San Francisco on February 21, 1914. Present were F. M. Smith, C. B. Zabriskie, Frederick Bradshaw (general superintendent of the Butler), and Clyde A. Heller (president of the Butler and also head of the Tonopah Belmont). As matters turned out, agreement could not be reached.[23]

On April 6, 1914, the Butler company filed suit against the West End in Tonopah District Court of the State of Nevada, asking for a perpetual injunction against further operations by the West End in the Butler mine.[24] According to the Butler company, it had always been the owner of the Eureka and Curtis lode claims; that the West End owned the West End lode mining claim, which was contiguous to the two Butler lodes; and that by means of shafts, winzes,[25] and cross-cuts the West End had trespassed upon the Butler property. By these allegedly illegal acts, the West End was charged with improperly extracting some 25,000 tons of ore, for a total value of $500,000. For remedy, the Butler company sought $500,000, a permanent injunction, and its costs of suit.

In its response, the West End asserted that at all times from December 30, 1912, until some time in January 1914, the Butler management was aware of the West End's operations. It even gave consent to them and at no time made any protest before January 1914. On April 6, 1914, Judge Mark Averill granted a temporary restraining order, enjoining the West End from conducting further mining operations in the disputed ground pending a trial on the merits of the case. In essence, the dispute centered around the West End's apex claim.

On July 6, 1914, the West End filed its formal answer to the original complaint of the Butler company. Acknowledging the Butler mine's ownership of the Curtis and Eureka lodes, the West End then brought up the apex concept as the source of its extralateral rights, saying that "no part of the top or apex" of certain veins to be found within these lodes was to be found within the bounds of the Jim Butler property. On the contrary, in these instances, each vein apex lay within the West End ground, with these veins descending downward and extralaterally into the Butler claim. It was these veins that the West End said it had been mining, claiming also that it had every right to do so. Almost incidentally, the West End also contended that the value of the ore in dispute was only $204,300, not $500,000.[26]

Judge Averill made the next move, directing the companies to allow certain geologists and mining engineers to examine the underground ore bodies. These investigations apparently greatly strengthened the West End's apex claims, extending them well beyond its original expectations.[27] The company immediately sought and obtained an injunction barring the Butler Company from further mining in the Fraction Ledge, as the disputed ground was known. The court also dissolved an attachment previously gained by the Butler company against the West End. In turn, the West End claimed $360,000 in damages from trespass by Butler miners.[28] On December 2, the Butler company responded by asking for treble damages of $3 million from the West End, together with an order of the court restraining the West End from paying dividends.[29]

At this point, both sides had wheeled up their big guns for the coming legal battle. The Jim Butler brought in Judge Curtis Lindley, a famous expert in mining law and its chief counsel, and he was assisted by William E. Colby and J. H. Evans. The West End employed Judge W. H. Dickson as its expert, and James F. Peck as its chief counsel.[30] Horace V. Winchell, W. H. Wiley, and Edward A. Jussen (all noted geologists) were called in as mining experts by the West End. The Jim Butler brought in Professor Andrew C. Lawson, a prominent geologist at the University of California; Fred Searls, an associate of William Boyce Thompson and of George Wingfield in Reno; Fred Siebert, of the Goldfield Consolidated Mining Company; and John W. Finch, a member of the Wingfield-Nixon mining group. As the *Tonopah Miner* described it, the stage was "being set for one of the greatest legal battles that has ever taken place over mining property. A great deal of money hinges on the outcome. . . ."[31]

The Butler-West End case depended upon the ability of the West End experts to prove that the veins in the Fraction Ledge had their apexes on the West End property. To make their case, the West End introduced a model of the disputed ground, illustrating the location, dip, top, and direction of the veins involved. W. H. Wiley then testified for the West End that the North and South veins were separate, not an anticline (going downward from the crest of a fold or arch). Even if the two were one, he argued, the apex would be at the highest point.[32]

Wiley was followed by Horace Winchell, testifying for the West End, who declared that the apexes of the North and South veins were as "definite and distinct as a dictionary is from a Bible. . . ." Winchell placed the origins of the two veins at different geological periods, rather than as a single ledge.[33]

Opening for the Butler company, Judge Lindley set out with an attack on the West End theory that its claimed extension of the north-dipping vein over the one dipping south was in fact an extension. He deemed it "broken cracks and stringers." Lindley also held that the West End vein ran north and south, not east and west. From these contentions, he argued that the West End had no extralateral rights.[34]

John W. Finch followed Lindley, using a series of colored diagrams to develop a theory of mineralization that was said to have fascinated the entire court room. Fred Searls followed up by contending that there was but one lead (ledge) involved, extending in a series of anticlines, rather than two leads joining up in a common vein below.[35]

Early in 1915, Judge Averill found for the West End. The Butler company immediately appealed the decision to the Supreme Court of the State of Nevada. Again the West End prevailed, but its funds were still impounded pending the outcome of the litigation, because the Butler group next took its appeal to the Supreme Court of the United States. There the long dispute finally came to an end in

1918, with a victory for the West End. F. M. Smith now had control of a mine with up to $6 million in liquid capital.[36] Even in 1916, well before the final outcome, Smith's active imagination had already begun to contemplate ways to use West End capital for new projects.

Deterioration of Relationships with Edwards, Zabriskie, and Baker

Ben Edwards, Chris Zabriskie, Richard C. Baker, and Frank M. Smith were a complex, interlocking group. Borax had united them all until 1914. Zabriskie was Edwards' brother-in-law. Both Edwards and Zabriskie had been friends and associates of Smith since the 1880s. Smith and Baker had joined forces in 1896. Zabriskie associated himself with Smith in the United Properties Company; indeed, he had probably instigated Smith's entry into that disastrous undertaking. All four were investors in the West End Consolidated Mining Company.

By 1913, F. M. Smith's financial troubles had pushed him into increasing dependence upon the development of the West End mine. These developments started to impose serious strains upon his relations with the others. It is clear from his letters that Zabriskie disapproved of the West End loan to Smith. But he was careful to add that "outside of that [the objecting stockholder] has not got a leg to stand on."[37] In fact, three months earlier Zabriskie had written Edwards expressing his anger at the "baseless charge" involving the purchase of the Halifax-Tonopah stock by the West End, which he considered was a "perfectly legitimate transaction."[38] However, Zabriskie admitted that his own affairs were "in a constant state of turmoil and fighting," presumably because of Smith's related troubles. This was the first overt sign of his disquiet over his relationship with Borax Smith. Estrangement from R. C. Baker probably began by October 1913, because Smith believed strongly that his borax stock deserved a better offer than the Baker syndicate was willing to make. By June 1914, Smith had resigned, and Zabriskie had taken over administration of BCL's American operations as a vice president, not as managing director as Smith had been.

The next development was both peculiar and interesting. The November 21, 1914, issue of the *Mining and Scientific Press* carried the following advertisement:

TO PROSPECTORS

BORAX MINE WANTED

You find it. I will find the buyer. Send me samples. I will test them and report without cost to you. I will assay your gold, silver or copper ores also without charge IF YOU ARE A PROSPECTOR. Send me a sample of any unfamiliar rock you are unable to classify, if you think from your experience it might have value.

F. M. SMITH

SYNDICATE BUILDING   *OAKLAND, CAL.*

This small notice indeed did set the dove-cotes to fluttering. Ryan probably called it to Zabriskie's attention, and Zabriskie fired off a copy to Baker in London, with the observation that there need not be "any grave concern," then adding his "great regret that Mr. Smith has adopted such a course."[39] Evidently the news reached Edwards by letter from Baker, who wrote inquiring,

How are you getting on with the West End and its dividend—I hope your influence has been effective. Our friend F.M.S. must be in a green state of mind—I see he is advertising for a Borax Mine—he cannot realize what such a course must mean in the mind of any decent person. I hope he will think better of it.

With kindest regards

Yours sincerely,
R. C. Baker[40]

The reactions of Zabriskie and Baker hardly seem to have been justified. F. M. Smith had just suffered the loss of an industry that he had done more than any other man to bring into being. He still had the energy and ambition of a man of 45, as a reporter had noted in Salt Lake City in 1911. What was more natural than a desire to get back into borax and to recover the fortune he had lost? Perhaps the simplest answer is the best: a mutual concern shared by his critics that Smith just might succeed in his new endeavor. In point of fact, that is exactly what happened.

On the eve of victory for the West End at the end of 1914, Ben Edwards wrote Chris Zabriskie approving the latter's intention to resign from the West End board, but asking him to hold off until Judge Averill had handed down his decision in the Butler apex suit.

Edwards went on to express confidence in the West End's case, adding that an underground tour had proved that the north vein in every uprise had extended "continuity to an apex at a point from forty to eighty feet higher than where the south vein ends against it." With "Wiley and Winchell we had two men that have no superiors, if equals, [and] Judge Lindley got into trouble every time he tried to bother them. . . ."[41]

A few months later, Senator Kearns wrote Edwards a highly complimentary letter about his success in handling his first apex case "to the 'queen's taste'," adding that he thought "Mr. Smith should appreciate your efforts in his behalf."[42] In his reply, Edwards revealed his inner feelings that F. M. Smith had failed to realize what Edwards had accomplished, and the hard work and close attention required.[43] Nonetheless, he stayed on as vice president of the West End for two more years. Even thereafter, he maintained his friendship with Smith, appearing as a witness in his behalf in the Baar case in 1925.

Not so with Zabriskie. In the spring of 1916 he wrote Edwards about West End matters, then went on to say that "Smith is in the East with an eye on Searles Marsh providing the Leasing Bill passes. This is confidential. I have not seen him and will not unless he calls on me or unless I run across him accidentally."[44] By 1917, Zabriskie could say that he had not been "an official or a stockholder" in the West End for a long time, which meant that he had severed his last link to Borax Smith. In the same letter, he refers favorably to Edwards' new Broadway Bank (at 22nd Street and Broadway in Oakland),[45] adding that he presumed that "this will mean your being released from your connection with 'F.M.' on which I most heartily congratulate you. . . . I would not go back to the old state of affairs for any amount of money."[46]

Admittedly, F. M. Smith was not an easy employer. As a rugged individualist and self-made man he liked to do things his own way, and often resisted sound advice. He was never a domineering man in his manner, or in any sense a braggart. But his will was strong and he could be stubborn. His was a complex personality and it had its kind and generous side, as Chris Zabriskie surely had had opportunity to know almost better than anyone else outside the family. And it was said that Chris was the only man who could keep F. M. Smith waiting and get away with it. After her marriage in 1907, Evelyn Smith came to consider Margaret Zabriskie to be her "closest friend;

but after Mr. Smith dropped out of PCB, it was never the same again."[47]

By 1917, Ben Edwards had left the West End. His banking business was now a full-time assignment of its own. Another factor was his conviction that as soon as the impounded funds of the West End became available, F. M. Smith would commence investing them in other projects, which would not be congenial to a banker's natural caution. His prediction turned out to be right, but not to the extent of foreseeing Smith's ultimately successful return to borax.

And so the four men, once so close and each so highly endowed with ability, finally drifted apart. Together they had accomplished great things. How would they fare now that only two were still working together, while their original benefactor was now on his own?

The West End Undergoes Diversification at the Hand of F. M. Smith

Francis Marion Smith was an old-fashioned mining magnate like Senators George Hearst or William Andrews Clark. He was not a trained geologist or mining engineer, and he never pretended to be. He was a mining entrepreneur, a man on the alert for properties with possibilities for paying off upon development, and a man capable of designing an organization, selecting competent subordinates, and providing the company with funds and leadership. He possessed much practical knowledge about mining. Frequently he went underground to see things for himself, and he had the experience and common sense to understand what was going on. Thus it was inevitable that he would get around to using the wealth of the West End for larger purposes. Ben Edwards was no longer there to urge caution. John Sherwin now had direct charge of the mine, but had moved his headquarters to Oakland, while Herman Budelman and Fred Ninnis had responsibility for mining and milling operations in Tonopah.

F. M. Smith's first move toward diversification came in 1918, when, on the advice of a mining friend, he bought the Opoteca mine in Honduras for $80,000 in cash. The Opoteca was a very old silver property, reputed at one time to have been a large producer—"the most important . . . between Mexico and Peru."[48] Smith sent Fred Corkill down for a survey, and his report was negative. Nonetheless, the West End Opoteca Mines Company was organized in 1918 to take over the property as a subsidiary of the Tonopah company. However, nothing further ever came of this project.

F. M. Smith's second venture into diversification had a rather complex history. It ultimately proved to be the means by which he built his second fortune. The story has three principal settings: Searles Lake, California; Callville Wash in the Muddy Mountains district of Clark County, Nevada; and Oakland, where F. M. Smith did business and made his home.

Searles Lake is a large dry lake in San Bernardino County, California. It is a treasure trove of saline minerals,[49] of which potash, soda ash, salt cake, and borax have been the most profitable commercially. As early as 1862, John W. and Dennis Searles had been prospecting in the Slate Range above the lake that bears their name. By 1874 the brothers had started borax production on the northwest corner of the lake, incorporating their venture in 1878 as the San Bernardino Borax Company. In his "Autobiographical Notes," F. M. Smith tells of an interesting visit to the company's works, which he ultimately acquired and then closed down. Between 1887 and 1896, a deep well was sunk into the bed of the lake, revealing a vast array of minerals, some found nowhere else.

About 1909, the California Trona Company was formed to extract potash from Searles Lake.[50] Subsequently this firm borrowed money from an English concern known as Foreign Mines Development Company. Through foreclosure, the latter company eventually gained control, after which it announced rather loudly that it intended to break Borax Smith's "borax monopoly" by developing production at its property.[51] In addition, Foreign Mines got into a cross-dispute with the German-owned potash syndicate in which actual warfare with the sheriff's deputies was a real possibility.[52] The following March, the Federal Government withdrew the land at Searles Lake from further entry and mining exploitation because of the many legal complications that had emerged.[53]

In mid-1914, the American Trona Company, successor to California Trona, announced its intention to build a branch railroad to Searles Lake, where it held title to 40,000 acres. Head of the company was the Baron Alfred Von Der Ropp, known in the chemical trade as simply "The Baron."[54] Two years later the government announced it was adopting a leasing system to control access to the lake. One of the two borax leases was expected to be granted to F. M. Smith.[55] There is every reason to infer that Smith acquired the lease through his control of the West End Mining Company. The first step in his return to borax had now been taken.

The second step followed in 1920, when the West End Chemical Company was incorporated in California to take over the Searles Lake leases from the mining company. In this transaction, the chemical subsidiary acquired a leasehold for 2,984 acres of the surface of the south end of Searles Lake, adding 800 acres adjacent to the lake for a plant site.[56] As part of the agreement, and perhaps to pacify the mining company stockholders for lack of dividends, one share of chemical stock was distributed for each of the 1,788,486 shares of the mining company's stock.[57] Because the Smith family held over 800,000 shares of the mining stock, it automatically acquired control of the new chemical company through this distribution.[58]

Smith's First Attempt Fails

The notorious secretiveness of mining men is based upon the very practical consideration that concealment protects potential and actual discoveries. However, this same secretiveness has more than once been the incentive for inquisitiveness and even the hiring of detectives and resort to espionage to "keep tabs on the competition."

In the borax industry, sensitivity to the entry of new producers was an added factor, going back virtually to Smith's beginning in the industry in 1872. For example, in the late 1890s Smith had followed the tracks of one of Max Calm's borax wagons near Borate, picking up bits of ore thrown by the mule skinners at their animals, so that he could have it assayed for grade. Even earlier, he had travelled by horseback across the broiling Mojave Desert, stripping himself completely to rest in the shade of a rock until the heat of the day had passed—all so that he could get a look at John W. Searles' San Bernardino Borax works on Searles Lake. He even contrived to interview Searles, without disclosing who he really was.

By the second decade of the present century, PCB was still the major producer, continuing to operate at Ryan in the Greenwater Range. But now the Baron's American Potash and Chemical Company had begun developing the original Trona property in earnest.

Because APC used brine rather than extracting the refractory cole-manite ore, its costs were potentially lower, thus presenting a competitive threat to PCB's very existence.

Then, too, there was F. M. Smith, who made no secret of his intention to get back into borax. He would present a competitive threat to an industry whose producers were already highly interdependent.

Borax Smith's activities following his advertisement for a borax mine in 1914 had immediately become a matter of keen interest to Chris Zabriskie and R. C. Baker. As noted, both men had taken the rather odd position that it was improper if not downright unethical for Smith to attempt to become a borax producer again. Now that he had actually acquired his borax leases at Searles, the threat he represented seemed serious. Zabriskie reported to Baker that "The Baron" (evidently Von Der Ropp) had told him that Smith "was anxious to get back into the borax game" and wanted to market the Trona company's borax. As Zabriskie told it, the Baron informed him that Smith "evidently feels" that Baker was the cause of his exile from the industry. Zabriskie then went on to tell Baker that he informed the Baron what a good friend Mr. Smith had always had in Mr. Baker—a declaration unlikely to do Zabriskie any harm in his relations with his chief.[59] Attached was a report to Zabriskie from G. Hecker asserting that as of October 9, 1918, F. M. Smith's Searles lease amounted to 1098.5 acres in his own name and 1060.8 acres in that of West End Mining. Full details about development of the property were included.

The initial chemical process used by West End at Searles involved a technique devised by a Dr. Morse. Under this method, brines were pumped to the surface and then placed in evaporating pans for eventual separation. Much material was lost through leakage and the method was obviously unprofitable.[60] In 1920, John Sherwin, managing the Searles Lake operation for Smith, encountered at a nearby mine a young German immigrant who had recently graduated in chemistry from the University of California. His name was Henry Hellmers, and Sherwin, who was a shrewd judge of men, hired him for the chemical company. This proved to be one of the most fortunate moves Sherwin ever made, for it was Hellmers who later worked out the West End Process through which the property ultimately became successful.

Smith was now in his 74th year, but he still retained his marvelous reserves of energy, his indomitable will, and a determined faith in his own judgment. Within a few months these qualities would enable him to rock the borax industry once more.

11

Francis Marion Smith Returns to the Borax Industry

I t is time to be old, To take in sail," Emerson wrote. It is all a question of what is "old." On February 2, 1921, Francis M. Smith was 75 years of age, a time when most men are long past the advent of retirement. But Smith was not an ordinary man. Physically, he was as active and energetic as ever. Emotionally, he lived for two objectives that were linked together. He had a devoted wife and a family of four handsome children, three of them girls in their early teens, and the fourth a boy of eight. He was determined to build an estate for them, to protect them after he was gone. At the same time, he was equally determined to regain a place in the borax industry. After all, it had been the source of his original wealth, and he knew the business better than anyone else, having devoted 40 years of his life to creating the industry and developing its world market.

In the West End Consolidated Mining Company, Frank Smith had control of a source of funds essential to his purposes, and of course he had no inhibitions about using it. The next step was to bring the West End Chemical Company into being. But before this development could acquire real significance, the chemical concern had to obtain a reliable source of borax. It would soon be at hand, almost providentially, even though the initial efforts to recover borax from the Searles Lake brines by the Morse process had proved a failure.

The Muddy Mountain Colemanite Deposit
On January 23, 1921, which happened to be the anniversary of F. M. Smith's marriage to Evelyn Ellis Smith, two prospectors found

246

Mr. and Mrs. Smith with Frank, Jr., and "Hooligan" at Arbor Villa, about 1921. (F. M. Smith collection.)

probably the richest colemanite deposit then known. The name of one of them, oddly enough, was Francis Marion Lovell, and the other, George D. Hartman. The site of the deposit was near the village of St. Thomas, Nevada, then about 46½ miles east of Las Vegas by the roads of that time. The location of the find was known as Callville Wash. Even at that late date, Smith was still known as the borax giant. Accordingly, Lovell sent him a telegram in Oakland, taking care to notify other bidders as well, among them representatives of the Pacific Coast Borax Company.

This was the sort of news that was made to order for Borax Smith—a sudden possible change of luck, after years of troubles, and an opportunity to make or lose a fortune with a single decision. In no time at all he had packed his bag and set out on the long train ride to Las Vegas. From Las Vegas he had to arrange for transportation to the site, and at this point the stories vary—some had him flying in by plane, others traveling by horse or horse and wagon, others even on foot. The truth seems to be that he rented an automobile, hired a driver because he had never learned the art, and then set out on the rough and dusty journey.[1] Still, the horse

The last official photograph of Francis Marion Smith, at about the time he bought the Anniversary Mine in his 75th year. (James T. White Company.)

version remains a distinct possibility, and wholly consistent with the man.

On arrival, Smith is said to have found his capable former chief engineer, Clarence Rasor of PCB, sitting on a nearby rock chatting with Lovell and Hartman. Smith began his inspection, finding from the outcropping of the colemanite that the bed was very extensive (later it proved to be 3,000 feet in length, 300 to 500 feet thick, and with a crude ore potential of at least 400,000 short tons).[2] It did not take Borax Smith long to take the plunge. To make the deal, he proposed that Rasor and he write out their offers on paper, put the slips under a rock, and let Lovell take them out and decide who was the winner. This was done. F. M. Smith turned out to have the higher bid: a check for $50,000 for a deposit, with payment of $200,000 more promised on the back of an envelope, to be paid immediately upon his return. After eight years in *borasca* (unproductive mining), he was in ore again at last. The next step was to hurry back to Oakland to arrange to develop what he immediately named the Anniversary Mine.

Using mining company funds, Smith made the necessary advances to West End Chemical, exchanging stock for cash. Engineers soon appeared on the site. They decided that the grade and quantity of ore were unbelievably rich, with a potential value of anywhere from 10 to 60 million dollars. Borax Smith could scarcely contain himself in his exultation, probably all the more so because he knew how little joy the news would bring to his former associates, Baker and Zabriskie, whose mines at Ryan were much more distant and probably not quite so rich. Zabriskie in particular had long been keeping a very close eye upon everything his old benefactor had been doing, all the more so now that it began to look as though Smith were about to make a dramatic comeback in the industry from which he had drawn his original fortune.

In a very lengthy letter to Baker in London, written but a few months after Smith had bought the deposit, Zabriskie told of a meeting with Billy Alberger, who still headed the Key Route. Although Zabriskie could only paraphrase a conversation with Smith about which Alberger had told him, the account sounds wholly authentic, for it was the way Smith used to talk. It reflects his long years of frustration along with his latent optimism, which came surging to the surface now that new wealth at last seemed at hand.

According to Alberger, Smith had sent for him ostensibly to learn about Key Route affairs. Then he finally came to the real point: "Well, I have a lot of borax again. I have a lot of it, and I am again going to be in the game. . . . it will take me some little time to get developed and thoroughly organized, maybe a couple of years, but I will be in it, and when I get around to it I will give the Borax Company [PCB] a whirl." Alberger replied that it ought to make "a merry fight," and Smith answered, "Yes, you can tell those directors of yours, or rather, the members of that committee of mine [the Advisory Committee], that if they only fool around a couple of years longer, I will pay off all my debts myself, and when I do, I will go down there and kick them all out, and then you and I will run the railroad." Alberger was somewhat puzzled, asking if Smith really meant to convey this message. He got a prompt affirmative reply. According to Alberger, the Committee laughed at the idea when he presented it to them, remarking that Smith would be doing them a large favor if he could pull off his scheme.[3] This reaction speaks volumes about the Committee's real attitude toward F. M. Smith.

The Committee never really understood Francis Marion Smith. He was an individualist, an old prospector, and a fighter—a man who thought in days rather than years, and who was always ready to take a risk when the prospective profit was large. For years he had been humiliated by his unfortunate excursion into high finance. He had reason to have many grievances against those whom he once thought were his friends. He had been treated shabbily by the banks, and his eight-year struggle to get back on his feet had been a very difficult one, beset by a dozen law suits and troubles of every kind. Renewal of his spirits by the Muddy Mountain discovery was surely a pardonable reason for his desire "to get his own back."

Developing the Anniversary Mine

The Muddy Mountain deposit was of the lenticular type; that is, it had the shape of a double-convex lens, with the colemanite embedded within a surrounding series of limestone, shale, and pumice strata. After careful investigation, Hoyt S. Gale, an outstanding geologist, concluded that the colemanite had been deposited by an ancient spring in the Tertiary period. It may well have been the leached-out remainder of a pre-existing bed of ulexite, left intact because colemanite is borate of calcium and is insoluble in water.[4] In any case, Gale concluded that 35.56 percent of the deposit consisted of pure colemanite. He also noted that the bed had a southward dip, ranging between 45 and 60 degrees. Because the lens was largely intact, and free of fractures and cross-veining, Gale decided "that the Callville colemanite will prove most unusually dependable as an ore body for mining. . . ."[5]

To exploit this valuable deposit, Smith invested an additional $800,000 of West End Mining funds, which were advanced against

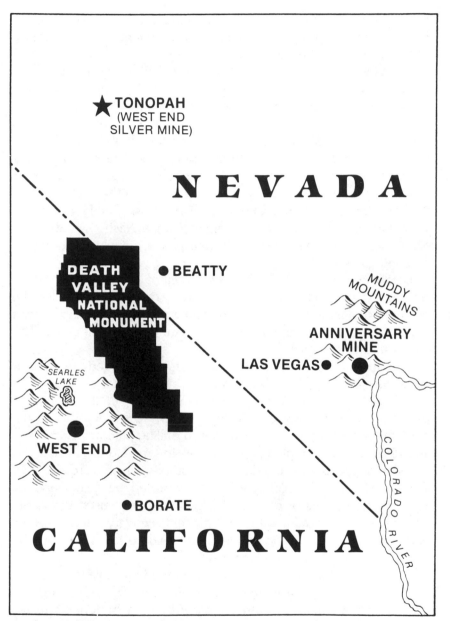

MAP 7. Last mining properties developed and operated by F. M. Smith: West End Silver Mine at Tonopah (1902-1926); Anniversary Borax Mine near Las Vegas (1921-1928); and Western Plant of West End Chemical Co., Searles Lake (1921-). Not to scale.

treasury stock turned over by West End Chemical. This money financed mine development, an overhead cable tramway, a primary crusher, and a rotary kiln for decrepitating the ore. Roads also had to be built to give closer access to the Union Pacific mainline. Always an innovator, Smith introduced some Caterpillar tractors to haul 10-ton trailers with steel wheels equipped with spokes and very broad treads. Thus the principle of the 20-mule team was revived in internal-combustion form for the 26-mile haul to the railhead at Dyke, Nevada. With this coup, Borax Smith had finally demonstrated the intrinsic correctness of his idea of some 20 years before for Old Dinah and a traction road. One of the tractors was a C. L. Best, made by a descendant of Daniel Best. One Holt and one Linn tractor were also bought, along with a Nash "Quad." The Quad was a wartime vehicle with four-wheel drive and four-wheel steering.[6]

Before commencing actual development of the mine, F. M. Smith accomplished another coup: he acquired an old biplane called the *Mercury* to survey the deposit and to fly executives and important visitors back and forth between the Anniversary Mine and Las Vegas and Los Angeles.

The mining method at the Anniversary involved an adit or downward-sloping drift driven into the deposit, with a form of shrinkage stoping for ore extraction. In principle, the technique called for drilling upward, which allows the colemanite to fill the bottoms of the stopes, serving also as a drilling platform because of the stability of its "angle of repose," as the mining men call it. No wooden supports were needed for the stopes, which were about 15 feet in width, and which could be supported by filling, and by leaving small pillars of ore behind. Scrapers were used to aid ore extraction into the adit, with a 90 percent recovery rate. Since the ore was mostly above the adit level, it could be fed down through chutes into ore pockets for removal.

At the mine entrance, the ore was trammed by cable in overhead buckets for 1,200 feet to the coarse ore bins. The tramming was electric and automatic, controlled by pushing a button. From the bins the ore was fed into the crusher, reduced to one-inch pellets, and then introduced into the oil-fired rotary kiln, where fine-screening yielded clean colemanite, ready for transport.[7]

For some years, F. M. Smith had enjoyed friendly relations with the Stauffer Chemical people—in particular, with John Stauffer, Sr. When times were difficult for Smith, he could count on a friendly hand from Stauffer. With the Anniversary Mine now in production, Smith had no refinery and no selling organization. Stauffer solved the problem by contracting to buy Smith's ore for refining in San Francisco, and sale in the United States and Europe. Soon the green bags of the "F. M. Smith Brand" borax became familiar in the trade. Indeed, at one point at the start Smith had written his foster daughter, Marion Oliver, that he was thinking of naming the product "Twenty Airplanes Borax," with a suitable design to go with it. "The name Smith," he added, "of course will be linked up with the brand, to make the article more saleable."[8] F. M. Smith was again confident and optimistic, right up-to-date in ideas, and unabashedly convinced that his name had sales value. It also must have provided him understandable satisfaction to contemplate flaunting the most famous name in the industry with a trademark to be used against his competition.

Describing his new property, Borax Smith told the press,

> The only other important known deposit of borate ore in the United States is the one I originally developed in Death Valley [the hillside claims]. The deposit our company has now acquired has the advantage that it can be mined very economically. The expense of marketing the mined ore will be very much less [than PCB's] owing to its proximity to the railroad. The distance from the Death Valley deposit to the main line railroad is about 150 miles, and in order to transport the product it was necessary to construct a branch connecting line costing millions of dollars. This was done after it was found the expense of transporting the product by means of the famous 20-mule team was prohibitive. Yet, notwithstanding this extraordinary transportation expense, the Death Valley mine has proved very profitable.

Smith went on to describe the many uses of borax, pointing out that at that time the fastest-growing one was in the manufacture of window glass, for which borax is a hardener, strengthener, and a way to increase luster.[9] And so, in 1922, the Anniversary was in production. Smith was "back in the game."

In 1925, there were three major borax producers: Pacific Coast Borax, which still mined colemanite at Ryan, although it was sitting figuratively on a gold mine in its unexploited deposit at Kramer; American Potash and Chemical, which obtained its borax from brine at Trona, on Searles Lake; and the newcomer, West End Chemical Company, which extracted colemanite at Muddy Mountain and also had over 2,000 acres of surface leases at Searles Lake, where it was initially engaged in experimental operations. With only three producers in the industry, it was predictable that each would be keenly aware of what the other two were doing, and would immediately have any marketing initiatives of either of the others reflected in its own sales and share of the market. In "co-respective competition" of this kind,[10] instability of price and sales is a constant threat. Such a threat invites the possibility of collusive price setting to procure stability and eliminate disagreeable surprises. F. M. Smith had instinctively grasped this principle at least 40 years earlier, forming the Borax Union in San Francisco to stabilize prices. But in the 1920s, Smith was in no mood to join forces with either concern, even if they had been receptive. His goal was a break-through to superiority, not a small company surviving under an umbrella provided by the larger two rivals.

The re-entry of Smith into borax in 1922 was a disruptive factor. The implications for PCB were far more serious than for American Potash. As Smith well knew, PCB was operating a colemanite property that required two railroads of its own of about 143 miles in total length to move its borates to mainline rail connections. By the UP route, the haul was 117 miles, as against 143 miles to the Santa Fe. Moreover, the Tonopah and Tidewater and the Death Valley railroads, although absolutely necessary in their time, regularly lost money, even on operating expenses. Borax Consolidated had to cover these losses. In comparison, Smith had a tractor haul of only 26 miles to a mainline railhead on the Union Pacific, and of course was not compelled to absorb the losses BCL had to endure to provide common carrier rail service. His ore body, although composed of colemanite, was rich and continuous, of a quality similar to the old Lila C, long said to be the best of the Death Valley properties. Once his marketing problem was solved, Smith had the competitive edge over his former company—at least at the beginning.

But both PCB and West End had a formidable rival in American Potash. Using the *Solvay* process, a Belgian innovation, APC had only to pump hot water down into the dry crust of Searles Lake, bring up the brine solution, separate the components, and thereby obtain borax—along with potash, salt cake, soda ash, and lime—together with some lesser known but valuable minerals. Given these important by-products, APC could assign its overhead costs any way it chose to, meaning that it was free to cut its price for borax. PCB and West End Chemical lacked these advantages; they had to get their product from colemanite, which was more costly to refine.

The result was a "borax war" that broke out around 1924 or 1925, driving the price from about $200 down to $16 a ton. West End survived because of the help provided by its Stauffer connection, aided by its ability to exploit its leases at Searles Lake, which enabled it to produce soda ash and carbonates. In this same period, furthermore, Henry Hellmers persuaded Smith and Sherwin to continue research into a carbonate process for recovering borates from the Searles Lake brines. Ultimately, the Westend process was perfected, and West End Chemical was able to survive this deadly price war. Indeed, its position was now substantially similar to APC's, except for its lack of adequate working capital. Gradually the company began to make a little money, compelling John Sherwin to find ways to conceal the profits from F. M. Smith because of a well-founded concern that Smith would divert funds into still other projects.[11] As soon as the Westend process was perfected the Anniversary Mine was closed down (in 1928) to be held in reserve for the distant future, when its ample reserves of colemanite would again find a market. West End now could get all the borax it wanted more cheaply from Searles Lake. In contrast, PCB was still dependent upon colemanite.

Hellmers' process, which is still used, called first for roasting lime in a kiln, to obtain carbon dioxide gas. Carbonation followed when lake brine was introduced into wooden towers with the gas. This precipitated the brine, producing bicarbonate of soda as a sludge at the bottom of the towers. The sludge then went to the classifiers for separation to extract the bicarbonates. These were diluted, washed, and filtered, then conveyed to feeder tanks that supplied the heated calcining units. This allowed extraction of soda ash. To obtain borax, the borax brine was separated, dried, cooled, and filtered, after which it was chilled. The concentrate was then put through ball mills for fine crushing, after which it was cleaned to grade by passing it through magnetic and centrifugal separations. The borax was then ready for packing and shipping.[12]

What about PCB, now that it faced two aggressive rivals, both with much more economical methods of production, extraction, and distribution? When Borax Smith first purchased the Muddy Mountain deposit, the press was full of talk about the return of the old, deposed borax king to his throne, his sudden acquisition of an alleged $20 million fortune in the deposit, and similar melodramatic observations. Zabriskie's initial reaction to these dispatches was to ridicule Smith's achievement as "rank stock promotion." But there is no doubt that he was deeply concerned for the future of his own company, as his letters of interminable length to Baker in the early 1920s all show. Zabriskie knew little about mining or geology, while others in the company were more fortunately prepared professionally. It was decided to look seriously at the old Suckow deposit acquired for PCB by F. M. Smith in October 1913. Experimental drilling began in 1925. It wasn't long before PCB executives realized that they had control of a huge deposit of borax in kernite form, perhaps 300 million tons. What was more important, it was extremely pure as well as water-soluble in nature. Preparation for the market required hardly more than crushing and grinding. And the Santa Fe mainline lay within five miles of the site.

PCB lost no time in getting into production at Kramer—later called Boron—starting in 1927. The great mines at Ryan were closed down in that year; the Death Valley Railroad was defunct by 1930; and that faithful old iron mule, the Tonopah and Tidewater, finally was allowed to quit in 1940.

PCB, too, was now "back in the game" with a vengeance. Ironically, it all became possible because three old Nevada miners—John Ryan, Fred Corkill, and Francis Marion Smith—had the foresight to acquire the Suckow property for the company in 1913, while Smith had made good on his personal vow to reestablish himself in the industry that he, more than anyone else, had created.

F. M. Smith Leaves the West End Mining Company

During the years after formation of the West End Chemical Company in 1920, the parent West End Consolidated Mining Company continued operations in Tonopah. F. M. Smith was the nominal head, but much of the executive work was done by John Sherwin, who acted in a similar capacity for the chemical company. As early as 1921, Zabriskie was predicting that Smith would fail in his return to borax, both because he did not go at things "in a businesslike way" and because Zabriskie no longer looked upon "Searles Lake as a menace in the Borax game."[13] However, he continued to keep a very wary eye on Smith and his business activities, particularly his use of mining company earnings for advances to the new chemical company.[14] Then, in 1924, when the news broke that the Smiths had sold a large portion of Arbor Villa for $350,000 for subdivision,

Zabriskie sent the information on to London, adding the handwritten comment that he did "not believe S. would cut up this property unless he is hard up for cash."[15] At least Zabriskie hoped that he was, if only for business reasons.

By June 1925, a group of minority stockholders headed by a man named John J. Gallois began an effort to oust Borax Smith as president of the mining company. The principal charge was that since 1920 the mining company had earned some $6 million in profits, of which Smith had diverted $5 million to other ventures, the present value of which was alleged to be only $353,000, while only $450,000 had been distributed as dividends. As it happens, the 1,700,000 odd shares of the chemical common that had been distributed as a dividend to investors in the mining company were ultimately to attain an aggregate market value of approximately $21.25 million (by 1956), while the total assets of the chemical company reached $22 million. Even more, net worth amounted to $21.2 million, including $9.75 million for the Anniversary property and $7.8 million for earned surplus.[16] To be sure, these rich rewards could not have been foreseen by Gallois and his associates in 1925, but they do show how wrong this group turned out to be.

It should be observed that F. M. Smith applied to the new mining company the same principle that he had followed in borax years before. The Tonopah property, like all mines, had a finite life. If the corporation that owned it wished to count upon a perpetual existence, then it had to invest earnings in new properties. The real basis of the dispute, allowing for but not conceding accompanying charges of mismanagement, concerned the *share* of earnings to be directed toward acquisitions, and the *choice* of new properties for such purpose. Smith controlled the company, was eager to buy a new borax property, and with his strong streak of independence to drive him, plunged into the West End Chemical project. Even by 1926 it was evident that the new company would become very profitable, but Smith no more than Gallois could foresee the outcome 30 years ahead. F. M. Smith had faith in the future. Gallois wanted dividends now. Posthumously, Smith proved to be right.

Smith's practice of diverting earnings to other properties actually was a sound one. Precisely because every mine has a finite life, a portion of its earnings are in fact consumed capital. The South African investment companies solve the problem by owning whole groups of mines, to spread the risk. There the custom is for the individual mine to pay large dividends (at 15 to 20 percent), which include capital consumption. Then the investment company pools these dividends to develop new properties, rather than passing them along in their entirety as dividends of the investment house. F. M. Smith was doing the same thing without an investment company, by building up the chemical firm with the earnings of the mining company. Neither Gallois nor Zabriskie even understood the principle. Their real motive was to destroy Smith.

Chris Zabriskie knew all about the Gallois–Smith controversy. Clearly he wanted Gallois to break Smith completely, and was on close terms with the former during the fight. In part Zabriskie's motive was simple hostility to his former friend and benefactor. In part he was particularly concerned about who might take possession of the chemical company, which also produced borax.[17] As for Gallois, it is probable that he wanted more than dividends, that his real goal was to capture the chemical company and then sell it for a big profit.

The battle began when the regular May meeting of the mining company stockholders was not held in 1924. In January 1925, Smith called a special meeting to ratify the actions of the Board of Directors for the past two years. Smith had 800,000 shares to vote on his side, although 600,000 had been pledged to J. F. Carlston of the Central Bank in Oakland as collateral for a $300,000 loan. Gallois had only 200,000 shares on his side. Smith prevailed in this meeting. Then Zabriskie made the interesting observation, "Carlson [Carlston] and Galloit [Gallois] are acting together"; their plan was to gain control of the mining company, which would also give them control of the chemical company. Then it was their hope, Gallois told Zabriskie, "that we [PCB] would take it [West End Chemical] off their hands."[18]

Gallois informed Zabriskie that, according to Smith's report, the mine had made profits of $200,000 in 1924. The real figure had been much larger but much had been drained off for West End Chemical, in which $3.5 million of West End mining funds had been invested. Zabriskie went on to tell Baker that Gallois would ultimately defeat Smith in court, but only after a long fight. He also reported that he told Gallois "that on account of former relations with Smith, we [PCB] did not wish to be placed in the position where we would appear as having conspired to bring about his [Smith's] downfall." Apparently it was the appearance, not the substance, that mattered.

This dispute went on for another 18 months, and on May 27,

1926, the Gallois faction succeeded in electing a new set of directors for the West End Consolidated Mining Company, with only F. M. Smith himself held over on the new board. The next step was a suit by Gallois to gain access to the books and records of the company. Zabriskie thereupon wrote Gallois congratulating him upon his victory.[19] He later followed this with a letter to Baker, telling him of Smith's initial defeat in the Baar suit, which Zabriskie thought would affect control of West End Chemical as well.[20]

However, this is not the way things turned out. First, Baar lost on a reversal by the California Supreme Court. Second, F. M. Smith voluntarily quit as president of the mining company in June 1926. (He did *not* resign as president of West End Chemical, and the mining company did not control the chemical company.) As part of his resignation, it was agreed that Fred C. Ninnis would become president of the mining company, while Herman D. Budelman would become general manager and John Sherwin would confine himself to managing West End Chemical.[21]

F. M. Smith's West End Chemical plant at Searles Lake, California, in 1953. (Courtesy of Caterpillar Tractor Company.)

West End Mining continued to prosper for a few years, although it closed its mill in 1927, and went on a leaser basis in 1928. At the end of 1930, the mine closed permanently. From 1906 to 1930 it had produced 774,011 tons of ore, for a gross yield of $14.5 million, which made it the fourth biggest property in Tonopah.[22] If it had not been for the several hundred thousand dollars that F. M. Smith had poured into its development in the years before 1913, it probably would not have achieved its outstanding success.

The Baar and Gallois fights took their toll of Borax Smith just at the time when the new borax company was beginning to come into its own. By 1928 his health was failing rapidly. He began to suffer a series of little strokes that forced him to quit as president of West End Chemical. John Sherwin took over, aided by Mrs. Smith and her brother, George C. Ellis. By 1930 Smith had lost the capacity of speech, although his mind remained clear and he was still able to walk with assistance and to take short automobile rides. A year later—on August 27, 1931—he died. A few months afterward, John Sherwin also passed away. By 1932, Evelyn Smith had taken over the presidency of West End Chemical.

Mrs. Smith managed the growing company successfully for several years. Eventually she was persuaded to step down, whereupon her brother, George C. Ellis, took her place. Her daughters still recall her efforts to train him in the production side of the business. They describe her climbing up ladders to the carbonation towers, exclaiming to Henry Hellmers, "Helm, tell George what happens here, and then what follows. He has to know everything so that he can run the plant."

Smith's Last Years

Through his successful re-entry into the borax industry, first with colemanite at the Anniversary Mine from 1922 to 1928, and then with the West End process at Searles Lake, F. M. Smith could draw immense satisfaction from an achievement that repeated the dramatic aspects of his 60-year career in business. Nonetheless the going was hard during the last decade of his life. There was the strain of turning West End Chemical into a success. There was the mortal threat to the new company latent in the borax war of 1925. There was the deadly harassment of the Baar suit, lasting 18 months. And finally there was Gallois' attempted take-over of both the mining and the chemical company.

Evelyn Smith seated in her husband's buckboard at the Furnace Creek
Museum in Death Valley, 1950. (F. M. Smith collection.)

In addition to these burdens, the Smiths found it increasingly
difficult to maintain their style of living, even after drastic economiz-
ing. To keep up Arbor Villa, they sold a four-block strip along 9th
Avenue between East 24th and East 28th Street. Very modest
California stucco bungalows were built there. Except for this con-
cession to necessity, the great estate and its gardens kept most of
their former splendor. But the squeeze from rising taxes finally
reached the point where the Smiths were forced to make a fundamental decision in 1924: should they give up the entire property
and move into a less expensive home, or should they slice off some
more of the magnificent gardens and try to hang on for a while
longer?

Because Oak Hall and Arbor Villa were F. M. Smith's pride, the
decision was a hard one. Finally it was decided to keep the great
house, surrounded by an island of land stretching from the west
front to East 24th Street between 7th and 8th Avenues, with a
somewhat smaller section to the rear. Eighth Avenue was then run
through to Park Boulevard, slicing off the south side some more,

while the entire section on the north was sacrificed all the way to the great gates and iron fence along Park Boulevard. The abandoned lands were sold to C. P. Murdock and Company, while the doomed observation tower that stood by the extension of 8th Avenue was deliberately set on fire and burned down one summer evening in August 1924, to commemorate the opening of the new subdivision. Watching from a window at Oak Hall, F. M. Smith must have reflected about how short an existence had been vouchsafed to probably the finest estate in the Bay Region. It is said that he would wince visibly as each of the great trees came crashing down from the subdivider's axe.

Fifteen years of adversity were simply too much. In 1928, F. M. Smith entered virtual retirement. As his strokes grew worse he became an invalid. Evelyn Smith then took over all of his business affairs. The final blow was the inevitable decision to give up Oak Hall. An attractive new home was found in Vernon Heights, in Oakland. It had a small formal rose garden and even a touch of Queen Anne in its two-story design, but it could not accommodate many of the elegant furnishings of the big house. The best that could be retained was kept, and an auction of the remainder was held in September 1930. By that time, Francis Marion Smith had left for the last time his home of almost 38 years.

A year later Smith suffered a fall on the stairs in his new home, breaking his hip. On August 27, 1931, he died at Fabiola Hospital, with his devoted wife at his side.

Within a day the name of Borax Smith was supreme for one last time in the headlines around the Bay—as the 20-Mule Team "Borax King," as the founder of the Key Route, as the region's greatest philanthropist, and as the man who had opened Death Valley to the world.

The passing of Francis Marion Smith reminded the leaders of the City of Oakland that they had lost the most distinguished citizen the community had ever had, a forgotten giant whose name for years had headed every subscription list and whose business contributions were the central factor in the development of his adopted city. On September 1, 1931, the City Council passed No. 227, "Resolution of Condolence on the Death of Francis Marion Smith." This resolution had been prepared by former mayor Frank K. Mott, who had held office during the years of Smith's prominence in the city. It reads as follows:[25]

Whereas, the City Council of the City of Oakland has learned with keen regret and sorrow of the death of our esteemed, kindly and public-spirited friend and citizen, Francis Marion Smith, and

Whereas, on behalf of this Council, as representative of the people of Oakland, we desire to record our appreciation of his worth and to testify to his many laudable services as a foremost and leading citizen of this community, and

Whereas, for many years a resident of our City and active in its business and public affairs, he unfailingly displayed throughout his life a fine civic spirit and loyalty that was not only helpful and inspiring, but contributed immeasurably to the advancement, up-building and welfare of the City and her people, and

Whereas, no enterprise, or project which had for its purpose the enhancement of the City's interests or the betterment of the community life escaped the notice of Mr. Smith and he always was among the first in active and substantial support of any beneficent measures and through his enthusiastic and generous impulses led others to join and participate in these worthy and meritorious undertakings, and

Whereas, his many benefactions, both public and private, are too numerous to record here, but mention should be made of his valuable contribution to the City of several park areas and a children's playground, as well as his generous subscription to the fund which initiated the establishment of the Public Museum, and throughout his life he filled the part of a forward-looking, outstanding, and good citizen and his memory is one to be long revered and respected, Now, therefore,

Resolved: That this Council extend to the members of his family its sincere sympathy in their bereavement and ask the people of this City to bear in grateful remembrance the many kind and noble acts of this generous-hearted man, and be it

Further resolved: That this Resolution be spread in full upon the minutes of this Council and that engraved copies thereof be forwarded to the members of the family.

> *I hereby certify that the foregoing is a full, true and correct copy of a Resolution passed by the City Council of the City of Oakland, California, on September 1, 1931.*
>
> > *Fred N. Morcom*
> > *Mayor of the City of Oakland*

This generous tribute was not to be the last. Two years later, the

Oakland Junior Chamber of Commerce set aside October 24, 1933, as Founders' Day. The choice of Francis Marion Smith as the first resident to be so honored and of the date were not accidental. No other man had ever equalled him as a civic leader, while October 26 was the anniversary of the beginning of operations by the Key Route 30 years earlier. At the commemorative luncheon, Mayor McCracken declared that Smith "was one of the first to envision the possibilities of the great East-bay region, planning how the city could be served by a local transportation system and by vessels plying from its docks to the four corners of the world." The former postmaster, William Nat Friend, credited Smith with having given thousands of dollars to Oakland churches, to the construction of the YMCA building and to other benefactions. The publisher of the *Oakland Tribune*, Joseph R. Knowland, acknowledged that Smith's "crowning achievement was his vision of a transportation system for the East side of the bay. He sowed the seed for the development of Oakland's great harbor." Knowland also said, on another occasion, "He was perhaps one of the first to envision a bridge to aid in crossing the bay. Out of his earlier dreams came the present reality—the huge San Francisco–Oakland Bay bridge." Finally, Alfred J. Lundberg, who had rehabilitated the Key Route and then headed it as a prosperous concern, proceeded to introduce the crew of the first Key train from Berkeley to San Francisco, and the captain and chief engineer of the ferry *Yerba Buena*.

Lundberg then presented a plaque bearing a profile in bas-relief of Borax Smith and the 20-mule team, followed by a brief description which read:

FRANCIS MARION SMITH
"BORAX SMITH"

Founder of the "Key Route"

Commemorating operation of the first train from Berkeley Station one o'clock p.m. on October 26, 1903—connecting with SS. Yerba Buena for San Francisco. Edward M. Boggs engineer of construction. James P. Potter superintendent.

PRESENTED TO KEY SYSTEM LTD ON THE THIRTIETH ANNIVERSARY BY

ALFRED J. LUNDBERG
PRESIDENT

The plaque was designed by Andrew T. Hass and executed by

William Gordon Huff. It was placed in the entrance of the Key System building on Broadway in Oakland, where it remained until the company was taken over by Alameda County Transit Lines.[27]

So ended the long and creative life of this remarkably interesting and very complex man. Ultimately, he had received a measure of the recognition and appreciation that lesser men and ill fortune had so long denied him. Even in finance he was restored posthumously to his rightful place. For through the leadership of Evelyn Smith, her brother George Ellis, and Henry D. Hellmers, the West End Chemical Company that Smith had founded survived to become a money-maker. On September 25, 1956, 25 years after Borax Smith's death, the company was merged into the Stauffer Chemical Company. The aggregate price paid for the outstanding West End common and preferred shares was slightly over $27 million.[28]

One likes to think that somehow, somewhere, Francis Marion Smith is aware that in the end his family was cared for, and that by his courage and foresight he had finally gotten back his own.

What Survives of the Physical Legacy of F. M. Smith?

As a builder, F. M. Smith had made a substantial impact upon his times. What remains a half-century later?

Within weeks of his death in August 1931, the long-abandoned borax refinery at West Alameda was torn down. Because it had been built of reinforced concrete, dynamite had to be used to accomplish the job. Next came Oak Hall and the remnants of Arbor Villa. In January 1932, the wrecking crew arrived with hammers, mauls, and axes. Within days, the magnificent house with all of the splendor of its interiors of rare woods was reduced to wreckage, with nothing saved in its original form. Today all that remains to remind one of the past is the great line of desert palms along 9th Avenue, and some of the former cottages of the Mary R. Smith Trusts. Where the beautiful gardens once surrounded the big house, there now exist countless shabby apartment buildings and small stores.

Presdeleau suffered a similar fate. The splendid barn and lookout tower burned in 1930. The house itself gradually became run down, and then was badly damaged by the hurricane of 1938. At that point, Evelyn Smith decided to have it torn down. After World War II the lands were sold and subdivided. All that now remains is the long sea wall that F. M. Smith had had built at the edge of Smith

Cove, the little Japanese bridge, and the tiny summer house at Cedar Island. Strangely, his boyhood home in Richmond, Wisconsin, still survives in excellent condition, while the "old red house" that once stood where Oak Hall was located can still be found on East 24th Street, near 8th Avenue.

Also within the Oakland area, the beautiful little Key Route Inn was torn down in August 1932. Its companion piece, the Hotel Claremont, still stands. On the grounds of Mills College, one can still see the handsome campanile designed by Julia Morgan, and given to the college by Mr. and Mrs. F. M. Smith in 1904. In the center of town, the sturdy old Syndicate Building still stands, newly renovated and in excellent condition.

The fate of the Key Route was a bit more complicated. Paving, road-building, and 20-cent gasoline in the 1920s doomed the financial future of Smith's old company. By 1930, when it underwent drastic recapitalization after sale at foreclosure, any equity held by the Smith Advisory Committee had been wiped out. In 1939, Key trains at last were operating through to San Francisco over the new bridge, just as F. M. Smith had intended when he started the project in 1902. The changeover made the old pier terminal and ferries useless, but because the original terminal had burned in March 1933, and the original rolling stock had been replaced by 1937, what remained to carry Smith's imprint was only the surviving rail system itself. Indeed, in 1941 the Key took over parts of the Southern Pacific electric lines when the major part of them was abandoned. Thus the Key Route finally won out in the long struggle that began back in 1910, in Borax Smith's time.

But the company could not withstand the floodtide of the continuing automobile revolution, which came surging in after World War II, inspired by continuing cheap fuel and the new freeway movement. The Key's local owners sold out in 1946 to National City Lines, a firm committed exclusively to motor buses. Within two years, F. M. Smith's well-planned and well-built street railway system was ripped up. The transbay lines were retained for a time, but they were allowed to deteriorate. On April 18, 1958, the last Key Route train departed for San Francisco, ending 55 years of safe and convenient service for countless millions of passengers. Borax Smith's vision proved to be right after all, for within four years the three major counties around the Bay joined to build a new and more extensive transbay interurban system.

As for borax, where it all began, one can still visit Teel's and

Columbus marshes, where he will find a few rock walls as the surviving artifacts. Within Death Valley itself, the ruins of the old Harmony Borax Works are protected as part of the National Monument, while the museum at Furnace Creek is the old bunk-house from Monte Blanco, built by F. M. Smith in 1882. The steam tractor, Old Dinah; the great borax wagons designed by J. W. S. Perry; the little Baldwin narrow-gauge consolidation locomotive that served the Death Valley Railroad; and the buckboard that Borax Smith used in his travels around the valley are all to be seen at Furnace Creek. One can drive up to Ryan, on the west side of the Funeral Mountains, and still see many of the buildings of the last camp Smith developed for PCB. Further east there are the ruins of the Lila C, while near Daggett, many miles south, one can take a rough ride up Mule and Eagle Canyons where Smith developed the first underground colemanite mines and the great camp of Borate. The Anniversary Mine is still held in reserve, while the plant on Searles Lake continues to be fully active.

Two other accomplishments of Smith's long career were less visible to the public and, unfortunately, are now forgotten. One was that by creating a first-class metropolitan transportation company, he made it possible for millions of passengers to travel within the Bay Region cheaply and in safety and comfort for many years, without a cent of subsidy from any public body. Here then was an intangible public benefit of large importance, stemming from the vision and initiative of a single exceptional man.

F. M. Smith's other great accomplishment was to make borax and its family of boron compounds a cheap commodity, highly useful to mankind. Before he had made his original discovery and had ex-ploited it fully to create a new mining industry, borax was a rarely used chemical, of interest to goldsmiths and makers of art glass, and selling at five times the price prevailing 20 years after Smith began operations. The highly imaginative Smith made a very useful prod-uct readily available for the benefit of millions of people, simply by mastering the art of producing it in volume and thereby making it cheap.

And so, after all, many things associated with Borax Smith *do* survive, although the most interesting ones are long gone. More than that, the rare kind of businessman that F. M. Smith was—part prospector, part miner, part magnate and industrialist, part sportsman, and part civic benefactor—is a species that today has become virtually extinct.

12

F. M. Smith as an Entrepreneur

*. . . to study the "entrepreneur" is to study the central figure in modern
economic history, and, to my way of thinking, the central figure in
economics.* [1]

hether one looks upon Francis Marion Smith exclusively as
a man of business or with regard to the entirety of his long
life and diverse activities, it will be seen that he represents an almost
perfect example of that least-understood figure in modern industrial
society, the entrepreneur.

Professor Cole of Harvard regards the entrepreneur as the real
leader in the building up of those comparatively few economic
systems that have achieved full industrialization and a high general
standard of life in the modern world. In a similar way, the late Frank
H. Knight of the University of Chicago viewed entrepreneurs as
possessed of a rare set of personal qualities: superior managerial
ability, foresight, capacity to direct others, and "confidence in their
judgment and disposition to 'back it up' " by assuming large risks.
Professor Knight emphasized strongly the large degree of uncertainty that surrounds business decisions involving the future. Men
who are willing, even eager, to engage in "uncertainty-bearing," to
take chances involving large sums, are indeed a rare type. [2] F. M.
Smith was such a man.

We must refer also to the views of the late Joseph A. Schumpeter
of Harvard, probably the foremost student of the theory of entrepreneurship. To Schumpeter, the entrepreneur provides a special
kind of leadership, that of "leading" land, labor, and capital into
new uses, not by persuading, or appealing to the owners of these
resources, but by *buying* these services from those owners. In other
words, he accomplishes his purposes through the market rather
than through politics. His activities, Schumpeter recognized, are
little known to the public, and therefore not much appreciated,
despite the basic contribution that entrepreneurs make to economic

268

growth and well-being. Indeed, one may add, the populist strain in the American tradition has often made the entrepreneur an object of suspicion and hostility.

Entrepreneurs, Schumpeter has noted, are leaders who seize the main chance to the exclusion of everything else. Their psychology is extremely complex. It cannot be said that mere money-making is their central goal. At the core of this peculiar psychology, Schumpeter thought, were "the dream and the will to found a private kingdom." Entrepreneurs' motivation includes "the will to conquer: the impulse to fight, to prove one's superiority to others, to succeed for the sake . . . of success itself." To such men, the will to win is a form of sport, not of gain-seeking. In addition, Schumpeter has argued, there is "the joy of creating, of getting things done," particularly when there are difficulties in the way. The entrepreneur delights in overcoming obstacles, in effecting change, in assuming large risks.[3]

There is no fundamental conflict among these three economists. Taking their views as a point of departure, it is possible to state what the entrepreneur is not. Above all, he is not a mere administrator, although he may direct large affairs from his top position in an administrative hierarchy. The administrator as such is a functional specialist in, say, finance, production, or marketing. He has responsibility for a given jurisdiction in a business organization and he may undertake initiatives within that jurisdiction. But he is not the free-wheeling leader of whom Schumpeter speaks. He does not take the large risks or assume the tasks of uncertainty-bearing that are the hallmarks of a true entrepreneur.

At the same time, the entrepreneur is not a capitalist, granting that some entrepreneurs also have been capitalists, as was F. M. Smith himself.[4] Strictly speaking, a "capitalist" is a person who invests substantial sums of money in a private business enterprise. But this makes him an investor rather than a true entrepreneur. To be an entrepreneur, he must also be the active leader who directs the enterprise, takes the risks, and shapes its destiny. F. M. Smith, for example, was an entrepreneur foremost, and also a capitalist in a substantial way—a *borrowing* capitalist.[5]

Some Aspects of Smith as an Entrepreneur

Before he left Wisconsin in 1867, Francis Marion Smith began to show the traits of a potential entrepreneur. In later life he spoke, guardedly, of having been sent to a second high school "for better discipline, I suppose." He told also of watching the sun setting over Rock Prairie and thinking of gold and of those who had struck it rich in California.

These two clues from early life reveal a streak of independence and a restless desire to try his luck in an unknown land. When he reached the age of 21 on February 2, 1867, he became free of parental control. Already he had been planning to strike out on his own by heading west. By spring he was on his way. He spent the next five years in fruitless prospecting at various locations, toiling as a cook when funds ran low. Here another notable factor emerges. Smith lingered in the regions where rich mines had been discovered. He avoided cities, in all probability because he could see no fortune for himself in such places. He even turned to wood "ranching" to survive in the desert. A strong sense of inner direction clearly was at work.

This subsequently found expression in the visit to Teel's Marsh, Nevada, a visit that probably can be attributed to more than idle curiosity. Already he was cutting wood for one of the tiny borax companies on Columbus Marsh. Why not see if this remote desert playa could be turned into a tangible opportunity? He made the trip, collected samples, took them straight back to Columbus, had them assayed, and learned that he had found the richest borate deposit then known in the region. Immediately he "seized the main chance," as Schumpeter called it, raced back to the site, made his locations, but then found they all had to be done again to comply with placer-mining law. With tireless energy and a readiness to fight for his claims as he had fought for his wood a few months before, Smith preserved his find from the claim jumpers.

The next step was to bring in his brother, obtain capital, hire labor, and set up a plant—all by early 1873. He was then 27 years old and was sure that he saw the future clearly. Borax had been selling for about 35 cents a pound. He could make money at far less because he had the largest and best deposit, and a big enough plant to capture the advantages of scale.

Smith never forgot those humble beginnings. Years later he told a reporter on a visit to Tonopah,

> I got off the train the other day at Coaldale and my first thought was of the old camp where I saw so many happy and hard-working days. There it was off on the horizon, seen as clearly and distinctly in the

mirage as though it existed in all the importance of its early youth. Of course, I knew the mirage covered a multitude of sins and glorified the ruins, for there is little there now but the crumbling adobe. In spite of this fact the town of Columbus will always have a tender spot in my heart, for it was the place where I got my start . . . .[6]

In short, even at the time F. M. Smith knew that he was "on to something big" at Teel's Marsh, for he had the unusual foresight of the entrepreneur as well as the drive to exploit his discovery to the fullest.

With the rush of additional production at Teel's, the price of borax soon collapsed to 10 cents a pound, and later dropped even lower. The little fellows went under, but Smith and his brother held on. His next move was to undertake the task of creating a national market by going on the road himself, selling his product in storefronts with the single-minded energy and self-confidence that typified his entire career. One by one he bought up the other small plants, then built a large one of his own at Fish Lake Valley. In 1888 his agent, Coleman, failed. Borrowing to the hilt (and to the unforgiving resentment of Joe Mather), Smith picked up the Harmony plant, the hillside claims, the Lila C, the Amargosa, the huge reserve of colemanite in the Calico Hills, and the West Alameda refinery. He had the vision and the courage that Mather so palpably lacked.

Smith now dominated the field. He had accomplished this feat by a gradual assertion of sheer business ability. He had recognized the importance of creating a market for his product. Within two years he was hawking the package trade himself. Almost instinctively, he understood the principle of economy of scale, which means, in many industries, that average cost per unit will fall as production increases. In these cases, the increase in resource inputs, particularly capital, will be relatively less than the increase in output obtained. Daniel C. Jackling, the copper magnate, had discovered this relationship in Utah while mining low-grade disseminated ore bodies: when the ore put through the fixed plant was increased substantially, the associated necessary increase in plant was proportionately less. Smith was doing the same thing years earlier, opening up his markets so that he could expand production and lower unit costs. By 1890, he had increased output by four and one-half times over 17 years.

Smith's second step to dominance lay in taking the huge risk of borrowing $400,000, to buy up the Coleman properties himself so that no rivals could enter the field. In the end, he had beaten them all. By doing so, he had converted what had been hardly more than an artisan trade into a national industry. His risk-taking had upset Mather, but without it he could not have become the magnate that he was by 1890.

Having "seized the main chance" and won out, Borax Smith could now indulge in what Schumpeter considered to be the ultimate goal of all great entrepreneurs: "the dream and the will to form a private kingdom." His kingdom had three components. First, it embraced a single great business, to be controlled exclusively by the man who had created it—F. M. Smith. Within a few years that company was to become a multinational firm named Borax Consolidated, Limited. Here again was a significant kind of pioneering by Borax Smith, as original in its way as was his transformation of marsh "farming" into underground colemanite mining at Borate in 1889 and 1890. The mines at Borate were the biggest technological innovation since the beginning of the borax industry. BCL was a major international innovation in business organization. Here Smith had the help of Baker, Gerstley, and Lesser, to be sure. But it was Smith who had the borates, and the producing and selling organization that made the entire venture possible. Significantly, too, he had majority control. Smith could subordinate himself when he needed capital, but underlying all was his unending determination to stay independent—or at least to retain as much power as possible.

Smith's foresight and determination to build his own private kingdom motivated his development of a whole series of new mines and mining communities; his efforts to find a way to conquer the transportation problem, first by steam tractor and then by a remarkable pair of railroads; and his building at Bayonne of a new refinery of the most modern type in every respect. As early as 1889 he had realized the basic superiority of reinforced concrete, used it to build the addition at West Alameda, and then joined forces with E. L. Ransome to form both a construction and a machinery company connected with this major innovation.

The private kingdom of F. M. Smith actually had three parts. Borax was one. Arbor Villa and Presdeleau were another, reflecting the expression of his personal life. The third involved his Oakland activities—business and philanthropic.

The two imposing estates have already been described. Puritans would have condemned them as examples of "baronial splendor" (which of course they were), while modern radicals would attribute them to the wickedness of a "robber baron." Both assessments miss the point. "Splendor" connotes costly magnificence, both quite unwelcome in our age so far as the popular view of businessmen goes. As F. M. Smith himself perceived his two homes and their gardens, they were an opportunity to create and to enjoy beauty in many forms, to give pleasure to others, and to remind himself that he had made a success of his life. However, he never forgot his origins, for the little cabin just adjacent to the big house was a carefully treasured survival of the year 1871.

As for "robber baron," Smith probably would not have understood the term, literally or figuratively. As applied to 19th century entrepreneurs like himself, the epithet suggests unscrupulous appropriation of the wealth of others. What people of Smith's type did was quite to the contrary: to pioneer the development of a society based upon private enterprise. They did not appropriate the goods of others; they added immeasurably to the world's stock of goods by their own activities. Whatever their faults, their contribution was central and basic. Without it the wealth of the United States could not have been created.

The third province of F. M. Smith's kingdom encompassed his Oakland activities. Here we have a mixed story, as often has been the case with entrepreneurs. His dream for metropolitan development was magnificent in scope, and in principle well conceived. He was sure of his own judgment, grasped the opportunity, and committed everything he had to bring his vision into reality. In part he succeeded, by providing the city with a modern, unified, and well-managed transportation system. But in part he failed, because he could not foresee that the pace of metropolitan development would be slower than he expected; because he relied too heavily upon short-term borrowing; because he encumbered himself with an ill-fated merger involving partners who contributed more scenery than they did either money or talent; and because he fell into the clutches of a group of bankers more noted for their narrowness than for their vision or their readiness to provide any real help to a creative leader who had suddenly been thrust into an extremely difficult financial predicament.

As far back as 1902, the plunger in him had led him to commit several hundred thousand dollars to the development of the West End silver mine in Tonopah. Eventually this gamble paid off. But it would by no means be his last. In October 1913, he jumped at the chance to buy the Suckow property for his old company, despite the perilous state of his own finances. Soon he would be gone from PCB, but his legacy of the Kramer deposit would prove to be the salvation of PCB itself—a rather ironic outcome in view of Chris Zabriskie's later openly hostile attitude.

And so, by late 1913, Smith had lost his first fortune. But he had learned a lesson all the same. He still had the will and the personality of an entrepreneur, but never again would he commit himself to any bankers in the pursuit of his surviving business projects. Stripped of his fortune when he was 67, Smith was ready and eager within a year to get back into what he used to call "the borax game." He wanted to redeem himself, to take on his former associates in a fight to the finish, and to regain his private kingdom in all of its aspects.

In 1918, when he was 72, Borax Smith had the foresight and the initiative to acquire over 2,000 acres of Searles Lake leases, on the hunch that this just might permit the best technology for producing cheap borax. He demonstrated his willingness to plunge again in 1921, to buy the Anniversary Mine and try his luck once more with an underground colemanite property. By 1928, after Smith had risked much more money, Henry Hellmers had repaid his faith in him, by providing the Westend process for the plant at Searles. Through the chemical company he had created a viable enterprise that would regain much of his fortune, unfortunately after his own life was over.

F. M. Smith was severely criticized for diverting silver profits into the development of West End Chemical. But it should be remembered that Mr. and Mrs. Smith had by far the largest holding in the Tonopah company, and that Smith as an experienced mining man recognized the continuing importance of committing earnings to development, against the day when the ore would run out. After all, the ore eventually did run out, just at the time that West End Chemical was beginning to make money. Those disgruntled stockholders who had held on to their chemical shares, paid out earlier as a stock dividend to placate them, lived to profit handsomely from the success that Smith's risk-taking had finally brought about.

F. M. Smith As A Manager

Borax Smith once wrote R. C. Baker early in their association that he was "not a detail man." By that time, Baker also had had to be very much aware of his partner's strong streak of stubbornness and independence in the conduct of his affairs. Smith was always his own man, completely inner-directed, at times even "bull-headed," as one of his close friends once said. F. M. Smith's aversion to detail and his determined insistence upon all of the independence he could extract from any business relationship had certain consequences for his managerial policies. His central objective was to be the entrepreneur, to make the big decisions, assume the large risks, play his hunches as they occurred. As an outgrowth of these traits, he always preferred to be the top man in his ventures. He was invariably uncomfortable with associates with whom he had to share authority, and typically his boards of directors, although a necessary encumbrance, were regarded by him essentially as a nuisance. As a result, he had a strong tendency to people them with "dummies" or deferential experts.

Yet Smith did not always make himself chairman or president of his many enterprises. On occasion he would exert his power either as a single director, as with the early Key Route, or even as an investing capitalist operating in the background, as with the early West End Mining Company. When he did assume the presidency, as in PCB, the Terminal Railways, or the two West End companies, he avoided the day-to-day problems as much as he could. His temperament inclined him exclusively toward major questions, projects, and decisions. At the same time he did keep a close watch on his companies, readily going down into his mines for inspections, or, in the early years, riding mile after hot and dusty mile across Death Valley in a buckboard to size up claims, scout out claim jumpers, check on company properties, and size up competitors' operations. In this way, he filled his head with the raw perceptions that eventually he would bring together in a synthesis. At that point he would take a primary course of action. His associates often thought him impetuous, and in a sense he was. But behind these sudden actions there usually was a lengthy process of information-gathering.

A second consequence of Borax Smith's traits in management was an often uncanny ability to select outstanding subordinates— the sort of men to whom he could entrust full authority within their assigned domains. With few exceptions, F. M. Smith was an excellent judge of men. One has only to consider the remarkable group that he brought down with him from Nevada—for example, John Ryan, Fred Corkill, Billy Smitheram, and Chris Zabriskie. It was Smith who put together the original PCB organization. He knew them all, dealt with them on a personal basis, often had them as his guests, and usually established a loyalty and respect toward himself that actually did make the old company a team.[7] In fact, for years after he left in 1914, former Smith men remained in key jobs. The same pattern was repeated on the Key Route, in West End Consolidated Mining, and with West End Chemical. It was a pattern that worked because it gave Borax Smith the freedom to be an entrepreneur, the occupation that he found most congenial and for which he was naturally equipped.

A Comparison of Three Western Entrepreneurs: W. C. Ralston, C. P. Huntington, and F. M. Smith

In bringing this account to a close, it is worthwhile to refer briefly to an observation made earlier: that Francis Marion Smith belonged to a small group of western business leaders that included William Chapman Ralston (1826–1875) and Collis Potter Huntington (1821–1900). The factor common to the three of them was that they were all great entrepreneurs. Thus they shared the traits and objectives illuminated by Cole, Knight, and Schumpeter. Yet they were different—in temperament, in method, and in economic base.

Ralston, like Smith, was a mining man.[8] He took a fortune out of the Ophir Mine in Virginia City. He then gained control of the entire wealth of the Comstock by acquiring the stamping mills, the timber firms, and the Virginia and Truckee Railroad. The Comstock Agency of his Bank of California in San Francisco was the key to his power because it financed the mine operators. Within San Francisco, Ralston soon made himself the most prominent banker in town, following this by financing a string of local enterprises extending from the original Palace Hotel to a carriage works. Billy Ralston loved fine horses, liked to race the train to his home in Belmont, and was warmly appreciated for his generosity and his civic leadership. His dream was to build San Francisco into a great city.

But eventually the ore ran out at the Ophir, and Ralston found his capital effectively frozen. A run followed, his bank was ruined, and he drowned the same day while taking his usual afternoon swim off the Golden Gate.

Ralston had built his business career on banking, and this gave him the key to control of the Comstock Lode. In the end, his strong optimism, his desire to build, and his willingness to plunge combined to destroy him.

Huntington began life as an itinerant peddler of tinware, following this with a hardware store in Oneonta, New York.[9] He, too, soon felt the call to the far west. He made the long trip across the Isthmus of Panama and landed in Sacramento, where he opened a branch of the Oneonta store to serve the mines. In time he became interested in railroads, through a local short line. His opportunity came when the transcontinental railroad project suddenly sprang to life with the Civil War. Joining with Leland Stanford, Charles Crocker, and Mark Hopkins, Huntington set out to capture the right to build the Central Pacific Railroad. Initially, his was the job of lobbyist and political fixer in Washington, shaping the drafting of a bill that would commit the federal treasury to financing construction through lending federal credit to the four builders' Contract and Finance Company. This was the same bill that provided for substantial land grants to the Central Pacific. During the construction period, Huntington was forced to devote much time to peddling the federal bonds granted to the construction company. Of the Big Four, as they were called, he was the one with the most real business ability.

Huntington's original base lay in political influence, exerted during the exigencies of wartime. Once the Central Pacific had been completed in 1869, he had the capital to display his skills as an entrepreneur. His first independent step was the building of the Southern Pacific from San Francisco to New Orleans. Because Huntington was a superb organizer and a skilled manager who had all the necessary talents, despite a complete lack of formal training, he carefully expanded his railroad empire until it traversed the entire continent—the only man who has ever done so. When he died in 1900, he left an outstanding group of properties, except for the Central Pacific, which seems to have been neglected because of its heavy indebtedness to the government.

In a word, Huntington became an entrepreneur through politics. Once started, he would carry on brilliantly from his own business base. But there was a caution about his business methods that distinguished him from both Ralston and Smith.

Looking at all three men, it can be said that all of them shared the entrepreneurial characteristics identified by Knight and Schumpeter. All of them made their contribution to economic growth and development. All of them left the American West a different place for their having lived and worked there.[10] Nonetheless, there were sharp differences among them. Huntington got his start through politics, although he soon proved his ability to carry on with his own resources. Both Ralston and Smith began their careers as small businessmen, then showed their capacity to build great enterprises.

Huntington's power rested upon railroads, which in those days were largely land-based transportation monopolies. Ralston employed credit to gain control of Virginia City, using the gains for risky ventures in San Francisco. Smith built an entire industry, and through it, a substantial fortune. The only help he ever received from government was a periodic protective tariff on borax. Smith developed his diverse Oakland undertakings by a method that would have horrified the case-hardened Huntington and probably even the more venturesome Ralston: extensive borrowing on short-term notes. Thus it is hardly surprising that Huntington left the largest fortune—about $75 million—for he exerted his entrepreneurship in a very secure environment. Smith was next in order, with assets that peaked at about $25 million, but as the boldest of them all, he risked his entire fortune and lost it. He was also unique among the three in making a dramatic comeback when he was 75 years old. Ralston had made the least, and then had lost it all practically overnight in the failure of his bank. In his case, there could be no subsequent recovery.

There were a few other differences as well. Huntington was thrifty and would never have been called a warm and outgoing personality, although he did practice philanthropy on a substantial but private scale. In contrast, Ralston and Smith were warm and generous men who loved the role of the lavish host. Smith, in particular, was a philanthropist who continually headed subscription lists in his home community. Like Ralston, he was a builder who had a deep personal interest in the development of his chosen city.

Finally, there is the matter of time. Ralston's period of prominence lasted less than 20 years, ending in 1875. Huntington began to emerge as an entrepreneur about 1860, achieved outstanding stature by 1870, and spent the last three decades of his life in the role for which nature and opportunity had fitted him best: as entrepreneur and top manager. Thus both Huntington and Ralston were typical captains of industry of the last half of the nineteenth century.

Smith was unique. He was active in business for an incredible 60 years, in a career that extended from the last three decades of the nineteenth century into the first three of the twentieth. In that long period he managed to build an entire industry in one of the world's harshest regions. He also developed an extensive urban and interurban transportation system, a large realty concern, the fourth largest silver mine in Tonopah, and a second successful borax company that is a producer of heavy chemicals as well. In addition to all this, he found the time to become an active sportsman—in yachting, golfing, fishing, hunting, and tennis. In sports, too, are to be found risk, competition, uncertainty of outcome, the opportunity to fight, the will to win, and the chance to prove one's superiority.

In bringing Borax Smith's long story to a close, one ought to ask whether entrepreneurship still has a function in today's economic world. Joseph Schumpeter thought that in an age of corporate management, decision by committee would take its place. Following Schumpeter, John Kenneth Galbraith has taken the same line, disposing of the entrepreneur with the contemptuous observation that he represents "the economist's only hero." For the static, no-growth economy many intellectuals favor today, this line of thinking stands up fairly well, provided that one accepts its other consequences—a falling standard of living and an end to all technological progress.

Short of this extreme position, it may be conceded that, unlike the relatively simple structure of authority established by F. M. Smith for the companies he controlled in his time, the modern corporation indeed does diffuse power to a greater degree. But innovation must still occur if the economy is to advance, and innovation is inseparable from uncertainty. The necessary capital, indeed, may be obtained from others, by borrowing or by sale of equities. Still, those in charge must take responsibility, for which they can garner the fruits of success or pay the price of failure, as the case may be. Either way, no corporation can stand still. It must innovate or it must quickly adapt to the innovations of others, if it is to survive. Those who do the innovating are the entrepreneurs, acting upon the same basic principles as did their predecessors in the nineteenth century.

Francis Marion Smith was unique and will not be seen again, but as long as the American people maintain an economy based upon growth and progress, they will continue to require the services of those who have the talents and drive that he possessed.

NOTES

Chapter 1: An Introduction to Borax and to "Borax" Smith

1. U.S. Borax and Chemical Corporation, *The Story of Borax* (Los Angeles, California, 1969), p. 45.
2. W. A. Gale, "Development and Present Status of the Borax Industry," in Robert F. Gould, ed., *Borax to Boranes*, vol. 32 of *Advances in Chemistry Series, American Chemical Society* (1961), p. 14.
3. Georgius Agricola, *De Re Metallica*, translated from first Latin edition of 1556 by Herbert Clark Hoover and Lou Henry Hoover, new edition. (New York: Dover Publications, 1950), pp. 110, 560.
4. This suggestion was made to me by Mr. Norman J. Travis of Borax Consolidated, Limited.
5. U.S. Borax and Chemical Corporation, op. cit., p. 45.
6. Virginia Bartow, "Pioneer Personalities in Borane Chemistry," in Robert F. Gould, ed., *Borax to Boranes*, op. cit., pp. 6–11.
7. Taken largely from U.S. Borax and Chemical Corporation, op. cit.
8. According to Gale, Marco Polo is believed to have brought tincal to Venice in the late thirteenth century, on his return from China. In this way the salt was introduced into the Venetian glass and gold ornaments trade, and then into modern Europe. (See W. A. Gale, op. cit., pp. 14–15.)
9. W. A. Gale, op. cit., pp. 14–15.
10. The huge underground deposit of kernite, near Boron, California, is something of an exception to the rule. It may be an ancient dry lake or the result of volcanism in ancient times.
11. Department of the Interior, United States Geological Survey, *Mineral Resources of the United States, 1915*, Part II, "Nonmetals" (Washington: Government Printing Office, p. 1017, note to table.)
12. W. A. Gale, op. cit., p. 15.

Chapter 2: A Wisconsin Farm Boy Goes West

1. In 1884, Henry and Charlotte Smith finally sold their farm and moved west to San Jose, California, where Henry Smith died in 1890 and his wife in 1893. When they moved, the house was sold to the Wendorf family, who have continued to live there for three generations. F. M. Smith financed the sale through his brother Byron. All family data are from the Smith family Bible, now in the possession of F. M. Smith's daughter, Mrs. Mildred Smith Nicholls, of Piedmont, California.

2. Archie D. Stevenot, "Cottonball Refinery in California," with a Foreword by James M. Gerstley, Vice Chairman of U.S. Borax and Chemical Company. Published in the company's house organ, n.d. It is significant that Fred Stevenot, a descendant of Archie's and Emile's, served as a director in Smith's West End Chemical Company some 70 years later.

3. All of the foregoing material has been based upon "Francis Marion Smith: Autobiographical Notes on His Early Life," dictated about 1925 but not published. Smith was always rather reticent about his life story, out of modesty, not secretiveness. For an example, see the interview in the *Oakland Enquirer*, June 23, 1911.

4. Two versions of his story are available, both recounted many years later. One is in Spears, op. cit., pp. 177–186; it contains more detail. The other is in "Frank M. Smith, The Financier–Philanthropist," by James King Steel, in Evarts I. Blake, ed., *Greater Oakland, 1911* (Oakland, Calif.: Pacific Publishing Co., 1911), pp. 274–282. There are no important discrepancies between the two versions.

5. For photographs, a brief history, and a map of the whole district, see "Borax Country," *Nevada Highways and Parks*, no. 2 (1959), pp. 18–22.

6. A quite thorough yet concise history of the modern borax industry is found in W. E. VerPlanck, "History of Borax Production in the United States," *California Journal of Mining and Geology*, 52:3 (July 1956), pp. 273–291. For a brief account of Smith's own involvement, see Carl L. Randolph, in Norman J. Travis and Carl L. Randolph, *United States Borax and Chemical Corporation: The First One Hundred Years* (New York: The Newcomen Society in North America, 1973), p. 12.

7. John R. Spears, *Illustrated Sketches of Death Valley and Other Borate Deserts of the Pacific Coast* (New York: Rand, McNally & Co., 1892), p. 177ff; Ver Planck, op. cit., p. 275.

8. *U.S. Geological Survey, Mineral Resources of the United States, 1903* (Washington: Government Printing Office, 1904), p. 1018.

9. The two Smiths apparently started business as Smith and Storey Brothers, but the Storeys, who had supplied the equipment and some capital, soon dropped out. Meanwhile, Smith Brothers also

operated as Blanco Vale Borax Company, and then as Teel's Marsh Borax Company.

10. *Scientific American* (September 22, 1877), p. 184. The process is also described by the State Geologist of California, Henry Hanks, in *California State Mining Bureau, Third Annual Report of the State Minerologist*, part 2, "Report on the Borax Deposits of California and Nevada," by Henry G. Hanks (Sacramento, California: 1883), p. 46.

11. No description of the design of the borax wagons is provided, but it is well-established that the famous ones used at the Harmony Works in Death Valley were specially designed about 1883 by Mr. J. W. S. Perry, superintendent of the plant. (For the method used by the Smith Brothers several years earlier, see *Scientific American* [September 22, 1877], p. 184.)

12. *The Story of the Pacific Coast Borax Company*, compiled by Ruth C. Woodman, with photographs by Ann Rosener (Los Angeles: The Ward Ritchie Press, 1951), p. 12.

Chapter 3: Branching Out: The Death Valley and Mojave Deposits

1. *The Borax Miner* (March 10, 1875). For a biography of Coleman, see James A. B. Scherer, *The Lion of the Vigilantes: William T. Coleman and the Life of Old San Francisco* (Indianapolis: The Bobbs-Merrill Company, 1939). On the Pacific Borax Company, see *The True Fissure* (Candelaria) July 29, 1882.

2. *The Borax Miner* (April 17 and September 25, 1875; January 29, 1876; and August 12 and November 4, 1876).

3. U.S. Borax and Chemical Company, *Annual Report 1971* (Centennial Edition, 1972).

4. *The True Fissure* (July 29 and August 26, 1882).

5. In 1888 Smith already dominated the industry. In 1884, Julius Smith had left the Teel's Marsh Borax Company. Smith had the two Pacific Borax plants, the Teel's plant, and an interest in Harmony and Meridian in Death Valley. (Robert Shankland, *Steve Mather of the National Parks* (New York: Knopf, 1951), pp. 20, 25; Ruth C. Woodman, op. cit., p. 30.)

6. Lillian Ninnis' lively and accurate account, "Cottonball for Rosie," tells the story very well, and is accompanied by some superb photographs of Death Valley by David Muench, *Nevada Highways and Parks* 26:3 (Fall 1960), pp. 24–33, 39–40ff. Mrs. Ninnis is the widow of Fred Ninnis, later an associate of Borax Smith in Tonopah.

7. It was said that the works were called "Harmony" because it was the result of collaboration between Coleman and Smith.

8. In the first careful geological account of American borax his-

tory, Henry G. Hanks refers in 1883 to "the discovery of a large and valuable tract of borax near Furnace Creek. This passed, by purchase, into the hands of William T. Coleman and Frank M. Smith, of San Francisco." Hanks adds, "Messrs. Coleman and Smith have not yet produced borax in Death Valley, but are engaged in putting up works on a ridge quite elevated, at which point they have sunk artisian wells." Hanks, op. cit., p. 36. John R.Spears writes in 1892 that Coleman and Smith, "being partners in some borax operations, started to work the deposit north of Furnace Creek," adding that they then established Greenland Ranch, which had 30 acres in alfalfa, an adobe house, and running water on all sides. This is now called Furnace Creek Ranch.

9. Ninnis, op. cit., p. 39.
10. U.S. Borax and Chemical Company, *100 Years of U.S. Borax* (1972), pp. 8–10.
11. Ibid., p. 9.
12. William Caruthers, *Loafing Along Death Valley Trails: A Personal Narrative of People and Places* (Ontario, California: Death Valley Publishing Company, 1951), p. 37.
13. Ibid., pp. 37–38.
14. California State Mining Bureau, Bulletin No. 24 (San Francisco, May 1902, *The Saline Deposits of California*, by Gilbert E. Bailey, Pt. II, "Borates," pp. 38–39; Hanks, op. cit., p. 29; Ver Planck, op. cit., p. 280. Ver Planck aptly describes the opening up of colemanite mining as the start of "the Colemanite Period" and the end of the "playa period" (marsh operations) in borax history.
15. Proof that Smith and Coleman operated separately as well as jointly exists in the former's exclusive control of Pacific Borax Company from 1880 and of Teel's Marsh Borax Company after 1884; and in Coleman's control of Amargosa Borax Mining Company and Greenland Salt and Borax Company by 1882. (Hanks, op. cit., p. 55.)
16. *Oakland Daily Evening Tribune*, May 8, 1888.
17. *Engineering and Mining Journal*, XLV:19 (May 12, 1888), pp. 349–350.
18. Ver Planck, op. cit., p. 280; *Oakland Daily Evening Tribune*, March 16, 1893.
19. Byron G. Smith, F. M.'s older brother, had a store of his own in Candelaria, where he made his home. He seems to have helped with the management of the other stores as well. *The Chloride Belt* (July 18, 1891). On some occasions this store was referred to as the "PCB store."
20. Lorena Edwards Meadows, *A Sagebrush Heritage: The Story of Ben Edwards and His Family*, with illustrations by Patricia Meadows Robertson (San Jose, California: The Harlan-Young Press, 1972), pp. 101, 111–114.

21. James King Steel, "Frank M. Smith, The Financier-Philanthropist," op. cit., p. 276.
22. C. B. Glasscock, *Here's Death Valley* (Indianapolis: The Bobbs-Merrill Company, 1940), pp. 124, 182ff. In my opinion, this is the best book ever written on Death Valley. Among other things, it is notable for the author's unusual recognition of the decisive role Borax Smith played in Death Valley history.
23. Fred Corkill's daughter, Mabel Corkill (Mrs. A. P.) Fulcher, provided me with much information and many photographs of her father's career. See also Lorena Edwards Meadows, op. cit., pp. 90, 118–119, 178, 180. Fred Corkill's wife's sister married James F. Peck, originally from Buffalo, New York, and later of Berkeley and San Francisco. During the last two decades of Borax Smith's long life—best called his "time of troubles"—Jim Peck served him brilliantly in several ways.
24. Meadows, op. cit., *passim*. This charming and very accurate book recreates the life of the Candelaria region, and also provides much insight regarding the personalities of the "Nevada Circle."
25. Meadows, op. cit., p. 85.
26. Ibid, p. 94.
27. *The Chloride Belt* (December 10, 1892). Two weeks later Zabriskie announced that he would have no further connection with PCB. However, it is highly likely that he continued his business association with F. M. Smith personally.
28. William E. Ver Planck, "Boron," in California Division of Mines, Bulletin 176, *Mineral Commodities of California* (no date), p. 87.
29. Ibid, pp. 87–88.
30. Ver Planck, "Borax Production in the United States," op. cit., pp. 280–281; *The Story of the Pacific Coast Borax Company*, op cit., pp. 27–28.
31. Ver Planck, "Borax Production in the United States," loc. cit., p. 280.
32. *The Story of the Pacific Coast Borax Company*, loc. cit., pp. 27–28. The machine, known as "Old Dinah," has been attributed to Smith, who tried it out again later without success at the Lila C. Other accounts say that he preferred a railroad but was talked into trying a tractor.
33. This was a minor and pardonable conceit of Smith's, for in personality he was generally modest and was not aggressive in groups. As C. B. Glasscock had noted 40 years ago, if one looked at a Tonopah and Tidewater Railroad time table, he would find the name of practically every important friend or associate Smith had ever had, from Baker through Ryan and Zabriskie—with each identified with a particular station.
34. Ver Planck, "Borax Production in the United States," loc. cit., p. 281.

35. Shankland, op. cit., p. 26.
36. Ibid., p. 28.
37. Ibid., p. 19–21.
38. Ibid., p. 34.
39. There is personal evidence that Smith later felt guilty about this. Also, it was quite uncharacteristic of him, for his public benefactions were numerous and large over most of his life.

Chapter 4: Creating A World Market: The Formation of Borax Consolidated, Limited

1. James M. Gerstley, *A Reminiscence of My Father*, privately printed and copyrighted in 1975 by James M. Gerstley, p. 2. I wish to express my warm appreciation to Mr. Gerstley for providing me with this very informative and charming memoir, and for many other kindnesses essential to the preparation of this book. (For the specific reference in his *Reminiscence*, see pp. 1–2.)
2. Gerstley, op. cit., pp. 2–3. U.S. Borax and Chemical Company, *100 Years of U.S. Borax* (1972), p. 20, in which the firm is called "Redwood and Sons."
3. Gerstley, op. cit., p. 4; Ruth C. Woodman, op. cit., pp. 31–32; U.S. Borax and Chemical Company, *100 Years of U.S. Borax*, op. cit., p. 20.
4. *Oakland Tribune*, April 28, 1896.
5. In his biography of Steve Mather, Shankland rather consistently emphasizes F. M. Smith's negative traits—real or supposed—perhaps because of his thoughtless act in severing Mather from the payroll as soon as the latter fell ill in 1903. (Even here there is another side to the story.) Thus Shankland portrays Smith as unimaginative, dominated by emotional torpor, and very slow to make any decisions. If these had been Borax Smith's actual qualities, he would never have left Richmond, Wisconsin.
6. James M. Gerstley, *Borax Years, 1933–1961: Some Recollections,* (Pasadena, California: The Castle Press, 1979), p. 81.
7. *Oakland Tribune* (November 19, 1896).
8. Ver Planck, op. cit., p. 281.
9. *Oakland Tribune* (August 5, 1897).
10. U.S. Borax and Chemical Company, *100 Years of U. S. Borax*, op. cit., pp. 20–21.
11. Letter, Smith to Baker, March 24, 1898. Among the properties under consideration were The Borax Company, Ltd.; the *Société Lyonnaise;* Larderello, in Italy; and Ascotan and Arequipa in South America (Letter, Smith to Baker, February 17, 1898).
12–22. Letters, Smith to Baker: February 17, March 12, April 15,

April 26, July 7, July 8, August 1, September 23, November 22, December 22, and December 23, 1898.

23. Data from James Gerstley, *Borax Years, 1933–1961*, op. cit., p. 9.

24-28. Letters, Smith to Baker: February 15, 1899; June 14, 1900; June 4, July 29, and December 7, 1901.

29. Letter, Smith to Baker, January 25, 1902. In 1904 Smith tried one more time. Responding to a proposal from Baker for merging "all our Oakland interests," Smith suggested formation of a New York company for this purpose. The interests were, presumably, the Alameda refinery and the Leona Chemical Company, which mined iron pyrites to make sulfuric acid (Letter, Smith to Baker, March 30, 1904).

30-33. Letters, Smith to Baker, November 29 and December 30, 1899; February 24 and March 1, 1904.

34. Interview in Oakland, Calif., December 26, 1957.

Chapter 5: Borax Consolidated Limited: The Period of Control by F. M. Smith in the United States

1. Ver Planck, "History of Borax Production in the United States," op cit., p. 283.

2-7. Letters, Smith to Baker, March 3, 1899; undated (March 1899); February 16, April 21, and June 14, 1900; May 5, 1902.

8. Hoyt S. Gale, "The Lila C Borax Mine at Ryan, California," in U.S. Department of the Interior, United States Geological Survey, *Mineral Resources of the United States* (Washington, 1911), p. 861.

9. U.S. Borax and Chemical Co., *100 Years of U.S. Borax*, op. cit., p. 24.

10. Hoyt S. Gale, op. cit., p. 864.

11. U.S. Borax and Chemical Co., *100 Years of U.S. Borax*, op. cit., p. 23.

12-16. Letters, Smith to Baker, April 21, 1900; April 5, 1901; May 5 and August 19, 1902; September 14, 1903.

17. L. Burr Belden, "Obscure Borax Chapter Found in Traction Road," *San Bernardino Sun-Telegram*, January 18, 1953.

18-19. Letters, Smith to Baker, April 29 and July 4, 1904.

20. L. Burr Belden, "Double Cross by Senator Delays Borax Railroad," *San Bernardino Sun-Telegram*, January 25, 1953. *See also* C. B. Glasscock, *Here's Death Valley*, op. cit., pp. 174–178.

21. Belden, "Double Cross by Senator Delays Borax Railroad," op. cit.; David F. Myrick, *Railroads of Nevada and Eastern California*, vol. 2, "The Southern Roads" (Berkeley, California: Howell-North Books, 1963), pp. 456–457, 460–461.

22. Myrick, vol. 2, op. cit., p. 489.
23. L. Burr Belden, "Double Cross by Senator Delays Borax Railroad," op. cit.
24. Myrick, op. cit., vol. 2, pp. 499, 502.
25. Ibid.,vol. 2, p. 511.
26. Ibid.,vol. 2, p. 557.
27. First noted by C. B. Glasscock, op. cit., pp. 149–151.
28. "B.F.E. and C.G.S.," *Eighteen Days in Nevada*, privately printed (Oakland, California, 1907), p. 5. "B.F.E." was Ben F. Edwards and "C.G.S." was Charlotte Grace Sperry.
29. "B.F.E. and C.G.S.," *Eighteen Days in Nevada*, op. cit., pp. 45–46.
30. Smith had a bunkhouse built at Monte Blanco in 1882 for his crews. The building now serves as a museum at Furnace Creek.
31. Dante's View has an elevation of 5,475 feet. (All topographical data are taken from the U.S. Department of the Interior, Geological Survey maps for Ryan, Furnace Creek, and Funeral Peak Quadrangles.)
32. Woodman, op. cit., p. 39; Myrick, op. cit., vol. 2, p. 608.
33. Ver Planck, op. cit., p. 286; U.S. Borax and Chemical Co., *100 Years of U.S. Borax*, op. cit., pp. 26–27; Woodman, loc. cit., p. 39.
34. Harrison P. Gower, *Fifty Years in Death Valley—Memoirs of a Borax Man,* with an Introduction by James M. Gerstley, Publication No. 9 of the Death Valley '49ers (San Bernardino, Calif.: Inland Printing and Engraving Co., 1969).
35. Shankland, op. cit., pp. 35–36.
36. Letter, Smith to Baker, April 12, 1904.
37. U.S. Borax and Chemical Co., *100 Years of U.S. Borax*, op. cit., pp. 29–30.
38. *San Francisco Chronicle* (October 24, 1913). According to James M. Gerstley, a second parcel was ultimately acquired from Dr. Suckow in 1941 (James M. Gerstley, *Borax Years: Some Recollections, 1933–1961*, op. cit., p. 24).

Chapter 6: The Diverse Personal Life of Francis Marion Smith

1. Letter from Marion Smith Oliver, the Smiths' foster daughter, to the author, January 24, 1961. Mary R. Wright, who was to become Mary R. Smith in 1875, was known to intimates as "Mollie" and always as Mary R. Smith to the public.
2. Information provided by Mrs. Anna Mae Burdge Miller (Mae Burdge), who was a ward of the Smiths and lived with them for over 10 years. (Letter sent to the author dated July 11, 1958.)
3. Letter from Marion S. Oliver to the author, July 1961.

4. Letter from Marion S. Oliver to the author, no date.
5. Notes of author from joint interview with Marion Oliver, Mrs. Sara Winifred Burdge Cole (Winifred Burdge), and Mae B. Miller, at Kingsley Manor, Los Angeles, November 2, 1957.
6. Letter to the author from Mae B. Miller, July 11, 1958.
7. *The Chloride Belt* (January 24, 1891).
8. Notes of author from joint interview with Mrs. Oliver, Mrs. Miller, and Mrs. Cole, Los Angeles, November 2, 1957.
9. Letters to the author from Marion Smith Oliver, January 24 and July 9, 1961. A letter to the author from Albert E. Norman (August 4, 1961) says that the Oakland Directory records F. M. Smith as residing at 456 East 17th Street (old numbering).
10. Notes of author from joint interview with Marion S. Oliver, Winifred B. Cole, and Mae B. Miller, Kingsley Manor, Los Angeles, November 2, 1957.
11. Information about Grace Sperry from Smith family Bible.
12. Two hold-outs on 9th Avenue never did sell out to Smith. Data concerning dates, owners, and acreage were provided by letters to the author from Albert E. Norman, dated December 6, 1960, August 4, 1961, and October 13, 1961.
13. Ernest L. Ransome and Alexis Saubrey, *Reinforced Concrete Buildings* (New York: McGraw-Hill, 1912), pp. 6–7. Ransome pays tribute here to F. M. Smith as his "associate for many years."
14. For an excellent history of this style, see Vincent J. Scully, Jr., *The Shingle Style and the Stick Style: Architectural Theory and Design from Downing to the Origins of Wright*, revised edition (New Haven and London: Yale University Press, 1971).
15. Mrs. Betty Scott of Los Angeles, a daughter of Mae Burdge Miller, very generously provided me with many news items about the house. These are mostly undated but include the years from 1895 to 1905.
16. Walter J. Mathews was born on May 2, 1850, and died in Oakland on November 20, 1947.
17. There is no record that Mathews ever had any contact with H. H. Richardson, but the shingle-style mansion was at its most prominent when Mathews began practice, and he obviously was fully familiar with it. Press Reference Library, *Notables of the Southwest*, vol. 1 (New York: International News Services, 1913), p. 890. See also J. E. Baker, *Past and Present of Alameda County*, vol. 2 (Chicago: S. J. Clarke Publishing Company, 1914), pp. 457–459.
18. It must be conceded that Bernard Maybeck was more original both in design and use of materials. But Mathews was an outstanding architect all the same.
19. Information from undated newspaper clippings provided by Mrs. Elizabeth Scott.
20. The best known fetes were the garden parties called the "Fetes des Fleurs," at which the young women would throw roses

down from the balconies at the young men—a medieval custom that Mrs. Smith brought back from France—and the May Day fetes for charitable purposes.
21. Information from undated newspaper clippings provided by Mrs. Elizabeth Scott.
22. Information provided the author through an interview with Marion Oliver, Mae Miller, and Winifred Cole, in Los Angeles, November 2, 1957.
23. Information provided by William Meringer, of Shelter Island, July 11, 1978.
24. Information provided the author by William Meringer, who checked the assessment records for 1891–1900 and also provided a map of the Smith properties.
25. Information provided Mrs. Dorothy Smith Bayley by Mrs. Gertrude Tuthill Robinson, January 26, 1962. Mrs. Robinson published a history of Shelter Island, but no copy is available for citation.
26. Information provided the author by Dorothy S. Bayley, at Shelter Island, July 19, 1978.
27. Told to the author by Ollie Wells, Shelter Island, July 19, 1978.
28. Borax Smith loved trees almost as much as he did his roses. Along 9th Avenue just above East 24th Street, there can be found a long row of very tall date palms, of the same type as Smith had planted at Greenland (Furnace Creek) in Death Valley. These great trees have now been brought under permanent official protection.
29. When F. M. would order "the best California wines" from Park and Tilford's for Presdeleau, invariably the shipment consisted of wines from the Olivinia Vineyard, whose proprietor was Julius Paul Smith. This information was provided to the author by Marion Oliver.
30. Much information was acquired from Marion Oliver, Mae Miller, Winifred Cole, and Dorothy Bayley and her son, Robert Bayley. The 50th Anniversary Edition of the *History of the Shelter Island Yacht Club* was also helpful.
31. Altogether there were 17 entries, from which there were eight subsequent withdrawals. Information from the *New York Herald*, *The World*, *The Sun*, and the *Newport Herald*, all for August 9, 1906.
32. Information provided by Robert Bayley, a grandson of F. M. Smith.
33. *The Herald*, August 9, 1906. Captain Howell also had charge of *Hauoli II* and served Smith until 1913, when Smith's trustees sold all of his boats.
34. As told to the author by Mrs. F. M. Smith, in Oakland, August 19, 1956. At the time of the race she was Evelyn Ellis.
35. Eleanor Farjeon, *Portrait of a Family* (New York: Frederick A. Stokes Company, 1936), p. 443.
36. For detailed accounts of the cottage plan, the author found the

San Francisco Chronicle for December 22, 1901, and October 11, 1903, very helpful.

37. *First Annual Report of Mary R. Smith's Cottages*, for the year ending February 12, 1903 (Oakland: Baker Printing Company, 1903), pp. 3–4, 7.

38. *Eleventh Annual Report of Mary R. Smith's Cottages*, for the year ending February 13, 1913 (Oakland: Carruth & Carruth Co., 1913), p. 10. It should be pointed out that following the death of Mary R. Smith at the end of 1905, Evelyn Ellis, who was to become the second Mrs. F. M. Smith in 1907, took over the management of the Mary R. Smith Trusts, a post that she filled with typical quiet competence for the next 50 years.

39. Eleanor Farjeon, *Portrait of a Family*, op. cit., p. 443.

40. Interview with Marion Smith Oliver, Mae Miller and Winifred Cole, in Los Angeles, November 2, 1957.

41. As told to me by Mrs. Betty Scott, letter, September 13, 1979.

42. *Oakland Tribune*, December 13, 1899.

43. *Oakland Tribune*, January 1, 1906.

44. As told to me by Mrs. Betty Scott, letter of August 28, 1979.

45. The result was a charming little typescript account, which she termed "The Travelling Bridesmaid's Report."

46. The entire line was completed on October 30, 1907, to Gold Center, just below Beatty, Nevada, where connection was made with the Bullfrog Goldfield.

47. Smith and his friend Mark L. Requa acquired extensive copper holdings around Ely, Nevada.

48. This information was confirmed to me by two of Evelyn's own daughters, Dorothy Smith Bayley and Mildred Smith Nicholls, and by Mrs. Betty Scott, who learned of it from her mother, Mae B. Miller.

49. According to Grace Sperry, Evelyn had the word "obey" left out of her marriage vows.

Chapter 7: The Oakland Ventures: The Tractions, The Realty Syndicate, and The Key Route

1. U.S. Geological Survey, *Mineral Resources of the United States, 1891* (Washington: Government Printing Office, 1893), pp. 587–588.

2. One highly significant measure of Smith's achievement is that when he began production at Teel's in 1872, borax sold for about 35 cents per pound. What Smith did was to build a huge market, and by increasing output enormously, he took advantage of the economics of scale as well as technological improvements, to cut costs to a trifling amount. By the early 1890s, the price was about seven cents per pound. Here is a

good illustration of Joseph Schumpeter's heretical thesis that monopoly can actually lead to a cheaper product.

3. George C. Ellis, who became Smith's brother-in-law and close associate, responded bluntly regarding this impressive vision by declaring, ". . . he always had it, and he never gave up on it to the day of his death, in 1931." (Interview with the author in Oakland, December 26, 1957.)

4. By 1895 he had moved PCB headquarters to 101 Sansome Street, also in San Francisco. After the earthquake and fire of 1906, he moved them again, to the Albany Block in Oakland. By 1912, they were placed in the Syndicate Building in Oakland.

5. Personal letter, F. M. Smith to R. C. Baker, his London borax colleague, December 16, 1901.

6. Data on the company and its predecessors are available in Dallas Walker Smythe, *An Economic History of Local and Interurban Transportation in the East Bay Cities with Particular Reference to the Properties Developed by F. M. Smith*, a dissertation in partial satisfaction of the requirements for the PhD in Economics (Berkeley: The University of California, 1937. Unpublished.), pp. 30–31. Smythe has performed a thorough piece of scholarship, providing an authoritative study of this subject. The description of the route of the California Railway is taken from a "Map of Oakland and Vicinity Showing Lines of the Oakland Traction Company, the San Francisco, Oakland and San Jose Consolidated Railway, and the East Shore and Suburban Railway Company," prepared by Gibbs and Hill in New York, and dated for July 1911. At that time F. M. Smith controlled all of these companies.

7. *Oakland Daily Evening Tribune*, April 29, 1893.

8. *Oakland Daily Evening Tribune*, April 29 and May 1, 1893.

9. During this same year, Chris Zabriskie left Columbus, Nevada (where he worked for Smith), moved to Oakland, entered the real estate business, and began offering lots in the Alden Tract, close by the C&N properties. His advertisements spoke glowingly of the new ferry terminal, which was to be built "immediately."

10. Smythe, op. cit., p. 67.

11. Ibid., pp. 67–68.

12. *Oakland Daily Evening Tribune*, January 11 and 12, 1894; Smythe, loc. cit., p. 68.

13. *Oakland Evening Tribune*, February 6, 1894.

14. *Oakland Evening Tribune*, February 15, 1894.

15. Frank C. Havens (1848–1918) was born in Sag Harbor, New York—five miles from the site of Smith's future estate, Presdeleau. He came to San Francisco in 1866, engaging in brokerage and real estate operations. He then moved to Oakland, and in 1895 joined with F. M. Smith in establishing the Realty

Syndicate. (Frank Colton Havens, Correspondence and Related Papers, ca. 1881–1962. Courtesy of the Bancroft Library, The University of California, Berkeley.)

16. Smythe, op. cit., pp. 69–70.
17. Ibid., pp. 79, 80, 80–124. The city of Hayward was referred to as "Haywards" in the corporate title of the company.
18. Smythe, loc. cit., p. 80.
19. Ibid., p. 74.
20. Ibid., pp. 125–128. This deal has the characteristics of a charade, in the sense that it was all prearranged from the start.
21. Smythe, op. cit., pp. 72, 128–129. "Par value" is the arbitrary nominal value assigned to a bond or a share of stock when either is issued for initial sale. For example, bonds are usually issued at $1,000 par on nominal value each, although they may trade subsequently at a higher or lower market price. In the same way, a share of stock may be assigned a par value of, say, $100.00. On the market, it, too, may trade at values above or below par.
22. As cited by A. S. Dewing, *The Financial Policies of Corporations* (2 vols.), vol. 1, p. 286.
23. Smythe, op. cit., pp. 104–109.
24. Mary R. Smith disliked him, viewing him as a bad influence on her husband.
25. *Oakland Daily Evening Tribune*, September 23, 1895; Smythe, op. cit., pp. 69–70; 69 n. 97.
26. *Webster's Third New International Dictionary*, ed. by Philip Babcock Gove (Springfield, Mass.: G. and C. Merriam Company, 1976), p. 2319.
27. *Oakland Daily Evening Tribune*, September 24, 1896.
28. *Oakland Daily Evening Tribune*, August 17, 1897; August 31, 1897; and November 16, 1897.
29. *Oakland Daily Evening Tribune*, October 6, 1898.
30. *Oakland Daily Evening Tribune*, November 19, 1901.
31. *Oakland Tribune*, December 12, 1901.
32. On January 13, 1902, the U.S. War Department persuaded Congress to deny the company all use of Yerba Buena Island. *Oakland Tribune*, January 13, 1902. William Fayette Boardman, first County Engineer for Alameda County and also City Engineer for Oakland, from 1866 to 1870, proposed an interesting variant on Smith's plan: let the state build the Yerba Buena Island terminal and open it up to all the companies. (*Oakland Tribune*, January 25 and November 29, 1902.)
33. Letter, F. M. Smith to R. C. Baker, December 16, 1901. (Courtesy of Borax Consolidated Limited.)
34. Plaintiff's Exhibit No. 7, in the Matter between *L. Baar v. F. M. Smith, et al.*, in the Superior Court of the City and County of San Francisco, #133,684, Department 3, heard between June

1925 and October 1926, before the Hon. Timothy I. Fitzpatrick, Judge.

35. *L. Baar v. F. M. Smith*, pp. 1400–1405, printed on behalf of appeal of defendants to California State Court of Appeals, ca. 1926. The word "unadjusted" reflects the action of Klink, Bean in writing off slightly over $3 million in value of certain assets.

36. The financial side of these two hotels is virtually impossible to work out because Smith and Havens had a pooled account that amounted to a kind of partnership. It was split so that Smith held ⅔ and Havens ⅓. Each deposited cash, securities, and notes, and also drew out assets in the same forms. This arrangement was separate from the Syndicate, yet the partners conducted transactions with the Syndicate as part of their personal arrangement as well. (Papers of Frank C. Havens, courtesy of the Bancroft Library of the University of California, Berkeley.)

37. Smythe, op. cit., p. 96 n. 10.

38. *Oakland Tribune*, March 6, 1902.

39. *Oakland Tribune*, March 7, 1902.

40. *Oakland Tribune*, March 21, 1902.

41. All the Key Route boats were elegantly finished in panelled mahogany, decorated with potted palms at the window ends of the benches, and initially were provided with orchestras. F. M. Smith liked to do things right and always preferred the best. To achieve these standards with his ferries, he had them designed so that no freight or livestock could be carried on the upper deck. Having traveled on the Huntington steamers for years, he held strong views about comfort, cleanliness, and attractive surroundings. Because he was an inveterate cigar smoker, he had to ride on the lower deck, with the fish and livestock.

42. The rock-filled mole came eight years later, in a different location because of tidal problems.

43. *Oakland Tribune*, May 30, 1902.

44. *Oakland Tribune*, December 27, 1902.

45. At the time, the *Tribune* was in warfare against Smith's Oakland Transit, and passed up the event with a brief paragraph.

46. As a commentary on modern times, let it also be noted that from the day that it opened in 1903 until the end of its operations in 1958, the Key Route functioned without technological difficulties, despite its use of four different sets of equipment and its adoption of moderately complicated signal systems in 1912 and again in 1939 for operations across the Bay Bridge. In contrast, one need only note the innumerable problems and breakdowns of the new BART system that replaced the Key.

47. The letters are part of Governor Pardee's correspondence in the Bancroft Library of the University of California, which kindly allowed me to read the Smith letters.

48. Letter, Smith to Pardee, January 16, 1903.
49. Letter, Smith to Pardee, January 28, 1903 (Bancroft Collection).
50. Letter, Smith to Pardee, September 30, 1903 (Bancroft Collection).
51. There is some conflict in dates between my two principal sources, Dallas Smythe (see footnote 6 for this chapter), and Peralta Associates and Vernon J. Sappers, *From Shore to Shore: The Key Route* (Oakland: Peralta Associates, 1948), p. 4. Mr. Sappers is a local authority on the Key Route, and I am inclined to accept his account in these matters.
52. The ultimate outcome was somewhat ironic, for 30 years later the SP would be ready to call it quits and the Key System would take over operation of several portions of these same SP lines.
53. *Sacramento Northern*, published by Interurbans Electric Railway Publications, edited by Ira L. Swett, vol. 20, no. 2 (September, 1962), p. 102.
54. The system failed only once, on December 4, 1924, when a Sacramento Short Line (formerly OA&E) train smashed into a stationary Key train, killing 10 people. The failure has never been explained, but probably occurred because the Short Line car was exceeding the set speed limit of 36 miles per hour on which the signal system was based. (*From Shore to Shore: The Key Route*, op. cit., p. 6.) Explanation is the author's own responsibility.
55. Ibid., p. 5.
56. *San Francisco Chronicle* (June 29, 1912).
57. *San Francisco Chronicle* (March 22, 1913).

Chapter 8:   The United Properties Company and Its Failure

1. Smythe, op. cit., pp. 96–97, 96 n. 12.
2. Ibid., p. 100.
3. Ibid., pp. 101–102, 101 n. 32.
4. *San Francisco Examiner*, December 9, 1910. Smith employed his nephew, Nat M. Crossley, and his associate, Dennis Searles, to represent him in the final negotiations for the separation of interests. According to a letter from Havens to Crossley dated November 29, 1910, Havens claimed $1,927,713 was due him from Smith, asking that it be liquidated through 11 notes at six percent, to be paid off over a period of 10 years (Letter Havens to Crossley, F. C. Havens Collection, Bancroft Library, University of California, Berkeley).
5. Following the death of Edward VII on May 6, 1910, Smith received an invitation from the King's Equerry, Lord Knollys, to

attend the funeral ceremonies in Westminster Hall. Probably
R. C. Baker arranged for this privilege.

6. L. Burr Belden, "Financial World Shocked by News of Smith
Crash," *San Bernardino Sun–Telegram,* February 15, 1953.

7. By December 31, 1911, Smith's debt was reckoned by his
accountant, S. K. Ballard, to have reached $8,694,940.95. *L.
Baar v. F. M. Smith, et al.,* Defendants' Exhibit No. 14, p.
1180.

8. Smythe, op. cit., pp. 150–153. After the collapse of the United
Properties merger and Smith's personal financial ruin, Zabriskie
and Smith gradually drifted apart, in the end to become bitter
enemies. According to Belden, Zabriskie never again referred
to his role in the affair, nor apparently admitted any responsibility for the disaster. But luck was with him, for he succeeded
Smith as head of the Pacific Coast Borax Company. (Belden,
San Bernardino Star–Telegram, February 15, 1953.)

9. In *A Line of a Day,* October 16, 1910. (Courtesy of F. M. Smith
family.) "C.B.Z." was Christian Brevoort Zabriskie.

10. *Baar v. Smith,* testimony of F. M. Smith, pp. 213–216.

11. *Baar v. Smith,* pp. 220–221; Smythe, op. cit., pp. 154–155.

12. *Baar v. Smith,* p. 222.

13. *Baar v. Smith,* pp. 218–220.

14. Smythe, op. cit., p. 156.

15. Neither company carried depreciation accounts in these years.
Instead they relied on routine maintenance and special sales of
preferred stock or bonds, frequently to the Realty Syndicate, to
replace and to add to physical plant and equipment.

16. David H. Moffat, Jr., encountered financial constraints of the
same kind when he tried to build a direct main-line railroad—
the Denver, Northwestern and Pacific—from Denver to Salt
Lake City. The Union Pacific, the Denver and Rio Grande, and
the Santa Fe naturally were all opposed. Consequently, the
New York banks turned a deaf ear to his pleas for financial
assistance. Moffat died in his hotel in New York City in March
1911, while trying in vain for financing.

17. Smythe, op. cit., pp. 159–160; and *Baar v. Smith,* p. 1222.
Under direct examination, F. M. Smith testified, ". . . I think
the principal reason was that I did not find the United Properties Company's collateral suited the convenience of the bank
for exchange. It was not a good liquid security, up to that time."

18. Moreover, "bond certificates" were issued in place of the
UPC's proposed first mortgage bonds, because insufficient
securities had been turned in to serve as collateral for the bonds
under the terms of their indenture. Smythe, op. cit., pp. 161–
162; 161 n.33.

19. Smythe, loc. cit., p. 162.

20. Smythe, op. cit., p. 164.

21. On direct examination, Tevis testified many years later that

Smith's note broker, Gerald C. Morgan, had told him that he had placed Smith's secured notes with some 285 banks, in amounts ranging from $5,000 to $20,000, as of that time. His floating indebtedness at the end of 1911 was well over $8 million. (*Baar v. Smith*, p. 104, testimony of W. S. Tevis.)

22. Smythe, op. cit., pp. 171–172.
23. Ibid., pp. 167ff.
24. Ibid., pp. 173–176; 177–178; 177 n. 72, 75. Notes Payable were accordingly reduced by $789,800; these included $674,100 to F. M. Smith so that OTC could reacquire 749 $1,000 bonds of Oakland Traction at $900 each. Smythe accepts Tevis' interpretation (*Baar v. Smith*, pp. 88–89) that this was illegal and also his claim that one of Smith's attorneys corroborated this view. Smith denied both the story and the interpretation. In his explanation, Smith said that he had used his private means to raise cash for the OTC; that he did so in the amount of about $675,000; that OTC gave him the bonds as security for these advances; that the final transaction retired this floating debt. On cross-examination, Tevis finally admitted that it was a loan transaction, not a sale of the company's bonds. Thus his charge against Smith was without merit. (*Baar v. Smith*, testimony of F. M. Smith, p. 1164; W. S. Tevis, pp. 282–285.)
25. Smythe, op. cit., pp. 189–190.
26. For example, Hanford took the very valuable tidelands from the Key by paying $1.55 million. W. R. Alberger said in July 1911 that they were worth $3.5 million, and that this transfer would "look very bad." (Smythe, op. cit., p. 178 n.75.)
27. Ibid., pp. 200–201.
28. Ibid., pp. 206–209.
29. Ibid., pp. 213–214. Stevenson was connected with the London house called Investment Registry. *Baar v. Smith*, p. 712.
29a. According to the *San Francisco Call*, May 8, 1913, only $3,750,000 in UPC securities ever reached outside investors.
30. *Baar v. Smith*, testimony of W. S. Tevis, pp. 113–119. The letter was dated October 14, 1912.
31. Smythe, op. cit., p. 218 n.39.
32. Agreement in Trust by and between F. M. Smith, W. S. Tevis, R. G. Hanford, and Hanford Investment Company, dated January 25, 1913. (Courtesy of Vernon Sappers, Sappers Collection.)
33. Smythe, op. cit., pp. 219–223.
34. *Baar v. Smith*, testimony of W. R. Williams, p. 1061.
35. *Baar v. Smith*, testimony of W. R. Williams, pp. 1061, 1064, 1068.
36. *Baar v. Smith*, p. 1068.
37. *Baar v. Smith*, Plaintiff's Exhibit No. 7, pp. 1367ff.
38. This excludes the current liabilities of the Realty Syndicate shown above.

39. *Baar v. Smith*, p. 1376.
40. *Baar v. Smith*, Plaintiff's Exhibit No. 6, pp. 1323ff.
41. In an interview in 1957, George C. Ellis told the author that Smith "was too proud to take it." *Baar v. Smith*, testimony of F. M. Smith, p. 620.
42. *Baar v. Smith*, testimony of F. M. Smith, pp. 457–459.
43. Smythe, op. cit., pp. 235–236.
44. Ibid., pp. 241–242.
45. Ibid., p. 249.
46. *Baar v. Smith,* testimony of William I. Brobeck, pp. 716–717.
47. Smythe, op. cit., Table 10.
48. Ibid., p. 261.
49. Agreement made on January 17, 1914, among the Realty Syndicate, George G. Moore, and the Mercantile Trust Company.
50. *San Francisco Chronicle*, January 20, 1914; *San Francisco Examiner*, January 22, 1914; *Oakland Tribune*, January 21, 1914.
51. *Oakland Tribune*, September 2, 1914.
52. It is worthy of comment that this syndicate called for another block of Smith's stock on July 15, 1914 (see *San Francisco Chronicle*). A final portion of the borax stocks was not sold until after the war.
53. *Baar v. Smith*, testimony of William I. Brobeck, p. 704.

Chapter 9: After the Crash

1. *Baar v. Smith,* op. cit., pp. 1174–1176, 1179.
2. The Realty Syndicate had $218,750.00 in UPC bonds as of April 26, 1913. *Baar v. Smith*, p. 1372.
3. *Baar v. Smith*, op cit., pp. 1371–1373. Klink, Bean estimated Smith's undelivered stocks to the UPC at $1,544,400, while also determining Smith's adjusted portion of the UPC partnership fund at $3,870,000. However, no value was assigned for this equity. *Baar v. Smith*, pp. 1376–1377.
4. Interview with George C. Ellis in Oakland, December 26, 1957. This was Ellis' opinion. Just a few months after Smith's assignment, Colonel J. W. Reid, Acting Chairman of Borax Consolidated, reported that for the company's fiscal year ending September 30, 1913, it had earned net profits of £361,920 (about $1.8 million at a conversion rate of $5.05 to the pound). At that time the company had outstanding 900,000 shares of common stock with a par value of $5.05 each, on which it had earned an astonishing $1.68 per share, for a return on equity of 33 percent. As of that date, the Smith interests held 500,000 of these common shares. If these are capitalized very conservatively at 10 percent, then Smith's shares actually were worth at least $8 million.

5. *Baar v. Smith*, testimony of W. S. Tevis, p. 276.
6. *Baar v. Smith*, testimony of W. S. Tevis, pp. 291, 294. Tevis admitted, under cross-examination by Peck, that he was selling UPC securities to buy other properties for which he did not pay Smith his 60 percent share. Pp. 298–9.
7. *Baar v. Smith*, op. cit.
8. Interview with Norman P. Ellis in Oakland, December 26, 1957.
9. From a document prepared by Tevis and Hanford and dated November 15, 1912. (Provided to the author by Mrs. Virginia Hanford Edwards [Mrs. Stewart Edwards], daughter of Albert Hanford, R. G. Hanford's brother. Mrs. Edwards has very kindly supplied me with numerous documents.)
10. *J. C. Settle v. F. M. Smith et al*, Superior Court of the State of California (July 1, 1913).
11. On the contrary, the deal later yielded a handsome profit to the West End because the Halifax had a large, undeveloped body of silver ore.
12. *San Francisco Chronicle*, August 2, 1913. Information provided to the *Chronicle* by Dennis Searles, a Smith associate.
13. *San Francisco Chronicle*, August 1, 1913. We shall defer examination of the West End matter until the chapter on that company.
14. *Frederick G. Cartwright v. F. M. Smith*, a complaint dated July 12, 1913, filed in the Superior Court of the City and County of San Francisco.
15. *In the Matter of F. M. Smith in Bankruptcy, No. 8199*, a petition filed in United States District Court by Leo R. Dickey, C. E. Gilman, Albert Hanford, and the Union Land Company on July 24, 1913.
16. *San Francisco Examiner*, July 25, 1913.
17. Peck was one of the ablest and most prominent lawyers in San Francisco. He had been born in Buffalo, New York, then was taken west at the age of six months, and grew up in Merced, California.
18. Information provided by Norman P. Ellis to the author. The trust was finally dissolved in 1956.
19. From a copy of the agreement kindly provided by Mr. Vernon Sappers of Oakland, California.
20. Hanford had died on January 25, 1920. The Hanford Investment Company had been dissolved in 1916, with Tevis, Hanford, and Hanford's private secretary, Miss Mary O'Connell, as Trustees for the concern. As late as 1918, Tevis and Hanford were still dealing with Elliott Stevenson, in the hope of obtaining financing for their water companies. At the time of Hanford's death he was on the edge of bankruptcy.
21. Zayda Zabriskie, daughter of Chris Zabriskie, married Frank Buck, a member of this family.
22. It is not certain that the note obtained by O'Connell was the

Havens-Ohlandt-Buck note, although mention is made of this sequence in various sources or by interested persons. The suggestion that O'Connell was partially paid with a defaulted F. M. Smith note was made by W. S. Tevis, in *Baar v. Smith*, p. 321.

23. *Baar v. Smith*, Opening Brief for Evelyn Ellis Smith, Defendant and Appellant, before the Supreme Court of the State of California, in prayer for a writ of *supersedeas*, San Francisco No. 12316, April 20, 1927, to set aside in its entirety the judgment of the trial court. *201 Whiting 87 (1927)*.

24. *Baar v. Smith*, testimony of W. S. Tevis, p. 322.

25. This was the basic case of *Baar v. Smith* in the trial stage, identified as No. 133,684, Department of Superior Court of the State of California, in and for the City and County of San Francisco, before the Hon. Timothy I. Fitzpatrick, Judge. The transcript of record is in published form, because F. M. Smith *et al* took appeal in the State Supreme Court. The published record is available in the library of the University of California Law School at Berkeley.

26. *Baar v. Smith*, testimony of W. S. Tevis, p. 321.

27. Of some related interest, Albert Hanford, brother of R. G. Hanford, filed a similar suit to Baar's against Tevis and Mary O'Connell in 1926, winning his case and obtaining judgment for execution in 1931. Around this latter time, Tevis filed for voluntary bankruptcy. He died in 1933, entirely dependent by that time upon a trust fund.

Chapter 10: F. M. Smith Rebuilds His Fortune with Tonopah Silver

1. *San Francisco Call*, October 18, 1913. The real figure was confirmed officially to be $4 million (*San Francisco Examiner*, June 26, 1914). Over 40,000 additional deferred ordinary shares in Borax Consolidated, Ltd., were not sold until about a decade later. Most of the stock, however, had been sold within a year to a British syndicate, after R. C. Baker came to San Francisco for negotiations for the agreement in October 1913. Apparently Baker did not acquire the shares for his own account. After the war, other smaller blocks were also marketed in England, and again apparently not to Baker personally. Although he acquired full control of Borax Consolidated in 1914, retaining it until his death in 1937, Baker had a broader basis of support than did Smith when he was in control. Evidently, too, Baker may have felt some continuing compassion for Smith, or at least a reluctance to take advantage of Smith's difficulties, despite their disagreements over business matters. (*San Francisco Chronicle*, October 1, 1913; articles in the *San Francisco*

Bulletin and the *San Francisco News Bureau*—also for October 1—suggest that Baker went home with the desired option to buy, but that the deal had not been finally closed.)

2. At one time, one of the town's bars boasted a famous picture of Jim Butler and his mule, bearing the title "Me and Jim Found Tonopah."

3. Russell R. Elliott, *Nevada's Twentieth-Century Mining Boom: Tonopah, Goldfield, Ely* (Reno: University of Nevada Press, 1966), pp. 3–6; and Byrd Fanita Wall Sawyer, "The Gold and Silver Rushes of Nevada," M.A. thesis in History, University of California (December 1921); published in Jay A. Carpenter, Russell Richard Elliott, and Byrd Fanita Wall Sawyer, *The History of Fifty Years of Mining at Tonopah, 1900–1950*, University of Nevada Bulletin, Vol. XLVII, No. 1 (January 1953); Nevada Bureau of Mines, Geology and Mining Series No. 51, pp. 1–5.

4. Sawyer, op. cit., pp. 3–5.

5. Lorena Edwards Meadows, *A Sagebrush Heritage*, op. cit., pp. 142–151.

6. Meadows, op. cit., pp. 145, 150–151, 155.

7. Ibid., p. 153.

8. Carpenter, op. cit. In May 1903, Zabriskie wrote Edwards that F. M. Smith would absorb the unsold balance of company treasury stock, paying for it at 50 cents per new share as the company required funds. In short, it was a drawing account. (Letter, May 12, 1903.) (Meadows Collection.)

9. *The Tonopah Miner* (June 14, 1913).

10. Carpenter, op. cit., *Tonopah Bonanza* (February 17, 1906). Chris Zabriskie was an eager buyer of West End stock, profiting from his friendship with F. M. Smith at that time. R. C. Baker also acquired some shares. In any event, it is noteworthy that Smith made his well-known trip to Nevada in March 1906, taking Baker and Zabriskie, along with Evelyn Ellis and Grace Sperry.

11. Letters, Zabriskie to Edwards, May 22, 1903. (Meadows Collection); May 2, 1903, and May 20, 1903 (BCL Collection).

12. *Webster's Third New International Dictionary*, p. 99. Apex disputes were complicated by the presence of branches from the main stalk. Moreover, these disputes were common in the old camps, because the properties were small and laid out in a patchwork. Today mining companies acquire properties in thousands of acres; thus the apex problem is now relatively rare in the United States.

13. Carpenter, op. cit. On June 15, 1908, Smith wrote Edwards urging him to replace a man named Solinsky with James F. Peck as counsel in the suit because Solinsky "has not the necessary snap to him in my estimation." (Letter, Smith to Edwards, June 15, 1908. Meadows Collection.)

14. Carpenter, op. cit., pp. 98–99. The cyanide process was in-

vented in 1887 and introduced first in South Africa in 1890. It uses cyanide of potassium as a solvent for the extraction of gold and silver from their ores. First the ore is crushed and pulverized, then dissolved in the cyanide solution, which is separated from the ore by filtration. The solution is then passed through zinc dust, which thereby acquires a black slime. This is purified and the gold or silver is then extracted by heating, followed by casting in bars. (*Encyclopedia Britannica*, 1950, vol. 6, pp. 916–17.)

15. *The Tonopah Miner*, June 14, 1913.
16. Letter, Zabriskie to Smith, July 2, 1913. (Meadows Collection.)
17. *The Tonopah Miner*, August 30, 1913. For a slightly different account, consistent with Edwards on the key points, see "Wallan Broad," *Oakland Tribune*, October 26, 1913.
18. *The Tonopah Miner*, August 30, 1913.
19. *The Tonopah Miner*, August 16, 1913.
20. *The Tonopah Miner*, November 8, 1913.
21. J. A. Carpenter, op. cit., pp. 101, 104.
22. Letter, Brady to Edwards (June 26, 1913). (BCL Collection.)
23. *San Francisco Examiner* (February 22, 1914). As early as November 3, 1913, Zabriskie wrote Edwards to make reference to a public charge by a Butler foreman named Pike that the West End was mining in Butler ground. Zabriskie noted that Heller had told him that he, Zabriskie, was correct; the West End was in the Butler zone by agreement between the two companies (Letter, Zabriskie to Edwards, November 3, 1913). (BCL Collection.)
24. *The Tonopah Miner* (April 11, 1914).
25. A winze is a downward sloping cut to provide access to a lower working place from above.
26. *The Tonopah Miner* (July 11, 1914).
27. *Goldfield News* (October 24, 1914).
28. *Tonopah Daily Bonanza* (October 16, 1914).
29. *Tonopah Daily Bonanza* (December 3, 1914).
30. *Tonopah Daily Bonanza* (December 7, 1914).
31. *The Tonopah Miner* (December 5, 1914); *Tonopah Daily Bonanza* (December 17, 1914).
32. *Tonopah Daily Bonanza* (December 9, 1914).
33. *Tonopah Daily Bonanza* (December 12, 1914).
34. *Tonopah Daily Bonanza* (December 14, 1914).
35. *Tonopah Daily Bonanza* (December 14 and 16, 1914).
36. Meadows, op. cit., pp. 218–219; Carpenter, op. cit., p. 107.
37. Letter, Zabriskie to J. C. Weir (a New York broker), November 6, 1913.
38. Letter, Zabriskie to Edwards, August 12, 1913.
39. Letter, Zabriskie to Baker, December 15, 1914. (Here he included Ryan as an ally, although Ryan's real view is unknown.) (BCL Collection.)

40. Letter, Baker to Edwards, January 14, 1915. (Meadows Collection.)
41. Letter, Edwards to Zabriskie, December 26, 1914. (BCL Collection.)
42. Letter, Thomas Kearns to Edwards, May 1, 1915. (BCL Collection.)
43. Letter, Edwards to Kearns, May 9, 1915. (BCL Collection.)
44. Letter, Zabriskie to Edwards, May 27, 1916.
45. Before 1913, Edwards had become president of the Berkeley National Bank, while as early as 1910 he had taken over as vice president of the Syndicate Bank in Emeryville at the request of F. M. Smith. Then he bought out Smith's interest in the Twenty-Third Avenue Bank, probably in 1913. (Meadows, op. cit., pp. 200, 206–07, 211, and 222.)
46. Letter, Zabriskie to Edwards, February 23, 1917. (BCL Collection.)
47. Interview with the author in Oakland, in 1955. Mrs. Smith also made the sage observation on that occasion, "Mr. Zabriskie made his choice"—meaning that he quit the service of F. M. Smith when he saw a better opportunity in the offing.
48. Letter, Herman D. Budelman to the author, August 20, 1962.
49. "Minerology of the Searles Lake Deposits," op. cit., p. 295; Ver Planck, "Borax Production in the United States," op. cit., p. 276.
50. According to Webster's Third New International Dictionary, p. 2451, "trona" refers to hydrous acid sodium carbonate in crystals or fibrous columnar masses. Potash actually is a potassium salt, but "trona" is widely used to refer to the liquor in which the various minerals are pumped to the surface of the lake.
51. San Francisco Chronicle (February 3, 1911); Los Angeles Times (ca. May 18, 1913).
52. San Francisco Call (December 23, 1912).
53. San Francisco Chronicle (March 10, 1913).
54. San Bernardino Sun (June 16, 1914).
55. San Francisco Examiner (June 3, 1916).
56. West End Chemical Company, "Special Report to Stockholders" (August 27, 1956), p. 22.
57. Carpenter, op. cit., p. 109.
58. Ultimately, West End Chemical issued 2,012,197 common shares at $1 par, and 1,609,241 cumulative preferred shares at $1 par.
59. Letter, Zabriskie to Baker, September 27, 1918. (BCL Collection.)
60. Interview with Henry D. Hellmers, vice president, production, West End Chemical Company; Los Angeles, November 19, 1957.

Chapter 11: Francis Marion Smith Returns to the Borax Industry

1. *Engineering and Mining Journal*, 111:14 (1921), p. 600.
2. Hoyt S. Gale, "The Callville Wash Colemanite Deposit," *Engineering and Mining Journal*, 112:14 (October 1, 1921), p. 526.
3. Letter, Zabriskie to Baker, June 9, 1921. (BCL Collection.)
4. Gale, op. cit., pp. 424–425; William E. Foshag, "The World's Biggest Borax Deposits," *Engineering and Mining Journal-Press*, 118:11 (September 13, 1924), p. 421.
5. Gale, op. cit., p. 529.
6. L. Burr Belden, "Smith Amazes All With Comeback in Borax World," *San Bernardino Sun-Telegram* (February 22, 1953).
7. George J. Young, "Mining Borax in the Muddy Range," *Engineering and Mining Journal-Press*, 117:7 (February 16, 1924), p. 276. Also interview with Henry Hellmers, Los Angeles, November 19, 1957.
8. Letter, F. M. Smith to Marion Smith Oliver, August 3, 1921.
9. L. Burr Belden, "Smith Amazes All With Comeback in Borax World," op. cit.
10. This term was devised by Joseph Schumpeter.
11. Interview with Henry D. Hellmers, Los Angeles, November 19, 1957.
12. L. Burr Belden, "West End Final Project Begun by 'Borax' Smith," *San Bernardino Sun-Telegram* (March 29, 1953); also interview between Mr. Hellmers and the author, Los Angeles, November 19, 1957.
13. Letter, Zabriskie to Baker, June 9, 1921. (BCL Collection.)
14. Letter, Zabriskie to Clarence Rasor, September 30, 1921. A copy went to Baker in London. (BCL Collection.) In this letter, Zabriskie says that the chemical firm had given the mining company 1,788,486 shares of its stock to cover advances, and that the mining company then distributed this stock, share for share, as a dividend to the mining company stockholders. "Smith received about 800,000 shares" of the chemical stock, which gave him practical control.
15. *Oakland Tribune*, June 16, 1924. Oak Hall itself was not involved at that time. Letter, C. R. Dudley to Zabriskie, June 17, 1924.
16. West End Chemical Company, *Special Report to Stockholders* (Oakland, August 27, 1956). Data for June 30, 1956.
17. Letter, Zabriskie to Baker, January 17, 1925. (BCL Collection.)
18. Letter, Zabriskie to Baker, January 17, 1925. (BCL Collection.)
19. Letter, Zabriskie to Gallois, May 28, 1926. (BCL Collection.)
20. Letter, Zabriskie to Baker, August 4, 1926. (BCL Collection.)
21. Carpenter, op. cit., p. 113.
22. Carpenter, op. cit., pp. 114, 149.

23. Dorothy Smith (Mrs. George T.) Bayley has spent many hours describing to the author family life during these years.
24. This story was told to the author by Gus Carlson himself, who stayed with the Smiths until F. M. Smith died in 1931.
25. From a copy of the resolution prepared in the handwriting of Marion Smith Oliver, who generously provided the copy to the author.
26. *Oakland Tribune* (October 25, 1933).
27. From a copy of the original proceedings, including a replica of the plaque, kindly provided by Frank M. Smith, Jr., who attended along with his mother, Mrs. Evelyn Smith, as guests of the Key System. For an illustration of this plaque, see frontispiece.
28. Calculated on the basis of an average market value per common share of Stauffer of $70 at that time. Part of the West End stock was already owned by Stauffer.

Chapter 12: F. M. Smith as an Entrepreneur

1. Arthur H. Cole, "An Approach to the Study of Entrepreneurship: A Tribute to Edwin F. Gay," *The Journal of Economic History*, Supplement VI–1946, p. 8.
2. Frank H. Knight, *Risk, Uncertainty and Profit*, No. 16 in Reprints of Scarce Tracts in Economics and Political Science, The London School of Economics and Political Science (London: London School of Economics and Political Science, 1933), p. 270.
3. Joseph A. Schumpeter, *The Theory of Economic Development: An Inquiry into Profits, Capital, Credit, Interest, and the Business Cycle* (Cambridge, Mass.: Harvard University Press, 1936), pp. 89–94.
4. In 1917, Smith described himself in *Who's Who* as a "capitalist," which indeed he was, although he was undoubtedly unaware of the Marxian origins of the term. Indeed, this self-description reflects pride.
5. For a different view, consider Samuel Insull. He, too, was an outstanding entrepreneur. In this respect he passed all the tests, as did Smith. But Insull was never a capitalist. His personal fortune even at its peak did not exceed $14 million, while he financed some $2.5 billion in public utility assets (1929) entirely through internal growth, corporate borrowing, and equity issues. For an absorbing study of Samuel Insull and the tragedy that destroyed him, see Forrest McDonald, *Insull* (Chicago: The University of Chicago Press, 1962).
6. *Tonopah Daily Bonanza*, June 23, 1916.
7. The remote desert locations in which PCB operated were, in a sense, a kind of feudal manor—like little kingdoms of their own.
8. George D. Lyman, *Ralston's Ring: California Plunders the*

Comstock Lode (New York: C. Scribner's Sons, 1937). The subtitle refers to the monopoly Ralston put together at Virginia City. Entrepreneurs have often created monopolies, but monopoly is a factor separate from entrepreneurship itself.

9. David Lavender, *The Great Persuader* (Garden City, N.Y.: Doubleday, 1970).

10. Huntington actually made his home in New York City and also spent much time in the Adirondacks, at his "Camp Pine Knot" on Raquette Lake.

Bibliography

Note on sources: There exists no central collection of materials concerned with the business career of F. M. Smith. Regarding his personal life, the four children of Borax Smith share a large collection of newspaper scrapbooks and photographs, together with some letters and documents. Under the expert guidance of Mr. Vernon Sappers, the California Railway Museum at Rio Vista Junction, California, has accumulated a large amount of material concerning the history of the Key Route, the various traction enterprises, and the United Properties Company.

The U. S. Borax & Chemical Company has considerable material about borax history and the place of Mr. Smith in that history, augmented by photographs. The parent company in London, Borax Consolidated, Limited, has extensive files of correspondence between Smith and R. C. Baker, and also between C. B. Zabriskie and Mr. Baker. The Bancroft Library of the University of California at Berkeley has material on the Pacific Coast Borax Company, and correspondence involving F. M. Smith and his early London representative, William Lovering Locke; letters from Smith to Governor George C. Pardee; and a substantial portion of the surviving papers of Frank C. Havens, including matters involving Smith. The Oakland History Room of the Oakland Public Library has an extensive newspaper file on Smith's later years as well as a rare copy of the large book of photographs, *Arbor Villa: The Home of Mr. and Mrs. F. M. Smith* (1902). Finally, the Library of the School of Law of the University of California at Berkeley has much material concerned with legal proceedings involving F. M. Smith.

Books

Agricola, Georgius (Georg Bauer). *De Re Metallica.* Translated from first Latin edition of 1556 by Herbert Clark Hoover and Lou Henry Hoover. New edition. New York: Dover Publications, 1950.

Baker, J. E. *Past and Present of Alameda County.* 2 vols. Chicago: S. J. Clarke Publishing Company, 1914.

Cardwell, Kenneth H. *Bernard Maybeck, Artisan, Architect, Artist.* Santa Barbara, California: Peregrine Smith, Inc., 1977.

Caruthers, William. *Loafing Along Death Valley Trails: A Personal Narrative of People and Places.* Ontario, California: Death Valley Publishing Company, 1951.

Chalfant, W. A. *Death Valley: The Facts.* Stanford, California: Stanford University Press, 1933.

Elliott, Russell R. *Nevada's Twentieth-Century Mining Boom: Tonopah, Goldfield, Ely.* Reno: University of Nevada Press, 1966.

Farjeon, Eleanor. *Portrait of a Family.* New York: Frederick A. Stokes Company, 1936.

Gerstley, James M. *A Reminiscence of My Father.* Privately printed, 1975.

———. *Borax Years, 1933-1961: Some Recollections.* Pasadena, California: The Castle Press, 1979.

Glasscock, C. B. *Here's Death Valley.* Indianapolis: The Bobbs-Merrill Company, 1940.

Gower, Harrison P. *Fifty Years in Death Valley—Memoirs of a Borax Man.* With an Introduction by James M. Gerstley. Publication No. 9 of the Death Valley '49ers. San Bernardino, California: Inland Printing and Engraving Company, 1969.

Knight, Frank H. *Risk, Uncertainty and Profit.* No. 16 in Reprints of Scarce Tracts in Economics and Political Science, the London School of Economics and Political Science. London: London School of Economics and Political Science, 1933.

Lavender, David. *The Great Persuader.* Garden City, N.Y.: Doubleday, 1970.

Lyman, George D. *Ralston's Ring: California Plunders the Comstock Lode.* New York: C. Scribner's Sons, 1937.

McDonald, Forrest. *Insull.* Chicago: The University of Chicago Press, 1962.

Meadows, Lorena Edwards. *A Sagebrush Heritage: The Story of Ben Edwards and His Family.* With illustrations by Patricia Meadows Robertson. San Jose, California: The Harlan-Young Press, 1972.

Myrick, David F. *Railroads of Nevada and Eastern California.* 2 vols. Vol. 1, "The Northern Roads"; vol. 2, "The Southern Roads." Berkeley, California: Howell-North Books, 1962 and 1963.

Press Reference Library. *Notables of the Southwest.* 2 vols. New York: International News Services, 1913.

Putnam, George Palmer. *Death Valley and Its Country.* New York: Duell, Sloan and Pearce, 1946.

Ransome, Ernest L., and Saubrey, Alexis. *Reinforced Concrete Buildings.* New York: McGraw-Hill, 1912.

Scherer, James A. B. *The Lion of the Vigilantes: William T. Coleman and the Life of Old San Francisco.* Indianapolis: The Bobbs-Merrill Company, 1939.

Schumpeter, Joseph A. *The Theory of Economic Development: An Inquiry into Profits, Capital, Credit, Interest, and the Business Cycle.* Cambridge, Mass.: Harvard University Press, 1936.

Scully, Vincent J., Jr. *The Shingle Style and the Stick Style: Architectural Theory and Design from Downing to the Origins of Wright.* Revised edition. New Haven and London: Yale University Press, 1971.

Shankland, Robert. *Steve Mather of the National Parks.* New York: Knopf, 1951.

Spears, John R. *Illustrated Sketches of Death Valley and Other Borate Deserts of the Pacific Coast.* New York: Rand, McNally & Co., 1892.

Walker, Jim. *Key System Album.* Glendale, Calif.: Interurbans, 1978.

Weight, Harold O. *Twenty Mule Team Days in Death Valley.* With Some Observations on the Natural History of Mules and Mule Skinners, and the Mining of Desert Borax, and a Reprint of Henry G. Hanks' Report on Death Valley, 1883. Twentynine Palms, Calif.: Calico Press, 1955.

Weight, Harold O., and Weight, Lucile. *Rhyolite, the Ghost City of Golden Dreams.* 5th ed., rev. and enlarged. Twentynine Palms, Calif.: Calico Press, 1970.

Articles

Bartow, Virginia. "Pioneer Personalities in Borane Chemistry," in Robert F. Gould ed., *Borax to Boranes,* vol. 32 of Advances in Chemistry Series, American Chemical Society (1961).

Belden, L. Burr. "Smith Amazes All with Comeback in Borax World," *San Bernardino Sun-Telegram* (February 22, 1953).

———. "West End Final Project Begun by 'Borax' Smith," *San Bernardino Sun-Telegram* (March 29, 1953).

———. "Financial World Shocked by News of Smith Crash," *San Bernardino Sun-Telegram* (February 15, 1953).

———. "Obscure Borax Chapter Found in Traction Road," *San Bernardino Sun-Telegram* (January 18, 1953).

Cole, Arthur H. "An Approach to the Study of Entrepreneurship: A Tribute to Edwin F. Gay," *The Journal of Economic History.* Supplement VI-1946, p. 8.

Foshag, William F. "The World's Biggest Borax Deposits," *Engineering and Mining Journal-Press,* 118:11 (September 13, 1924), pp. 419–422.

————. "Francis Marion (Borax Smith) Smith," *The National Encyclopedia of American Biography,* Vol. XXVIII, 1940.

Gale, Hoyt S. "The Lila C Borax Mine at Ryan, California," U.S. Department of the Interior, United States Geological Survey, *Mineral Resources of the United States* (Washington, 1911).

————. "The Callville Wash Colemanite Deposit," *Engineering and Mining Journal,* 112:14 (October 1, 1921), pp. 524–530.

Gale, W. A. "Development and Present Status of the Borax Industry," in Robert F. Gould, ed., *Borax to Boranes,* vol. 32 of Advances in Chemistry Series, American Chemical Society (1961).

Ninnis, Lillian. "Cottonball for Rosie," *Nevada Highways and Parks,* 26:3 (Fall 1960), pp. 24–33, 39–40ff.

Steel, James King. "Frank M. Smith, The Financier-Philanthropist," in Evarts I. Blake, ed., *Greater Oakland, 1911* (Oakland, Calif.: Pacific Publishing Co.), pp. 274–282.

Stevenot, Archie D. "Cottonball Refinery in California," with a Foreword by James M. Gerstley. U.S. Borax and Chemical Company, Los Angeles, California (n.d.)

Travis, Norman J. and Randolph, Carl L. "United States Borax and Chemical Corporation: The First One Hundred Years." New York: The Newcomen Society in North America (1973).

Unsigned. "Account of Process of Borax Production at Original Smith Plant," *Scientific American* (September 22, 1877), p. 184.

Unsigned. "Borax Country," *Nevada Highways and Parks,* 2 (1959), pp. 18–22.

Unsigned. "News Account of Failure of W. T. Coleman & Company," *Engineering and Mining Journal,* XLV:19 (May 12, 1888).

Unsigned. "Twenty Mule Team Borax," *Fortune* (November 1931), pp. 40–43, 122.

Ver Planck, William E. "Boron," in California Division of Mines Bulletin 176, *Mineral Commodities of California* (n.d.).

————. "History of Borax Production in the United States," *California Journal of Mining and Geology,* 52:3 (July 1956), pp. 273–291.

Young, George J. "Mining Borax in the Muddy Range," *Engineering and Mining Journal-Press,* 117:7 (February 16, 1924), p. 276.

Monographs

Adams, Ansel, and others. *Death Valley.* San Francisco: 5 Associates, 1954.

Bailey, Gilbert E. *Borates*, in California State Mining Bureau Bulletin No. 24, *The Saline Deposits of California*, Pt. II (San Francisco, May 1902).

Carpenter, Jay A.; Elliott, Russell Richard; and Sawyer, Byrd Fanita Wall. "The History of Fifty Years of Mining at Tonopah, 1900-1950," *University of Nevada Bulletin*, 47:1 (January 1953), Nevada Bureau of Mines, Geology and Mining Series No. 51.

Clark, William D., with Muench, David. *Death Valley: The Story behind the Scenery*. Las Vegas, Nevada: KC Publications, 1972.

Hanks, Henry G. "Report on the Borax Deposits of California and Nevada." California State Mining Bureau, *Third Annual Report of the State Minerologist*, part 2 (Sacramento, California, 1883).

Hanson, Erle C. *East Shore & Suburban Railway: Along the Eastshore of San Francisco Bay*. San Marino, California: Golden West Books, 1977.

Peralta Associates and Sappers, Vernon, J. *From Shore to Shore: The Key Route*. Oakland, California: Peralta Associates, 1948.

Sawyer, Byrd Fanita Wall. "The Gold and Silver Rushes of Nevada," in Jay A. Carpenter, Russell Richard Elliott, and Byrd Fanita Wall Sawyer, "The History of Fifty Years of Mining at Tonopah, 1900-1950," in *University of Nevada Bulletin*, 47:1 (January 1953), Nevada Bureau of Mines, Geology and Mining Series No. 51.

Swett, Ira L., editor. "Sacramento Northern," *Interurbans Electric Railway Publications*, 20:2 (September 1962).

Unpublished Manuscripts

Smith, Francis Marion. "Autobiographical Notes of His Early Life." Ca. 1925.

Smythe, Dallas Walker. "An Economic History of Local and Interurban Transportation in the East Bay Cities, with Particular Reference to the Properties Developed by F. M. Smith." A dissertation in partial satisfaction of the requirements for PhD in Economics. Berkeley: The University of California, 1937.

Sperry, Charlotte Grace. "The Travelling Bridesmaid's Report," 1907.

Pamphlets

U.S. Borax and Chemical Corporation. *The Story of Borax*. Los Angeles, California, 1969.

U.S. Borax and Chemical Company. *Annual Report 1971. Centennial edition*. Los Angeles, 1972.

U.S. Borax and Chemical Company. *100 Years of U.S. Borax.* Los Angeles, 1972.
West End Chemical Company. *Special Report to Stockholders.* Oakland, California, August 27, 1956.
Woodman, Ruth C. *The Story of the Pacific Coast Borax Company.* With photographs by Ann Rosener. Los Angeles: The Ward Ritchie Press, 1951.

Newspapers and Periodicals

The Borax Miner (Candelaria, Nevada).
The Chloride Belt (Candelaria, Nevada), 1892.
Department of the Interior, United States Geological Survey. *Mineral Resources of the United States* (Annual). Part II, "Nonmetals." Washington, D.C.: GPO.
Engineering and Mining Journal.
Goldfield News (Goldfield, Nevada).
Los Angeles Times.
Newport Herald (Rhode Island).
New York Herald.
New York Sun.
New York World.
Oakland Daily Evening Tribune (later *Oakland Tribune*).
Oakland Herald.
Oakland Post-Enquirer.
San Bernardino Sun (San Bernardino, California).
San Bernardino Sun-Telegram (San Bernardino, California).
San Francisco Bulletin.
San Francisco Call.
San Francisco Chronicle.
San Francisco Examiner.
San Francisco News Bureau.
The Tonopah Daily Bonanza (Tonopah, Nevada).
The Tonopah Miner (Tonopah, Nevada).
The True Fissure (Candelaria, Nevada).
The Walker Lake Bulletin (Hawthorne, Nevada).

Legal Proceedings

J. C. Settle v. F. M. Smith et al., in the Superior Court of the State of California (July 1, 1913).
Frederick G. Cartwright v. F. M. Smith, A Complaint dated July 12, 1913, and filed in the Superior Court of the City and County of San Francisco.
In the Matter of F. M. Smith in Bankruptcy, No. 8199. A Petition filed

in United States District Court by Leo R. Dickey, C. E. Gilman, Albert Hanford, and the Union Land Company, July 24, 1913.

L. Baar v. F. M. Smith, et al., in the Superior Court of the City and County of San Francisco, No. 133,684, Department 3, before the Hon. Timothy I. Fitzpatrick, Judge (1925–26).

Baar v. Smith, Prayer for a Writ of *supersedeas* by Evelyn Ellis Smith, Defendant and Appellant, before the Supreme Court of the State of California, San Francisco No. 12316, April 20, 1927, to set aside in its entirety the judgment of the trial court. *201 Whiting 87 (1927).*

INDEX